THE
IMPOSSIBLE

THE
IMPOSSIBLE

THE MIRACULOUS STORY OF A MOTHER'S FAITH AND HER CHILD'S RESURRECTION

BY JOYCE SMITH
WITH GINGER KOLBABA

New York Nashville

FaithWords
Hachette Book Group
1290 Avenue of the Americas, New York, NY 10104
faithwords.com
twitter.com/faithwords

First Edition: November 2017

FaithWords is a division of Hachette Book Group, Inc. The FaithWords name and logo are trademarks of Hachette Book Group, Inc.

The publisher is not responsible for websites (or their content) that are not owned by the publisher.

The Hachette Speakers Bureau provides a wide range of authors for speaking events. To find out more, go to www.hachettespeakersbureau.com or call (866) 376-6591.

Library of Congress Cataloging-in-Publication Data has been applied for.

ISBNs: 978-1-4789-7695-0 (hardcover), 978-1-4789-2253-7 (audiobook, downloadable), 978-1-4789-2260-5 (audiobook, CD), 978-1-4789-7694-3 (ebook)

Printed in the United States of America

LSC-Willard

10 9 8 7 6 5 4 3 2 1

CONTENTS

CONTENTS

CHAPTER 1

A Bad Feeling

Sunday, January 18, 2015

The air hung thick with tension. Usually Living Word Christian Middle School's gymnasium echoed with a cacophony of yells and cheers of students and siblings, parents shouting out advice, refs blowing whistles, and coaches screaming directions throughout a basketball game. But this game was quiet. No one was shouting or cheering. We heard only the sounds of the players talking with one another, the bounce of the ball hitting the wooden floor, and the screech of the players' shoes as they maneuvered around the hoops. Our Eagles eighth-grade A team were deadlock-tied with the Duchesne Pioneers. We just couldn't get enough ahead. So far this season our team hadn't been doing well, so we had to get a win under our belt. But Duchesne's team didn't seem to want to let us win! For every point our team made, the Pioneers tied it. Eleven, eleven. Fifteen, fifteen. Twenty-two, twenty-two.

My eyes stayed glued to the black-haired, handsome, olive-skinned young man wearing the black, teal, and white uniform, with the number 4 displayed across his back. As the point guard and shooting guard, my son John called the plays, controlled the tempo of the game, and talked to the ref if one of the players had an issue. He was also the leading scorer for the team.

Not bad for a kid standing tall at five feet four inches. To say I was proud of him would be the understatement of the year. I thought he hung the moon. Actually, I didn't think that; I knew it. But that wasn't to say I overlooked his quirks. And one of those—his penchant for arguing with his coach over plays the coach called and then rolling his eyes in disgust—had gotten him benched the game before.

While I was glad he was back playing in this game, I knew John was still stinging from the previous game's tension. But he stayed focused. His competitive streak was in full gear as he cut in and out, maneuvered, and ran around the floor with a vengeance. Basketball was his life. From the time he was three he had a basketball in his hands. All of his games were do-or-die for him.

Finally the game was nearing its end—and still the teams were tied. My husband, Brian, and I were exhausted from the game's tension, so I could only imagine what John and his teammates felt. The scoreboard read thirty-three to thirty-three, while the clock showed forty seconds left in the fourth quarter. All of a sudden, from out of nowhere, John captured the ball and ran down the court, dribbling toward the hoop. He pulled out a breakaway layup and shot. The ball soared through the air and landed with a swish.

Thirty-five to thirty-three.

Brian and I were on our feet, along with the other fifty to sixty people in the stands, erupting with the loudest cheers. Our Eagles were going to pull this off!

The clock ticked down while the Pioneers struggled to land a tying score, until finally the horn blew loudly, announcing the end of the game. Christian Middle School had won. And my son had made the winning basket.

The whole team jumped on one another—hugging and shouting and laughing. They'd worked so hard for this win; now it was time to celebrate. And they had Monday off school for the Martin Luther King Jr. holiday to do just that.

Brian and I walked down off the bleachers. We knew it would take time for the boys to settle enough to head back to the locker room and get changed before they were ready to leave, so we patiently waited off to the side. But John and two friends and teammates, Josh Rieger and Josh Sander, beelined straight toward us.

I groaned inwardly, knowing what they wanted. All weekend long, John had talked to me about wanting to go to Josh Rieger's house to spend the night after the game. And all weekend long I'd downplayed it, because I didn't want him to go. I couldn't explain why; I just had a weird feeling about it.

I didn't get ominous feelings often, but when I did, I'd learned to listen to them because they always meant something bad was going to happen. One time in particular, when one of my older sons, Tom, was a freshman in high school, his football coach showed up at our front door and asked if Tom could join the team on a camping trip. Something about this coach did not sit right with me. He seemed nice enough, but I couldn't shake the uneasiness I felt about the situation, so I said no. Several months later the coach was arrested for molesting boys.

"Please, Mrs. Smith! Please can John go? Let him spend the night. *Pleeeease!*" The two Joshes had ganged up on Brian and me. They knew Brian was a pushover, so they had to lay it on thick to Mama.

"Can I, Mom?...Can I?"

Everything within me wanted to shout no, to encircle his sweaty body in my arms and whisk him home to safety—from what, I didn't know. But I looked into my sweet boy's big, beautiful, dark eyes filled with excitement. How could I say no to him? They'd just won the game. They were good kids. He'd spent the night at Josh Rieger's house plenty of times. Josh's family were good people, and his parents, Kurt and Cindy, were responsible and attentive. I liked them and trusted them with John. And John loved going over there.

I'm sure I'm just being overly protective, I decided. I looked at these fourteen-year-old boys who stood in front of me, so eager to extend their celebration and have a little fun down time. *Joyce, you cannot be a stick in the mud. You can't be that mom.*

"Mom?" John needed an answer.

I sighed and nodded, against my better judgment, knowing I couldn't deny that kid something so simple, and sure I was overreacting to the uneasiness I felt. "Okay. You can go."

The boys all shouted their relief. "Ah, thanks, Mrs. Smith. This is great! We're going to have—"

"Just make sure you're safe. And don't do anything stupid." *Ha*, I thought. *They're fourteen. They're boys. Of course they're going to do something stupid. Just as long as it's not dangerous stupid…*

"Thanks, Mom! Thanks, Dad!"

"Make sure you stay in touch," I told him, as Brian and I gathered our coats to leave.

"I will. See you!" He turned and ran back to his team, still celebrating with their coach.

True to his word, John texted me later that night to let me know they were having fun hanging out with Josh Rieger's family, eating pizza rolls, drinking soda, and playing *Call of Duty*. No big deal.

I smiled and felt relieved. They were good boys. I didn't know why my spirit had been so troubled about John spending the night over there. *Nothing to worry about*, I reminded myself.

What John *failed* to mention to me was that earlier that evening, the boys had gotten bored and wandered two blocks away to Lake Ste. Louise, a small lake in the Riegers' neighborhood that they liked to visit. They saw that the lake was iced over, so they got the harebrained idea to walk out onto the ice, squat down, take a photo of themselves, and then post it on Instagram. The boys were dressed lightly. No coats. John wore shorts and a sleeveless T-shirt. Yes, it was unseasonably warm for January in the St. Louis area, but still…shorts and a sleeveless T-shirt? Had I known about his attire—or, more important, about his ice capade adventure—I would have driven straight over and hauled him home. But I didn't know. Parents so rarely know everything fourteen-year-olds do, unfortunately.

So that night, after we texted that we loved him, Brian and I went to bed blissfully unaware of anything other than John eating pizza and playing video games.

Monday, January 19, 2015

The next morning passed uneventfully. Brian headed to his job as a corporate media event specialist at Boeing, since the Martin Luther King holiday wasn't an official day off for his company. I fed and petted our dog, Cuddles, talked to my sister, Janice, and then grabbed some breakfast, along with my Bible, and sat in the kitchen to spend some quiet time with God.

I glanced at my phone's clock. It was almost twenty after eleven. Josh Rieger's mom, Cindy, and I were scheduled to do the "child exchange" sometime in the afternoon, so I still had some time before I picked John up. Cindy had said she'd call when they were on their way. Usually I'd meet Cindy and the kids at a mall or someplace in the middle between our houses, since we lived in St. Charles, Missouri, and they lived almost twenty minutes away in Lake St. Louis, about forty miles outside of St. Louis. Meeting in the middle allowed us to do the handoff without either of us having to drive the whole way.

Once I picked up John, I figured he'd want to go to the local recreational center to shoot some hoops and work out, since that was his routine on his days off from school. I wasn't sure if he'd want to go straight there or stop off at the house first, so I decided to check in with him. The phone's clock told me it was now 11:23 a.m. so I needed to figure out what we were doing. I texted him. "Hey, are we still doing the rec plex or are you coming here first and what time?"

John answered right away, "Text Cindy, idk" which I knew, was short for "I don't know."

What does Cindy have to do with John going to the rec center or coming home? I wondered. "No," I texted back, "I am asking you what you want to do about the rec plex. yes or no?"

"Idc." I don't care. "Is Dad going?"

I smiled. John and his dad loved hanging out together. They played sports together, went to the recreation center together. They even had a long-standing Saturday-morning-breakfast guy time at the local Waffle House, which they'd kept since John was eight years old.

"No, he is at work right now. He won't be home till later. He might go then. Don't know."

"Okay," he wrote back. That was it, nothing else. I sighed, feeling frustrated. I didn't know what he was saying okay to, and I didn't have an answer about whether we were going to the rec center or coming home. "That kid will be the death of me," I griped to myself. "I'm just going to call him."

At 11:26 a.m. I dialed my son's number, determined to get an answer to my question.

He picked up right away. "Hey."

"You didn't answer my question," I told him. "Do you want to go to the rec plex or not? If you do, I can have Cindy drop you off there and I'll pick you up later."

"Um, yeah, that sounds good," he said. He sounded cheerful, as if the day had been a good one for him so far.

"Okay, then, I'll see you there. Love you."

With that issue now handled and our game plan set, I turned my attention back to my phone, but this time for a different—more calming!—reason. I opened the Facebook app and found Mark Callaway's page. Mark was my older sons' former youth pastor at a church our family attended years ago, when we lived in Indianapolis. We considered him and his wife, Leslie, to be dear friends. Mark posted daily devotional writings on Facebook, and I tried to read them every morning. His writing always seemed to connect with exactly what I needed for that day.

What do you do when you are in a crisis, whether self-made or caused by other's actions. We can sit & fume, thinking of how we were cheated or what a failure we are . . . & that will do NOTHING (except put off dealing with it). David wrote, "My God, My God, why have you forsaken me? Why are you so far from saving me," yet hardly a breath later he said that GOD is enthroned [in the praises of HIS people] (Psalm 22). Later Scripture says to "thank God in all things." Worry/discouragement is a natural first response, but it is what we do next that matters. Do we stay there or do we move forward? By moving forward from a big problem to our BIG GOD begins bringing perspective and moves us past an emotional myopia. Then taking it further by thanking God for the challenge begins the process of conquering. When we see God as BIGGER and begin to thank God for the challenge, we are accepting the challenge as something we and GOD can handle. . . . That we will know more of GOD coming out of this than we did going in.

At that moment the phone rang. It was 11:51 a.m. and it was Cindy.

John's day had started well. The country was celebrating Martin Luther King Jr.'s life and civil rights accomplishments on the holiday named after him. But for John and his two friends, it was simply a fun and welcomed day off of school. They arose late in the morning and decided that since the ice on Lake Ste. Louise had proven thick enough the previous night when they had taken their photo, they, along with Josh's older sister, Jamie, would trek back down and check it out. The lure of a frozen lake—something that rarely happens in our area—was just too much to pass up.

The sun shone brightly on the ice, covering it with a look of pure glass. The day was unseasonably warm, promising to make it up to fifty degrees. A perfect day for the middle of January and a welcome reprieve from a cold snap that had been in the low twenties.

Dressed only in tank shirts and shorts, the boys first picked up some rocks at the shoreline and dropped them on the ice to see how strong it was. Satisfied that it was still solid enough to handle them again this day, they headed out, each step leading them farther offshore, while Jamie chose to play it safe and stay on land. They laughed and slid and enjoyed their ability to "walk on water."

The community of Lake St. Louis, Missouri, is home to two lakes in close proximity, Lake St. Louis being the larger at 650 acres. Even though its sister lake, Lake Ste. Louise, is not very large, at only seventy square acres, it still runs deep, measuring in most places between fifty and sixty feet, and with a muddy bottom covered with silt and sludge. Size doesn't seem to matter where water is concerned. Given the right conditions, a person can get into just as much trouble in a pond as they can in the ocean. John had discovered this just the previous summer when he and Josh Rieger had gone swimming out in the middle of *this same lake* and needed help when they were unable to swim back to shore.

But today John wasn't considering that warm summer day's troubles as he continued to glide over the surface. As he and his friends skidded around and jumped up and down on the ice, daring it to break, and feeling challenged to see how far toward the middle they could go, inside the Lake Ste. Louise's association club, mere yards away on the west side of the shore, manager Ron Wilson glanced through his office window, saw what the boys were doing, and came outside to confront them.

"Hey!" he yelled. "You kids need to get off the ice. It's too dangerous out there. Get off the ice!"

They acknowledged his warning, but they didn't seem to be in any great hurry to comply, so Ron returned to his office. In the meantime, I'd begun texting with John. When I called him to strategize on going to the rec plex, unbeknownst to me he was standing about fifty feet from shore.

A trait that all four of my sons share is that they constantly walk or pace when they're talking. Get them long enough on the phone, and they could probably make it to California on foot! So at 11:26 that morning, as I was talking to John and seated firmly on solid ground, he was pacing, mindlessly moving toward thin ice.

Within moments of hanging up the phone with me, ominous cracking noises thundered across the lake. The ice broke beneath his feet and the water devoured my son. Josh Sander dropped to his hands and knees, but as he was grabbing John's hand, the ice fell away beneath him. Josh Rieger, who was farther away, immediately ran over to help his friends. Lying on his stomach, he tried to pull John out but still fell in himself. The boys splashed frantically, desperately trying to escape the dark and cold water's grasp.

At 11:33 a.m. once again Ron Wilson glanced through his office window, but this time it was to witness the ice tear open and swallow the boys. Immediately he called 911, which in turn notified the Lake St. Louis police department.

"Call 911!" John yelled to Jamie Rieger. "I don't want to die!"

CHAPTER 2

On Thin Ice

Monday, January 19, 2015

At 11:35 a.m., the alarm went out to the Lake St. Louis fire department as well as to the neighboring community fire department of Wentzville.

As first responders headed to the lake, Josh Sander was able to grab on to a solid piece of ice, pull himself out, and half-crawl, half-slide toward the association's dock, which sat closest to the boys. John and Josh Rieger were still flailing in the water, bobbing up and down; John was pushing Josh onto the ice ledge while trying to get himself out as well.

Meanwhile, police officers Rick Frauenfelder and Ryan Hall were seated at their desks in the Lake St. Louis police department, writing reports and catching up on paperwork, when they got the dispatch call that three teens were on Lake Ste. Louise and had fallen through the ice. Immediately, they dropped what they were doing and ran to their squad cars. Flipping on the lights and sirens, both officers sped the short distance to the lake. Officer Hall rounded to the far side of the lake, and Officer Frauenfelder headed toward the dock by the Lake Ste. Louise club association building. Neither knew exactly where the boys had fallen in, so by splitting up they hoped one of them would find the spot quickly.

As the officers arrived at the lake, Wentzville Fire Protection District chief Mike Marlo, along with his wife, Kathy, were in their car, heading toward downtown Wentzville for the Martin Luther King Day parade. They were scheduled to represent their community's first responders, whom both Mike and Kathy loved supporting. Almost at the parade lineup, the fire tone announced the call, and Mike listened carefully to the dispatch: "Ice rescue, three thirteen- to fifteen-year-old boys, Lake Ste. Louise." Normally Chief Marlo wouldn't go out on calls, but something in his spirit moved him to think differently about this one. He couldn't explain why; he just knew he had to be there.

He looked at his wife. "We're going to this call."

Meanwhile Tommy Shine, an eleven-year veteran of the Wentzville Fire Department, had just started his forty-eight-hour shift with his unit, so it was the perfect time to hit the grocery store to shop for their rotation time at the firehouse. They had no sooner entered Dierbergs Market and walked down the produce aisle when they received the call that kids were in the water and one had completely submerged.

Tommy and the three others abandoned their cart and raced out to the truck.

Within minutes of the 911 call, Officer Frauenfelder was the first on scene at 11:38 a.m., with officers Ryan Hall, Tyler Christeson, Cody Fry, and Detective Sergeant Bret Carbray close behind. Josh Sander was sliding his body on the ice, already nearing the dock, wet and cold but safe. The officers saw Josh Rieger clinging desperately to the ice shelf—the largest and sturdiest mass of ice—but was struggling to hold on, as he was getting weaker and weaker. John was bobbing in and out of the water, flailing, flapping his arms, splashing, and grabbing for anything solid. But with each grab at the ice, a chunk would splinter off, leaving him still with nothing stable to hold on to.

"Help! Help us!" Josh and John yelled, as soon as they saw the men.

Immediately Rick Frauenfelder and Ryan Hall tore off their gun belts, vests, and other gear and raced toward the lake's edge. With no time to waste, Rick and Ryan immediately headed onto the ice, knowing that Bret Carbray would throw life jackets and ropes from their squad cars' trunks. As they were about twelve feet out, Bret tossed them the life vests and ropes. They hurriedly put them on and began crawling farther out, but Rick noticed that the ice was sloshy—not a good sign. With each movement, the ice was starting to give way. In his fifteen years as a police officer—eight of those with the Lake St. Louis police department—he'd answered plenty of calls regarding trouble on this lake, but nothing this bad. These boys were in real danger, and he wasn't sure he could help them. But he was going to try.

"Roll on your backs and lie flat!" he called out to the boys. "Stay calm and don't try to get out." He was worried that by panicking, they were actually doing themselves more harm. He could tell that hysteria had set in and the boys were unable to listen to his commands. He tried crawling more quickly, but the water was pooling on top of the ice, which became thinner the farther out he went.

By this point, John, having grown so weak and cold in the barely forty-degree water, was slipping under the surface for longer periods until finally he disappeared completely.

The St. Charles county ambulance Medic 9 and Lake St. Charles Unit 9224's firefighters arrived at 11:43 to find one boy with only his head above water and weakly holding on to the thin ice as it threatened to break away from the ice ledge. Having been in the water for ten minutes by this point, his muscles were weakened, his coordination and strength had quickly diminished, and his blood had begun to move away from his extremities toward the center of his body, his core, to keep him alive. But within a matter of seconds he could go under. Meanwhile, the EMTs worked on Josh Sander, who had made it back to shore, warming him with a Bair Hugger—a special heating blanket—and treating him for hypothermia. The firefighters dressed in ice floatation suits, grabbed a rescue wakeboard, and headed toward open water. Officers Frauenfelder and Hall, now themselves wet and cold, were still only about halfway to the other two boys.

"We've got to go back," Rick told Ryan when he saw Ryan's legs now covered with water as they were still trying to reach John and Josh. They slowly turned around and returned to shore.

Within moments Chief Marlo pulled up and navigated through the growing crowd of first responders and onlookers to take command. As he scoped out the lake with the broken ice and open water everywhere, his heart sunk. One boy was being treated. One boy was barely alive but hanging on. No sign of the third boy. If the lake just had one hole in the ice, he could have figured out that John must be in that area, but he didn't have that. He had a huge area of ice that was broken and no clue where John was. He could be *anywhere*, having been whisked away by any underwater waves. And now going on twelve minutes being submerged...

Chief Marlo *had* to figure out where that third boy was. He called for Ron Wilson to give him more details about what the association manager had witnessed. "Where did you see these kids? Especially the last time you saw them?"

"Out that way," Ron said, pointing out over the lake.

"Obviously out that way!" Chief Marlo said, feeling frustrated. "But *where* out that way?" A hundred yards? A hundred feet?

Officer Frauenfelder reached Chief Marlo and pointed out the direction. Then one of the firefighters called out, "Chief, when fourteen"—the Wentzville unit—"gets here, have them search out there." He pointed out about seventy-five feet from the dock. "We think we have nine to ten feet of water in that area."

Ten feet of water was definitely better than fifty feet. In an emergency situation where a teen has drowned, it might as well have been five hundred feet.

The chief wasn't ready to consider this a retrieval yet. Still, that reality was rushing toward them, and the dive-and-retrieval team was on its way. If there were any chance that this boy could still be alive, the first responders were going to do everything possible to find him and rescue him.

Chief Marlo radioed his guys with instructions. "Bring the ten-foot pike poles. You're going to search in an area that's nine to ten feet deep. And get your ice suits on now!"

Already en route on the Wentzville fire truck, Tommy Shine heard Chief Marlo, grabbed his ice floatation suit, and began to change. He didn't want to waste even a second at the scene, so as the truck sirens blared and the vehicle sped to the scene, off came the fire uniform and gear. In its place Tommy tucked himself into a bright yellow, rubberized, waterproof, and coldproof suit that looked as though he were headed to outer space.

Tommy was grateful that just a week prior, his unit had taken ice rescue training on Lake St. Louis. That training kicked in, and he focused his breathing and nerves to remain steady. He had a job to do. He wouldn't think about his own teenage son who, only a week before, had played ice hockey on a private lake. His son could have very easily been at this lake with these boys. He wouldn't think of all the noise and activity going on around him. He wouldn't think about the pressure that would weigh on him as soon as he entered that water—pressure to find that boy *alive*. And he refused to consider that the recovery dive team was also headed to the lake and would be there within moments of his arrival—waiting, preparing.

When the Wentzville fire truck pulled up to the lake, more than a dozen first responders were on scene working, guiding, coordinating, and preparing to resuscitate the boys and transport them to the local hospital, St. Joseph West. With the pike pole in hand, Tommy jumped off the truck before it had even stopped completely and, like a roadrunner, rocketed past Chief Marlo and the others.

The ice in many places was less than two inches thick, so Tommy knew as quickly as he wanted to get out there, he still had to be careful not to fall in and lose precious time rescuing himself. With each step he could hear the crackle of the ice beneath his feet. Twenty feet turned to fifty feet turned to seventy-five... until Tommy stopped 150 feet out. Although the boys fell into the water in the same area, the hole had become bigger and bigger as they worked to get out.

Meanwhile, firefighters Joe Marrow and Mike Terranova from Lake St. Louis had already reached the opening in the water. While Joe began searching for John, Mike handled Josh's rescue. Josh Rieger by this point was confused and disoriented from the cold. He had no strength to pull himself up to safety or to grab on to a rope or anything else, because his dexterity was gone and he could no longer hold on. Mike Terranova eased into the water, got behind Josh, and gave him a bear hug from behind. He rolled the boy onto the ice and then onto the rescue board. Once Mike was also out of the water, he secured Josh, and the officers and other firefighters pulled Mike's safety rope to glide them both back to land and the waiting EMTs, who immediately went to work on Josh.

The second boy was safe. But still no sign of the last one. No sign of my son.

Tommy cautiously dropped onto his stomach and rolled into the water, where the ice around him kept breaking apart. He cringed. Those movements were disrupting the environment, and as the ice broke, his search area kept expanding.

His buoyant suit bobbed him up and down slightly for a moment until he settled farther down with the water lapping at his shoulders. Then he began his methodical hunt on the opposite side of the hole from where Joe Marrow was searching. Joe, who had done his training in this very lake, knew what the floor of the lake was like. In many places it was muddy, filled with sludge. But in some places, it was rocky. Tommy and Joe were in the rocky area, for which they were grateful. They hoped they would locate John in this section, where it was more shallow; it would be easier to retrieve him from the bottom than having to deal with pulling up a body covered in mud.

"You're going to know the difference between a rock and a person," Joe told Tommy.

Even with the time pressure, they had to work slowly. The rubber suits and bulky rubber, oversized gloves were difficult to maneuver, but also, the men needed to disrupt the water as little as possible—not only because of visual issues caused by disturbing the muddy bottom, but also because even the slightest movement or wave could push John's body away from them. Slowly and meticulously they worked in about a one-hundred-foot circumference to find my son. Because of the size of the search area, Tommy and Joe divided the ring in half and began their hunt.

Tommy searched blindly, but the water gave up no visibility, just offered murky, dark swirls. The glare of the bright sun shining on the ice and water didn't help, either. He took his pole, which bore two large hooks—one at the end and another, slightly smaller hook a few feet up from the end—and pushed it to the bottom of the lake. Some of the water splashed on his face, and the frigid temperature reminded him of the urgency of his job. The water came up all the way to the top of the pole. Over and over, with painstaking precision and slowness, Tommy jabbed at the bottom, unable to see anything but darkness.

Mike Terranova returned to assist them, staying on the surface with the rescue wakeboard so that when they found John they could quickly get him to shore—*if* they found him, *if* they were even looking in the right place.

Every jab, every poke produced only hard rocks. And with every empty jab, another precious second of life was slipping away. In life-and-death rescue situations, first responders refer to this time as the Golden Hour—the theory that patients who receive definitive care within the first hour have a much greater chance of survival.

John had now been in the water more than fifteen minutes.

Tommy Shine breathed in deeply, forcing himself to remain calm and focused, shutting out every noise and commotion from the rest of the scene. *Come on,* he told himself. *You can do this. This is what you trained for just last week....Come on, kid. Where are you?*

John had everything going against him. Conditions. Time. There was no way he could survive having been in the water this long—even if he weren't completely submerged—but Tommy refused to let those thoughts enter his mind.

Both he and Joe worked the outside of the perimeter and moved inward toward the middle of the hole. But as Tommy continued to stab at the bottom, he continued to reap nothing.

Come on, he thought. *Where are you?* The divers on the recovery team were just minutes from arriving.

Suddenly something in Tommy's spirit—a feeling as though someone were next to him guiding him—prompted and almost pushed him to move in a different direction, straight toward the ice shelf.

Why would I go that way? he wondered. *I'm right here. If that kid's over that way, he's not going to make it.*

The feeling persisted, so Tommy inched his way farther from the middle and closer to the ice ledge, where he knew no one could survive if their body had washed under it.

He poked down with his hook. Nothing.

He moved within inches from the ice shelf, placed his back against it, and poked again. The hook hit something that definitely felt different from rock or mud. His heart pounded with hope.

Don't get too excited, he thought. *That could be my boot. . . . No, wait, that can't be it because I'm not standing on the bottom!*

He slowly started to lift his pole, and the hook resisted.

Please be this boy. Please don't be a tire or something.

He pulled hand over hand against the heavy resistance, willing himself not to lose what he'd hooked. As the pole rose slowly, Tommy caught a glimpse of something bright white.

John's shirt.

It was 11:51 a.m.—more than twenty minutes since John had fallen in.

"Got him!" Tommy yelled out to shore as he lifted the lifeless form of my son from the water. The hook had captured John in the middle of his body and had pulled him up by his shirt.

John had been one foot from the ice shelf. Any disturbance, even a light one, would have pushed John under and it would have been over. The recovery divers would have done the rest of the work. And they had just arrived on the scene as Tommy pulled John out.

Mike Terranova loaded my frozen child onto the rescue board, got on with him, and the guys on the dock pulled him back to shore with the speed of a jet engine. Everyone raced into action as they lifted the board onto the nearest dock and began CPR. His skin had a grayish-blue tint. His body was as limp as a noodle, yet was quickly becoming frigid from the conditions. His nostrils and mouth cavity were full of lake debris. His hair was rigid with icicles, his fingers and extremities were stiff and unyielding, and his skin was so frozen that the paramedics were unable to get any lifesaving device to stick to him.

They threw a warming blanket onto him, stuck an IV in his arm, and began chest compressions. With their first push against his chest, John's lungs gave up water as though a fountain had been switched on. Dirty lake water gushed from his mouth and nostrils. The paramedics worked to clear out his lungs and to get massive amounts of air back into his system as quickly as they could, knowing that if they could force oxygen back to his heart and his brain, it could potentially kick-start his body back to life.

Nothing worked. No pulse. No breath. No heartbeat.

My John was dead.

CHAPTER 3

A Race to the Hospital

Hi, Cindy!" I said cheerfully into the phone, surprised that she was calling
sooner than she was supposed to.

"Joyce." There was something odd about Cindy's voice. It sounded hollow,
shocked, but I didn't think much of it.

"I've been expecting your call."

"There's been an accident," she said.

"Oh no." My stomach lurched. *That feeling . . .* "Did you have a car accident?
Are you okay?"

Cindy's voice choked up. "The kids were out on the ice. John fell through
the water, and they've just pulled him out. Joyce . . . he doesn't have a heartbeat."

The room began to spin as my stomach lurched violently.

John fell through the water . . . he doesn't have a heartbeat. But that wasn't possible. I'd just talked to him.

"Joyce," Cindy said. "Come to the lake."

"Okay, I'll . . . yes." I don't remember if I even said good-bye before I hung up
the phone and was immediately on my feet. I suffer from rheumatoid arthri-

19

tis and my swollen, achy joints often won't let me move the way I want to—especially when the weather changes. But that day, my body kicked in, and I dashed around the house as though a raging fire were at my feet.

I grabbed my phone from the kitchen table and raced to the family room to pick up my purse and keys. They were gone.

My eyes shot around the room. Nothing.

I pulled throws and couch pillows off of every piece of furniture and pushed around newspapers, books, and the TV remote. "Where are my keys? Come on!" My ears pounded with the ticking of seconds racing by. *He doesn't have a heartbeat. . . . He doesn't have a heartbeat. . . . Where are my keys?*

I moved into the kitchen and scanned every counter, every chair. I threw open closets.

My stomach lurched again, threatening to give up its recent contents. And my brain went into a scrambled mode—it kept replaying Cindy's words over and over, along with my desperate mental plea to recall where my purse and keys were.

"Get a hold of yourself," I finally said aloud against a sob. "Breathe. The keys are here somewhere. Just slow down." I went back over the places I'd already looked. "God, you've got to help me," I begged as I headed toward my bedroom.

There on the back of the bedroom doorknob hung my purse. I seized the bag, shook it to make sure I could hear the keys jangling, then I jammed my hand in grabbing for anything that remotely felt like it had a jagged edge. *There!* With my car key firmly in my grasp, I headed toward the garage. Only, my feet felt as though I were racing through Jell-O—I couldn't move fast enough. And the ticking in my ears seemed to get louder and faster. I jumped into our Nissan Quest and peeled out of our driveway.

I had a twenty-minute ride ahead of me with about thirty seconds to make it in. Since it was a holiday, I prayed the traffic would be light. I prayed that the stoplights would all be green. I prayed that I wouldn't encounter any drivers who had a light foot on the accelerator or who got in my way. But mostly, I prayed for John.

As soon as I could safely pull out my phone, I called Brian at Boeing. It rang and rang and finally went to voice mail. I swallowed a sob, hung up, and tried again. After several rings, I heard a click and Brian's voice telling me, "You've reached the voice mail of Brian Smith..." Usually he answered his phone unless he was in a meeting or deeply involved in editing video footage for a promotional video or something. If that were the case, he might not be available for a while. The last thing I wanted to do was leave a message, but I had to do something.

"Brian, John's had an accident," I told his messaging system. "You need to call me right away."

I merged onto Interstate 70 and dialed my sister's number. I needed to hear Janice's calming voice. Instead, I got her voice mail as well. Next I tried my brother-in-law Don's phone. No answer. Another sob escaped my lips as I tried desperately to reach somebody, *anybody* to get the word out for people to pray, but also just to have another person to share my grief.

"God, I need you to handle this," I prayed out loud. "God, don't let me lose my son!"

The cops are going to pull me over because I'm on the phone and I'm screaming at God, I thought. I wasn't mad at God. I was making sure he heard me. I was getting his attention. *Oh well, I don't care if they pull me over. I can just get to the hospital faster.*

"Move it!" I said to a driver in front of me. He was going the speed limit, but to me he was driving entirely too slowly. "This is an expressway. It's seventy through here, not forty-five." I pulled into the passing lane and sailed by him.

My phone came to life. I grabbed it, hoping it was Brian or Janice. It was Cindy. I glanced at the clock on the dash. It registered about ten minutes after noon.

"They've taken John to St. Joseph West," she told me. "I'll meet you there."

"Okay, I'm on my way."

St. Joseph Hospital West was less than a mile from Lake Ste. Louise, and directly off I-70. It would be a straight shot for me now. Both of my son Charles's boys, Ben and Bryan, were born at St. Joseph West. Those had been joyous occasions. This most definitely was not.

I decided to call Charles, who still lived in our area. Surely he would pick up. But just as with the other numbers, this one, too, went to voice mail. "Ugggh!" My frustration and hysteria were getting the best of me.

"It's the pedal on the right that moves that thing, lady. Use it!" I called out to another driver as I willed her to speed up.

Next I tried Brian's side of the family. His sister, Miriam, had just started a new job, so I didn't have her number. Another strike. I decided to try her daughter, Jane—and of course, I reached a voice mail.

Having run out of options, I dialed Brad Carriger, a friend of our family's who used to be on staff at our church. "Please pick up, please pick up," I said through every ring.

Once again I heard the familiar click and inwardly groaned that this, too, had gone to voice mail.

"Hello?"

I paused a second to make sure it was an actual person.

"Hello?" the voice said again.

"Brad!" I gushed into the phone.

"Oh, hi, Joyce," Brad's chipper voice greeted me.

"There's been an accident!" My hysteria got the best of me and I blathered inarticulate words, but I couldn't make my tongue sync up with my brain for my words to make sense.

After several rounds of Guess Joyce's Message, Brad was finally able to piece together the news. "Okay, I'll call people," he promised me.

I felt so grateful and relieved and I wanted him to know how much I appreciated his help, but I could only mumble a sob-filled thanks before I hung up.

One more call, I thought, although after how badly I'd explained the news

22

to Brad, I wasn't sure I could do it over again better—even if somebody answered.

"All right, mister, you don't have to do thirty miles an hour to get on an exit. What is wrong with these drivers?"

I called my daughter-in-law Krista, Charles's wife. I was positive she would answer. She did, on the second ring. But hearing her sweet and warm voice didn't help me articulate anything any better.

"Oh no!" she cried, as soon as she grasped the news. "I'll get a hold of Charles. We'll be there right away."

Brian still hadn't called back, so I decided to try him one more time. He answered, and by his calm tone, I knew he hadn't gotten my earlier message. "You need to come to St. Joseph West. It's John. He's had an accident."

"What? What are you talking about? What kind of accident?"

"Just come to the hospital."

"Is he—"

"Get there as soon as you can. I'm on my way there now."

His voice turned unsure, questioning, as though he couldn't comprehend what I was saying. "Um...okay."

I knew that even if he wasn't fully connecting with the news, he'd drop everything and rush to the hospital. He was about fifteen to twenty minutes away. I just prayed he didn't encounter the kind of *slow, insane* drivers I had on my route. "Seriously, people! This isn't sightseeing time."

In between all the calls, I prayed. With each passing mile, I prayed. With every fearful, threatening thought that entered my mind, I prayed. But now I turned my *full* attention to God. No more phone calls. No more backseat-driving comments to other drivers. It was time for God and me to have a serious, no-holds-barred conversation. I thought about the Facebook devo I'd read less than a half an hour before: *There are times when you need God to just be God.* That's exactly who I needed—who John needed—right then.

"Lord!" I called out loud. "You can't do this. You can't take my son. Please do not take my son from me. Lord, just..." I was desperate. "You *can't*. You gave him to us, Lord," I reminded our sovereign God, thinking back fourteen years to when Brian and I had traveled the long journey to Guatemala and took this quiet, undernourished, dark-haired, dark-skinned little boy home with us. "You can't take him away from us. You can't. Not now!"

Finally, I spotted the exit for Veterans Memorial Parkway, the road that runs directly parallel to I-70 and, more important, the road that the hospital is on. My stomach clinched up again. I couldn't get there fast enough. But fear began to overtake me. What would I find? What would they tell me?

As I headed southwest toward the hospital, my eyes soon landed on the giant cross affixed to the orange brick side of the emergency room visitor's entrance. St. Joseph Hospital West came up quickly on my left, and I turned into the parking lot directly next to the emergency room.

Of course, there was not a parking space in sight. Around and around I drove, scouting out any opening. I didn't care if it was only half a space; even if I had to use a can opener to pry myself out, *I was going to park my car.* I was about ready to pull up under the carport at the front of the building where cars can drop off visitors, and just leave it there. Did no one understand that my son was in serious trouble and I had to get to him immediately? Was nobody actually *leaving* the hospital?

I glanced at the dashboard clock again. Twelve thirty. It had been just about an hour since I'd spoken with my John. *Will I ever hear his voice*—no, I wouldn't let my mind go there.

I forced my brain instead to focus on finding a parking spot. Finally! An older couple emerged from the hospital and walked toward a truck parked in one of the spots close to the front of the lot. I sighed out loud and pulled my car around to get into position to pull in as soon as they moved. But they didn't move. They were clearly taking their good old, sweet time.

What are they doing? Camping? I was ready to step out of my car and move their truck for them. Finally, I was in such a state that I rolled down my windows and yelled, "Are you going to move that truck before Jesus comes back?"

Just then, and probably fortunately for that couple, Cindy Rieger appeared out of the emergency room entrance and came running toward my car. She looked pale and her eyes were huge. "Here, I'll park the car for you," she told me, opening the driver's door. "I'll take care of this. You just go in."

I was so relieved to see her, I wanted to kiss her. But a wave of nausea hit me full force with a single realization: If she was coming outside to me, then whatever was inside that building wasn't good.

CHAPTER 4

A Mother's Prayer

The emergency room doors swung open wide to welcome the ambulance team and John. Typically paramedics will work on a person on-site for up to thirty minutes before transporting the victim to the hospital. They stayed on-site for less than half that time with John, however, because they were unable to attach the medical devices to him; his body remained so frozen they struggled to get anything to stick.

The paramedics had done all they could to provide lifesaving CPR to John, including inserting a breathing tube and IV line, with no results. Now it was the ER staff's turn.

Fortunately, the drive from Lake Ste. Louise to St. Joseph Hospital West was a brief five to six minutes. When the paramedics pushed John into the hospital, the ER team had been prepped and was waiting.

The EMTs handed John off to the medical team, who got him situated in Trauma Room A and immediately set to work.

John's body was cold and lifeless. His pupils were giant, fixed, and dilated from having no brain stem function. His temperature read eighty-eight degrees—ten degrees below a person's normal body core temperature of 98.6

and ten degrees into full-on hypothermia. As they attached his bloated, water-logged body to the monitors, Dr. Kent Sutterer and Dr. Nancy Bauer, along with a team of nurses, respiratory technicians, a pharmacist, and a half dozen other trauma care personnel saw with their eyes what they already knew: John Smith was dead—and had been dead for at least thirty minutes.

The monitors didn't blip, beep, or whine. They were simply silent, showing no pulse, no breath, no heartbeat. No signs of life.

No, no, no! Dr. Sutterer thought as he commanded the team to start CPR and grabbed a defibrillator with the paddles.

"Clear!" he said as he stepped toward John with the paddles and shocked his chest.

He quickly looked at the monitors again.

Nothing.

They began forcing oxygen into his body, along with the necessary heated IV fluids to warm his blood and organs, while trying to remove the lake water that had saturated every pore.

He directed a nurse to start John on epinephrine, hoping that the drug would be more successful in starting John's heart. The pharmacist readied the dosage and offered the syringe to a nurse, who stabbed John in the thigh. Nothing. "Let's up the dose and do it again." Typically, they would give two doses of the drug. Anything beyond that rarely proved successful. John received eight.

Dr. Sutterer's daughter, Anna, was John's age. In fact, they were classmates (although he didn't know that at the time). He knew only that he could not let this young man so full of promise expire on his watch. He had every life-saving medical prescription available to him. But he was not God. He could not bring a dead body back to life—and no medical intervention could change that reality.

"Let's get the Bair Hugger on him," he told the staff. They covered John's body with a forced-air warming device, like a blow dryer, to bring his temperature back into normal range, hoping that would help shock his system into restarting. But all of his organs had shut down. His body slowly rose in temperature but offered no other response.

After about twenty minutes of intensive CPR, Dr. Sutterer looked at John's temperature. There's a saying in emergency medicine: *They're not dead until they're warm and dead.* In other words, Dr. Sutterer needed John's body to come out of a frozen state, show no signs of life, and then he could officially give the word. His body was now lingering around ninety-five degrees.

Dr. Bauer, watching what was going on, broke the silence. "What's your goal temperature?"

Dr. Sutterer knew she was basically asking what he considered "warm and dead" so they could make the pronouncement. Dr. Sutterer finally had to admit the truth aloud. "This is it. He's up to ninety-five. I doubt if he's going to get any warmer, and he has shown absolutely no signs of coming back." With a sigh and feeling the heartbreak of a dad, Dr. Sutterer looked at the clock on the wall.

"His mother is on the way," a nurse said as she entered the room.

Dr. Sutterer nodded and stepped away from John. Time of death is time of death. The fact that I was on my way should have made no difference. But for some reason, his spirit felt unsettled about officially calling it, as though something was nudging him to wait. So without understanding why, he made the unusual decision not to call time of death until I had the chance to say my final good-byes.

Dr. Sutterer glanced over at Keith Terry, a twenty-something technician and a gargantuan man of about 280 pounds, standing at six feet seven inches. Keith was the one who had been giving John CPR. "Let's keep working."

Keith immediately went back to performing CPR in earnest while they waited for me to arrive. Only, Keith wasn't interested in just marking time. He was determined to get John's body to respond.

He pumped and pounded on John's chest, working his frame and maneuvering on and around my son. "Oh no, you don't," he told John over and over.

"You are not going to die on me." John was Keith's first adolescent patient, and Keith wasn't about to have a fourteen-year-old ruin his good CPR record.

But with each push and count and forced breath in, the monitor continued to show nothing but a flatline.

"I'm John Smith's mother. I'm here!" I said as soon as the sliding doors of the ER's visitor's entrance opened. I barely passed through them when a tall, heavyset firefighter with a thick crop of reddish-blond hair approached me. The shiny name tag pinned to his chest said, JEREMEY HOLLRAH.

"I'm waiting for you," he said. "Come with me." He smiled tightly. I think he was trying to comfort me, but it came off more as a grimace.

This can't be good, I thought. *The firefighters stuck around?* I swallowed hard, sniffed, and told myself to hold it together.

I barely registered the waiting area to my left filled with soon-to-be patients and their families as the firefighter directed me to the right and through the locked double doors into the emergency room hallway. On the right side, sliding glass doors for each separate room spanned the length of the hall-way. I glanced around, wondering which bed John was in. Instead, we made it perhaps ten feet when Jeremey turned left into a small closet of a private consultation room. The beige walls were stark except for a single crucifix that hung mournfully above several guest chairs.

I looked questioningly at Jeremey. Why was I in this room? Where was my son? Why did I have to wait?

Jeremey offered no answers or explanations as he said simply, "They'd like you to wait in here."

As soon as I nodded my agreement, Jeremey turned and exited the room, leaving me alone.

My heart thumped wildly against my chest and my knees grew weak. I dropped into a chair and clenched and unclenched my fists as I continued to pray. *Lord, please. Please, don't take my son. Oh, God. Oh, Jesus. You can't take John. Please, please. Oh, God, please. Let him be okay.*

I began to shake and I closed my eyes and willed myself not to pass out, not to vomit, not to start screaming at the top of my lungs.

Within a couple minutes, a slightly stooped, very thin and frail, five-foot-nothing nun stepped into the room. Donned in her gray-and-white habit, she looked to be in her sixties. Her face registered concern and her eyes glowed with compassion.

"Oh, honey, I'm just so sorry," she said in the kindest and sweetest tone. She sat in a chair next to me and took my hand in hers.

My eyes filled with tears and I inhaled deeply. *Lord, please don't let him die*, I prayed silently over and over. *Please do not let him die.*

After another few moments, Joseph Britain and his wife, Rebecca, popped their heads into the room. Joseph was the music pastor at our church, First Assembly Church in St. Peters. As soon as my eyes locked with theirs, they slowly entered and sat quietly with me.

What about John? Why was I still stuck in this cramped room? An overwhelming urge to scream rose up within me again, and I fought to maintain some semblance of control. My prayers became sobs to God.

I've heard about these scenes. I've seen them in plenty of movies. But never would I have imagined that the one sitting in a hospital waiting room and needing consolation would be me. I didn't want their pity, I didn't even want their words of comfort. I yearned for—*I needed*—their prayers.

As footsteps approached the room, I held my breath, hoping it would be someone from the medical staff to give me information. But each time, the footsteps found their way into other rooms, leaving us waiting, wondering. I thought about Brian, willing him to arrive soon. I knew he was rushing to get there, it just seemed to take too long.

Another ten minutes passed, and Jeremey finally reentered the room. "You can come back now."

It had been almost forty minutes since Cindy had given me the news. Now I rose slowly, desperate for an update but fearful of what that update might be. As a group, we exited the room, turned left, and followed Jeremey halfway down the hall, where we turned left again by the nurses' station. I sensed rather than saw their looks of concern and sadness. We passed another room and another room. At the end of the hallway, outside a doorway by the ambulance entrance to the ER, I saw a half-dozen first responders all milling around. They were quiet and seemed uneasy. Finally, when we reached them, we turned left into Trauma Room A.

The room was packed. About twenty medical personnel were there, looking fatigued and dejected. I spotted Cindy Rieger off to the side. She must have parked my car and headed straight for this room. That must have meant that her son was okay. Then my eyes landed on the gurney straight ahead of me against the far wall. Medical equipment hung from the walls and a large spotlight device dangled over the bed. John's body lay very still and was covered with tubes and blankets, and all I could see were two ashen gray feet.

A nurse, Alex Gibbons, stood at the head of the bed, squeezing a big black bag, which I assumed was forcing air into John's mouth and lungs. She didn't glance at me, keeping her concentrated focus on my son. The monitors were there but strangely silent. But it was the giant of a man with wide shoulders and bulging muscles intensely performing CPR on John who caught my attention. Keith Terry. His face was fiery red as perspiration dripped off of him. The front of his smock and under his arms were soaked. He didn't slow down for a second.

They found the biggest guy in the hospital to do CPR on my son to crush him, I thought. I knew under normal circumstances CPR is one of the most brutal things someone can do to a person. Oftentimes, in an effort to resuscitate someone, the administrator will inadvertently break ribs, bruise the chest, and essentially beat the person to a pulp. If the lake water didn't kill John, I was afraid this guy probably would.

Jeremey led me to a chair about halfway into the room and encouraged me to sit. The nun stood behind me and placed her hands on my shoulders. I sensed Cindy step beside the nun. Within moments, Mary Sander, Josh's mom, entered the room and squatted next to me. She placed her hand on my arm. The support from these women warmed and comforted me as much as it could. I appreciated their presence. But I didn't want to be there! I didn't want to need comforting. I didn't want my son lying lifeless in this room. With a steady stream of tears washing over my face and dropping onto my chest, I sat quietly and watched Keith determinedly work. Time seemed to stop, as though the minutes didn't matter anymore. I could vaguely hear the ambient noises of others in the room.

Lord, I need You right now. I need You more than anything right now.

It was too surreal, and I couldn't stop crying. *Those feet…they don't look right. Oh God, please don't let him die. Lord, not my son. Don't take my son.*

To my left I caught a glimpse of a bald man in a white coat pacing back and forth and staring at me. I decided to ignore him, as I kept my eyes glued to Keith and John's gray feet peeking out from under the large blanket.

Finally the man stepped next to me and squatted. He placed his hand gently on my knee. "I'm Dr. Sutterer," he said calmly and kindly. He inhaled deeply and paused uncomfortably. Then he quietly continued, as though he were going to say something else, but then changed his mind. "You can go up and talk to your son."

That's strange, I thought. His comment threw me. I was expecting this doctor to give me news, update me on the situation, tell me what else they were doing to help John.

I wiped my eyes and nodded hesitantly. Then I rose.

One step. I swallowed hard.

Another step. Keith and Alex stayed focused on their CPR work—pumping and pushing and counting.

Another step and I stood at the foot of John's bed. I could barely see his face; it was covered with a breathing mask and tubes. The blanket and Bair Hugger covered everything else, with tubes and wires coming out from underneath and winding their way to a half-dozen different machines.

I reached out my hands and placed them on John's feet. They were like ice.

In that moment I knew I had to be desperate with my Lord. I had to get a hold of God and get a hold of Him fast.

In my Bible study group we were working through Beth Moore's *Believing God*. In it Beth encourages Christians to embrace the faith statement "I believe God is who He says He is, and I believe He can do what He says He can do." I knew that the Holy Spirit had raised Christ Jesus from the dead and that the power that was there was also available to us, God's children.

All of a sudden, everyone and everything in that room faded away and it was just me and John and God. With a voice that I thought was quiet, but that actually bellowed through the room, down the hallway, and throughout the entire emergency room, I declared, "I believe in a God who can do miracles! Holy Spirit, I need You right now to come and breathe life back into my son!"

I sobbed an exhale and closed my eyes.

And in that instant, I heard the sound of a miracle.

Beep . . . beep . . . beep . . .

John's heart monitor—and John's heart—sprang back to life.

CHAPTER 5

The Most Beautiful Sound in the World

W e've got a pulse. We've got a pulse!"

Everyone in the room sprang into action as the heart monitor started its rhythmic beat.

And my knees gave out.

I stumbled backward toward the chair and dropped into it.

John had been in the water for close to thirty minutes, under the water for more than twenty minutes, had received CPR for about forty-three minutes, and had been dead for more than an hour. My son was dead and then . . . he *wasn't* dead!

The silence and heaviness of the room had lifted, replaced with a steady buzz. Commands shouted out, sobs heaved, and stunned gasps echoed. Everyone in the room was shocked. God was in that room, He had heard a desperate mother's plea, and He breathed life back into my boy.

Dr. Sutterer came back over to me. His face was pale and wore an astonished look. I think it matched everyone's face there!

"Once we get him stable, we can't care for him here," he explained. "We'll need to airlift him to Cardinal Glennon. My staff will get the paperwork together for you to sign to okay that."

I could see his lips moving. I could hear his voice. But nothing registered in my brain. I sat dazed and wide-eyed as he continued to speak. I opened my mouth but nothing came out. It felt like time had sped up from zero to a hundred, and I just couldn't keep up.

A nurse stepped over to me and suggested that we move back to the consultation room so she could talk to me privately about next steps and the logistics of the life flight. I nodded, still feeling foggy, as though I'd just witnessed the most surreal movie I'd ever seen.

Back to the consultation room we went, where she began to explain the reasons for the move and the details of the helicopter ride that would move John the forty miles from St. Joseph West to Cardinal Glennon Children's Medical Center, where he could receive better treatment.

As I listened, I choked up.

"If they ask me to ride in that chopper," I told her, "the answer is no. Oh no. No, no, no, no. I don't want to do that." The thought of flying in some contraption that could crash was too overwhelming for me. No, I couldn't do that. I wouldn't do that. No, thank you very much.

"Mrs. Smith?" Another nurse had popped her head into the room. "Would you come back down the hall with me for a moment? Dr. Sutterer has a question for you."

I stood immediately and followed, grateful to get back to my son. I became so consumed, though, with the possibility of having to ride in a helicopter that I informed that nurse en route, "I would prefer not to ride in the helicopter." She simply nodded her understanding.

Dr. Sutterer stepped out of the room and saw me just as I made it to the nurse's station. "What do you know about the appliance he has in his mouth?" He was referring to a dental piece John wore on the roof of his mouth to separate his back teeth.

I was so relieved they weren't asking me to ride in the helicopter that I blurted out, "The only thing I know about it is that it cost seventeen hundred dollars, and you can take it out of his mouth if you need to."

Everybody in the emergency area laughed. Well, that's all I *did* know about it.

As I thought about what this poor kid had just endured, though, I felt ashamed. *If my son can go through this and go through the horror of drowning, I can ride in that helicopter.*

In the flurry of activity I didn't notice that our church's children's pastor, Rob Purcell, had arrived, followed by Brian, my son Charles, and my daughter-in-law Krista. John's room was already so packed that I'm still not sure how we all squeezed in, but we managed. I looked at them, extremely grateful for their presence, but I was unable to say anything because by this point people began to swarm around me, handing me paperwork to sign. Everything looked so official and filled with legalese. More and more papers found their way into my hands—everything from insurance forms to permissions to airlift forms. They all blended in, and I had no idea what all I was filling out or signing. I autographed so many sheets, my fingers started to cramp.

Soon the pilot entered the room and brought more papers for me to sign.

"I've changed my mind," I told him, assuming they had informed him of my initial response not to ride along. "I'm going to ride in the chopper with my son."

He looked confused, and then with wide eyes and a furrowed brow, he announced, "Oh, there's no way. We aren't going to have room hardly for the stuff that we need now."

Relief flooded my spirit and I burst out, "Thank you, Jesus!"

My dazed brain began to wake back up and I was ready to get moving. *Let's get him to Cardinal Glennon and do what we need to do to get him up and back home,* I thought. To my mind, the work was done. God had brought my son back to life, he had finished the work, and that was that.

With the team prepping John for transport, and with our church pastors and friends already alerting others in our church community about the news, we all headed out to the parking lot.

I was in no shape to drive, and neither was Brian, who seemed shell-shocked by the news, so Charles offered to take us to Cardinal Glennon. I hopped in the front seat next to my son, while Brian and Krista got into the back, and off we went. Like a rocket.

I'd barely clicked the seat belt into its holder when Charles whipped out of the parking lot and zoomed into traffic. Even for a holiday, driving in rush-hour traffic was no easy task. From Interstate 70, we took a short ride on Interstate 170 and then turned onto Interstate 64, a main artery to St. Louis, which is normally bumper-to-bumper with heavy traffic. Charles slammed his foot down on the accelerator and refused to ease up. He was determined to beat the helicopter to its destination. If we'd traveled any faster, we would have been airborne as well. For forty minutes, we endured heart-pounding, whiplashing adventure as Charles whipped and weaved around traffic. Stop-and-go, bumper-to-bumper, was only a challenge to Charles as he fought to keep the vehicle at a consistently fast speed.

At one point, during a particularly scary maneuver, I stole a glance toward the backseat. Brian's eyes were so big and his face so pale, I thought we might need to usher *him* into the emergency room once we arrived. Krista was cringing—but not from the driving. Brian was holding her hand and crushing it.

Dear Lord, why didn't I take the chopper ride?

After the scariest ride I've ever taken in my life, Charles pulled up to the front door of Cardinal Glennon, where we almost fell out in our desire to escape from the car. We rushed through the doors and to the information desk.

"I'm John Smith's mom. He was airlifted here from St. Joseph West."

The volunteer smiled and, as though she had all the time in the world, casually typed into her computer. With a slightly furrowed brow, she looked at me and apologetically stated that he had not arrived yet.

No, how can that be? We left him forty minutes ago! I thought, as concern grew in the pit of my stomach. *That flight should have taken mere minutes.*

Something was wrong. Terribly wrong.

CHAPTER 6

A Heartbeat—but Nothing Else

John's heart had restarted, but the rest of his body had yet to get the message that he was alive. The medical team at St. Joseph West worked hard to ensure that his body *would* get that message. Yet some—including Dr. Sutterer—believed that they were just transferring him to another hospital to die.

Fortunately, their job wasn't to worry about that; their concern was to do everything within their human power to help his body recover. That was exactly what they did. They continued pumping his lungs and blood with oxygen, clearing out his body of the lake and other toxins, and now re-lowering his core temperature again in order to protect his organs.

They finally had him stabilized enough to load him on the helicopter, but almost immediately after that, John's body went into major failure again, so Dr. Sutterer rushed out to the chopper where he worked to keep John alive for the takeoff and ride.

Dr. Sutterer thought it would be another miracle if John even made it into the air alive.

★　★　★

Nearly three hours after the accident, John was ushered into Cardinal Glennon's emergency room. Pediatric critical care physician Jeremy Garrett had the updates on John's condition and held out little hope for his survival. He looked over the reports from St. Joseph West: CPR in progress forty-three minutes, eight epinephrine doses to get John's heart started, a weakened heartbeat that returned, lab work that showed terribly low body pH, massive metabolic acidosis, and no signs of neurologic function. He sighed heavily and shook his head. Realistically, the chances of John making it were slim. Dr. Garrett was an international hypothermia and drowning expert. He taught and lectured on it. He had worked on multiple cases. And *no one had ever survived* this kind of catastrophic experience to this extent before.

To Dr. Garrett, the *one* good thing John had going for him was that he had drowned in cold water. Dr. Garrett had worked on and heard about a lot of victims of that type of accident who'd recovered well—of course, none of them had been dead for more than an hour. Plus all of those victims had survived because of a special combination of factors—none of which John had—except that he had fallen into winter water. Even that wasn't good enough, though, since the water was cold but not *cold enough*. In other words, the water needed to be at a low enough temperature that it could essentially chill the brain before it froze the blood circulation to the brain. That way, John's brain could preserve its function. But that didn't happen. The lake temperature hovered around forty degrees, and John's body size was much larger than the typical survivor's, so John's blood flow to his brain had stopped before his brain froze enough to protect itself.

Dr. Garrett had to admit that the mere fact that John's heart had restarted after more than an hour *was* miraculous, but that simply wasn't enough to get John on the road to life. The odds were 99 percent against him. Too many challenges and issues faced my son's body. They were already six hours into the body's breakdown, and he knew that the first six to twelve hours were the real test of time. *If* John could survive twelve hours, then the next challenge was to get him to sixteen hours. But with such little brain stem function and with no neurological activity...

It was as though John were standing in the middle of a rope bridge high above a rocky gorge, and all the ropes had frayed apart except for one thin strand.

But John had a heartbeat—and that was something—and so with the overwhelming challenge ahead of him, Dr. Garrett rolled up his sleeves and got to work on my boy.

They did a number of CAT scans to see the condition of his lungs, organs, and brain.

They removed the breathing tube and the manual ventilation and transferred him over to a mechanical ventilator that breathed for him. But the staff had to keep adjusting the oxygen levels, because John's body was having a catastrophic inflammatory response to his initial and continuing injuries. He was swelling; fluid, acids, and toxins were building up in his system, and he had little ability to fight them off. Since being injured doesn't help the rest of the body get better, the team faced the real possibility of cascading failures.

Even though John's heart was beating, it was not supporting itself. It wasn't strong, so he still had inadequate blood and oxygen circulation and blood pressure—or what they called profound circulatory shock, which can cause death. So the team placed him on a continuous adrenaline infusion to help it do better than just limp along. John's heart needed to sprint.

Because of his heart's inability to push blood out with the force it needed, acid had built up in John's tissues, and his vital organs were unable to work—and each of those separately could cause death.

John's organs and tissues were so severely impaired that his muscle cells began bursting open and dumping their contents and acid into his bloodstream. (This death of muscle fibers is called rhabdomyolysis.) All of this "garbage debris" was flowing into his injured kidneys. They couldn't handle or keep up with the excess, so the kidneys' tubules, which filter out the toxins, started to plug up. That meant the kidneys were moving into renal failure. Another potential cause of death.

As the muscle cells exploded, they also released large amounts of minerals, which created something similar to a medical condition in oncology called tumor lysis syndrome. He had high levels of potassium, phosphorus, uric acid, calcium, and nitrogen. With these free-floating minerals no longer contained within cells, they obstructed vital passages, such as within the kidneys, which could cause acute kidney failure, seizures, cardiac arrhythmias, and death.

John remained comatose with no brain activity. He showed only minor neurological function in that he was able to breathe a little, but Dr. Garrett considered it rudimentary breathing—not the type that could support regular life. Basically it's the body's last-ditch efforts to deliver oxygen to vital organs before death. Every other neurological function—strength, coordination, reflexes, sensation—was gone.

Then there was the lake water that had filled John's lungs. Most drowning victims typically don't inhale water. They die by asphyxiating themselves—in other words, their air passages reflexively shut tight to keep water from entering. Or even if they do inhale water, it doesn't take much to massively harm them, so the air remaining in their lungs will keep them afloat. John, however, was on the bottom of the lake—and his lungs *had* filled with water.

But even pumping out that water didn't markedly make a difference, because he was also struggling with acute respiratory distress syndrome. John's lungs, filling with his own body's fluid from the inflammation, had put him into massive or acute pulmonary edema. Basically, the membranes and cells in his lungs began "weeping" plasma contents (fluid) into the lungs' air sacs. It accumulated and impaired John's ability to breathe and the body's ability to handle vital gas exchanges (oxygen to carbon dioxide). So even though the medical staff was forcing oxygen into his lungs, very little air was actually getting where it needed to go. And because the heart was beating so weakly, it was unable to remove fluids and carbon dioxide from the lung and blood circulation. And this, too, could cause death.

As Dr. Garrett considered their options with this massive fluid and gas buildup, he and the team weighed putting John on extracorporeal membrane oxygenation (ECMO), also known as extracorporeal life support. It's a continuous bypass machine that removes blood from a person's body to filter out the carbon dioxide, thus providing pure oxygen to the red blood cells. This treatment is considered a last-ditch effort to treat someone with heart and lung failure. Someone like my John. But as they discussed this option, they realized that it carried with it a huge risk of John bleeding to death, since they'd have to put him on blood thinners in order to keep any of the blood from clotting as it moved through the process.

"No," Dr. Garrett finally decided. "I'm worried that we would do more harm than good. His chances of survival are already tenuous enough. Let's not add to it."

Potentially bleeding to death was a very real concern with John because his blood system was already severely debilitated. His blood wasn't coagulating or thickening properly. Normally, a person's blood clotting system works by having a bunch of enzymes standing guard, ready to go if something triggers them. For instance, if you get a paper cut, those enzymes are alerted and rush to the area, where they form clots to stop the bleeding. Because it's confined to a small area, your system is able to create new enzymes and white blood cells for the next round of trouble.

John's blood coagulation system was off balance and had disrupted his white blood cell production. His blood and his immune system went into a huge inflammatory response to all the different layers of injury, but at the same time they were weakened to all the bacteria that live on and around the body and some that were in the lake water. John's white blood cells and enzymes had been triggered by the inflammatory response (the muscle cells ripping apart, the buildup of fluid and gases, the acid and toxins spreading through his body, not to mention the infection caused by the bacteria from a man-made, self-contained lake filled with silt, mud, duck excrement, and any other number of disgusting elements). His body was using the white blood cells faster than he could make them, which caused his blood to become neutropenic—his blood platelets were getting destroyed, his red blood cells were bursting apart, and his blood was struggling with coagulation. His white blood cells simply couldn't keep up. They were like a small battalion of soldiers who get ambushed by an entire army. You fight the good fight, but you can't take them all out. And eventually death results.

But there were also the blood pH levels. A normal blood pH is neutral and runs between a 7.35 and 7.45 level. The lower the pH, the more acidic the blood is. John's pH was at 6.5—and that was after he was getting oxygen. That meant he had too much acid—or lactic acidosis—brought on by heart failure, liver failure, and prolonged lack of oxygen. That also meant that he could not survive long. Anything below 6.8 is considered incompatible with life.

Another system that needed immediate attention was his gastrointestinal tract, which was swollen from the presence of the lake water. But worse, when blood stopped flowing into his intestines, the tissues there began to die, causing intestinal ischemia. Everything that was in his bowels, including dead tissues from the intestine walls, were breaking down and decomposing, ready to spew out of his body. Another issue that can cause death.

With his liver also suffering from lack of blood and oxygen flow and in acute failure, John got ischemic hepatitis (or shock liver). And since his pancreas lacked blood flow, he was developing acute pancreatitis.

John's digestive tract was a mess, and digestive enzymes, which should remain in that tract, weren't. They had entered the bloodstream, another potential way to damage the lungs and the linings of the blood cells.

So every part of his body that contained blood vessels (that would be everywhere) was severely sick. All the cells that work as natural barriers and linings were severely sick.

As the team worked, John's body took another bad turn. The heart was still slowly and weakly pumping blood, but now his blood pressure soared. As his lungs tried to combat his sick cells, they responded with pulmonary hypertension—his blood pressure in the arteries in that organ went off the charts. The team put him on monitors for beat-to-beat measurement of his blood pressure, gave him medication to try to combat it, and hoped for the best. But everything they did—all the medications, monitors, machines—weren't helping John's body to respond positively to this catastrophe.

We have a heartbeat and the circulation going, Dr. Garrett thought as they kept at their lifesaving work. *But can we continue it? Can this boy's body survive all of this? If it does, will there be a brain? Will this kid be any semblance of who he was before the accident?*

He feared he knew the answers. And they were all no. He'd had many drowning victims whom he'd saved from death, but they were never the same. They never woke up, never interacted.

We hear great stories of patients in comas who wake up months later and lead wonderfully normal lives—teens who go to their prom, who play basketball, who fall in love and live to a ripe old age. This wouldn't be John, Dr. Garrett believed. Those patients had suffered from traumatic brain injuries where just portions of the brain were hurt and other portions were never injured and never stopped getting blood flow.

One bodily failure was enough to bring death. John had them all. Every organ was in catastrophic failure. *Every cell* in his body was without oxygen long enough that his heart stopped because it lacked air. And then when his heart stopped, it was without blood flow. Without blood flow, *no* organ can survive. His heart, his organs, his brain, his *everything*, were overdrawn on oxygen. Even with all of Dr. Garrett's expertise and his team's medical knowledge and state-of-the-art equipment, they couldn't get those oxygen-deprived cells out of debt. No one could.

CHAPTER 7

"I've Heard Enough!"

My husband, Brian, my son Charles, my daughter-in-law Krista, and I sat in the emergency waiting room, waiting an achingly, eternally long time for word that John had arrived. Eventually after about forty minutes, the ER receptionist informed us that he'd made it. The staff was working on him and prepping him for a move up to the Pediatric Intensive Care Unit, and the doctor wanted to talk with us.

After securing our visitor badges, we got onto the elevator and hit the button marked "2." Crowded into the small space, I felt agitated and concerned. John's heart had started beating! So why the delay in getting here? What was the problem?

I know You've got this, Lord. You brought him back to life. I mean, seriously! You restarted my boy's heart! There's nothing You can't do! So keep it up, God. Thank You, thank You, thank You. You've got this. You've got this!

The elevator doors opened to showcase a brightly lit hallway leading to the PICU waiting room. As we walked quietly down the hall, I spotted a painted wooden arrow next to painted large gray rocks, grass, and happy yellow flowers dotting the wall. The arrow said simply, PICU, and pointed the way to the waiting room's entrance. Inside the waiting room, it looked like a wonderland of wooded creatures, with hot air balloons floating peacefully over rocky mountains and meadows covered with green grass and pine trees. I felt like I was standing in Colorado rather than in midwestern Missouri. In the middle of the room, next to some tables and chairs, stood a life-sized animated scene right out of a Disneyland adventure ride. A giant chipmunk carrying an over-sized camping backpack and dressed in a red hat, red jacket, blue jeans, and hiking boots stood with a tall walking stick and smiled his greeting. Just below him on a tiered rock formation stood a happy mountain goat with purple hooves, blue eye shadow, and a pink bow above her right ear. Chairs lined the walls, and the room was designed in such a way that you could find a corner or cubby area and get some privacy.

There would be no privacy for us, however, because by now, about twenty-five people—including John's classmates, church friends, and pastors—had arrived and congregated there. Thanks to my call to Brad Carriger, made when I was first on my way to St. Joseph West, he'd alerted anyone and everyone about John's situation. Many of them were here or on their way to offer prayer and support. But they didn't know what exactly had happened to John. Initially nobody knew he'd fallen through the ice or that he'd died. They knew only that he'd been involved in an accident and it was serious. Slowly the word seeped out that he'd drowned. Shock and fear registered on every face I looked at in that room.

But scanning over the crowd, looking at these people who loved John and my family—our faith community doing what the church has been called to do, to weep and mourn with one another, to bear one another's burdens—I felt such peace and strength. They didn't know yet that John had died and come back to life. But *I* knew.

Lord, do Your thing, I prayed, filled with a sense of strength and sureness. I didn't care why John was late getting to the hospital. I knew everything was going to be okay.

It was *going to be okay*.

We greeted as many people as we could, hugging and thanking each one for being there. And as grateful as I felt for their presence, my mind shifted to the doctor. When would *he* arrive? When would he give us the news that John had made a remarkable recovery and they were just keeping him in PICU overnight to watch him?

Finally at around 4:00 p.m., after we'd been in the waiting room about thirty minutes, a door opened on the other side, opposite the hallway entrance. A nurse walked in and started scanning the crowd. I tugged Brian's arm and, like a wide receiver who's just caught the football and is racing toward the end zone, I made my way to her.

"Mrs. Smith? Mr. Smith?" she said.

"Yes," I answered for both of us.

"Dr. Garrett, our pediatric critical care physician, would like to speak with you. Would you come with me? We have a conference room just outside here where you can talk."

I nodded. Charles and Krista followed us as we walked through the door that she'd entered and immediately turned right into a room filled with a long conference table.

She let us know that they had moved John into a PICU room and were getting him settled, so we should be able to see him soon. "Dr. Garrett is just finishing up with him and he'll be here in just a few moments."

We filed down the left-hand side of the table and each took a seat. Brian sat nearest the head of the table, then I sat next to him, followed by Charles and Krista. Brian looked dazed and unsure, as though he didn't really want to meet with Dr. Garrett. Charles and Krista were crying and upset. I just wanted to get it over with so I could see my son.

True to the nurse's word, within only a few moments, a dark-haired man with glasses and wearing a shirt and tie but no formal white medical jacket walked into the room. "I'm Dr. Garrett," he said softly and calmly.

You've got this, Lord, I prayed again, reminding God of what He'd already done.

He took a seat at the head of the table, next to Brian, and folded his hands together. "I have good news and not-so-good news," Dr. Garrett began. "What do you want to hear first?"

I didn't wait for anybody else to speak. It was as though it were just the doc and me in that room. "I'm a bottom-line girl," I told him. "I want the bottom line."

"Okay," he stated, still calm, still soft-spoken. He looked me straight in the eye, inhaled deeply, and stated, "Your son has no brain activity, only rudimentary brain stem function. His heartbeat is very weak and he is breathing, but barely. He's been without oxygen for more than an hour. We're doing everything we can, but realistically, it's doubtful that he will survive through the night. He's gone into catastrophic multisystem organ failure, which can bring on such things as seizures and death. His body is filled with bacteria that his cells can't fight. The first sixteen hours are crucial if there's even a hope that he survive." He paused and inhaled again. "If he *does* survive...he will be severely neurologically impaired." In other words, he was telling us that my son was either going to die—again—or he would be a vegetable.

With each phrase, I found myself getting more and more tense. This was not the conversation we were supposed to be having. *Oh buddy, you are wrong,* I thought at him. *This is not how this is playing out.*

"How far do you want us to go?" he said and then looked at Brian and me as he waited for us to respond.

And respond I did.

"How far do you want this to go?" I said, my anger at the boiling point. Dr. Garrett clearly didn't understand that when John's heart started, God had already done the work. My God had healed my son, and now the rest of his body just needed to catch up. I was livid that he was doubting what God had done.

His kind, quiet, gentle way of breaking the news to us felt arrogant and cold to me—because he was saying things I did not want to hear. I didn't care that he was some expert doctor. I didn't care that the previous year he'd been awarded doctor of the year in the St. Louis region. I. Did. Not. Care.

How dare you question what my God has already done? I thought. I expected this doctor to be up to speed to where I was. What was his problem?

I was so angry I was ready to cold-cock him. With a clenched jaw, fire rising in my cheeks, and tears of anger welling in my eyes, I slid my chair back, stood, and leaned over the table until my face was a ruler length away from his. I had heard enough, and I was done hearing any more. He asked me how far I wanted him to go, and I wanted him to have not a shadow of a doubt how far I wanted him to go.

"I've been told that you're the best," I stated firmly and loudly. "So this is what I want you to do. I want you to do your best in what you know to do, and my God will do the rest."

His eyes gave a momentary glint of shock.

"And no more of this death stuff," I continued, still in his face. "None of this negative talk will be spoken around him *ever* in his room. We will only speak life." I stood up straight, grabbed my purse, and without giving him a chance to respond, I marched out.

CHAPTER 8

We Will Only Speak Life

I was fuming and crying the tears of a woman who was ready to take on the world and rip it to shreds. I knew what I *knew*. And it didn't matter what the entire medical community believed. They were wrong. I didn't want to hear how bad they believed John was. I didn't want those words of death spoken about or over him. We would only speak words of life.

I'd lived a lot of my life allowing negative words to cover me. But no more. Scripture tells us that "death and life are in the power of the tongue" (Prov. 18:21). What we say is what we believe. And when we verbalize something, we give it power. If I said that John wasn't going to survive, then I believed it. The Bible says from the heart the mouth speaks (Matt. 15:18). And my mouth—and everyone else's around John—was going to speak only the truth of who God is.

As I stormed out of that conference room and back into the PICU waiting room, I was surprised to see our senior pastor, Jason Noble, standing nearby, looking concerned and anxious. Several other pastors had arrived earlier, but I hadn't seen him before when we'd been in the waiting room. I felt a source of strength flow through my body. A spiritual partner and warrior had arrived.

Pastor Jason had been at our church, First Assembly Church of St. Peters, only six months, and he was just the age of my older sons, but he had already cemented a place in my heart as a great spiritual leader. During the previous fall, I'd gone to him for counsel about some challenges I was having. Pastor Jason had listened and then shared hard truths with me, which changed my life, my marriage, my attitude, my faith. He hadn't patronized me. He hadn't tickled my ear with niceties. He'd respected and honored and loved me enough to tell me difficult things that hurt to hear, but that I knew I needed to heed. After that, I trusted him and knew that he loved and followed Jesus in a way that I wanted to love and follow Jesus.

As soon as people caught sight of me, the noise level hushed.

"I will not speak what we were just told by the doctor. But if all the pastors will come with me, we'll go back to John's room and pray."

I didn't know how much Pastor Jason and the other pastors knew of John's situation, but I was sure it couldn't have been much. His face turned determined as his jaw set. He nodded. "Okay," he said firmly. "We need to pray. Let's go. It's time."

My soul and spirit cheered. I had another fighter by my side. "This is not going to happen," I told him, to make sure he understood my stance. "John's outcome will *not* be what the doctor says."

"I agree," he told me. "It's not going to happen."

By this point Brian, Charles, and Krista were by my side, looking shell-shocked and uncertain of what to do next. They'd just experienced a surreal scene: An expert physician had just informed them that there was no hope for John, and their crazed wife and mom insisted—forcefully—that he was flat-out wrong. They were trying to come to grips and process everything. I wasn't. I'm not suggesting that I was better in my faith or a stronger person. I just knew what I knew. I had been in that room when John's heart started. They hadn't. I'd watched the Holy Spirit breathe life into my boy. They hadn't. I knew they needed to figure out where their faith stood. And frankly, I didn't have the time to wait on them to do that. I needed someone who was already up to speed and ready to go boldly before God's throne to plead our case and to stand on what we already knew to be true. And Pastor Jason was there, ready to go.

I turned back and pushed the security intercom button to the left of the door. As soon as the nurse responded, I informed her that I was John Smith's mother and that I wanted to go to his room. "I have my pastors with me and we're going to pray."

The door immediately buzzed, and I, along with Jason and five other pastors, stepped into the PICU and as a group headed to John's room. I was immensely grateful for this group of God-honoring men. Each one had a special relationship with our family and to have them all here, ready to pray over my son, meant the world to me.

There was Mark Shepard, John's former children's pastor, who had just had John at his house the previous week; Brad Riley, of Faith Chapel, whom my family has known for years (his daughter, Emma, is John's best friend); Al Edney, from Willet Road Church in St. Peters, and his dad, another of John's friends; Josh Cosby, our church's youth pastor; Rob Purcell, our current church's children's pastor, who had also been at St. Joseph West with us; and, of course, Pastor Jason.

A nurse met us halfway down the hall and offered to escort us to John's room. As we made our way, I couldn't help but notice the happy-blue ceiling covered with big, puffy white clouds. It was so cheerful, it felt more like we were walking into *Romper Room* than a hospital children's intensive care area.

We approached a glass-encased nurses' station and turned left. Three long sliding-glass doors down, she stopped in front of a corner room, number twelve. "This is John's."

I thanked her. "We will only speak life," I reiterated to the group. "This is not going down any other way." Then we descended on him.

I stepped up to his bed, put my hand in his, and looked at him. I knew he was in a coma, but the sight of him took my breath away. He was still an ashen gray-blue and his face was swollen so badly—even his eyes—that I could barely recognize him. It wasn't just that his eyes were shut tight because he was unconscious; they were unusually puffy.

He was wrapped in Arctic Sun wraps, because they were still keeping his temperature cool to ensure that his brain wouldn't swell. His arms, upper body, and legs were now exposed and I could see that they were scratched and ripped up from his battle with the ice shards. That sight alone stunned me. He had fought for his life, and that ice must have felt like glass scraping against him.

Then there were all the tubes and monitors. He had a clip on his thumb to monitor his heart rate. He had IVs in both arms giving him saline and numerous drugs. He had a central line, a deep big plastic tube in his groin area that measured pressures inside the heart and the vascular system. He had an arterial line, also in his groin, to measure his blood pressure as well as the heart's every beat. It also allowed the staff to draw samples of blood as it came out from the lungs to the body. He had a bladder catheter so they could follow his urine output hour to hour and know what the kidneys were making moment to moment, which also indirectly monitored cardiac function.

He wore a large, sturdy neck brace, since they feared he might also have neck injuries. The lower half of his face, except for his lips, was covered with breathing tubes, and those were attached to two giant tubes, the size of which could be used on astronauts—each was about the diameter of a half-dollar. They had a feeding tube down him as well. Essentially every place that he could have something in him, he had something in him.

I watched as the PICU nurse, Wendy Hof, hooked him up and checked his levels, and then I looked outside the large window at the far side of the room. Sunlight had fled this winter day, and a heavy darkness seemed to fill every space around us. It was time to pray.

As Wendy continued her work trying to get his levels stabilized and within normal ranges, the pastors inserted themselves into the mix and stood around his bed. I walked out to the hallway. I had battled fiercely, now I needed others to help me. The apostle James wrote, "Is anyone among you sick? Let him call for the elders of the church, and let them pray over him, anointing him with oil in the name of the Lord. And the prayer of faith will save the one who is sick, and the Lord will raise him up" (James 5:14–15). So that was exactly what we were going to do.

Brad and Jason stood at the head of John's bed, Brad on the right and Jason on the left, while the rest of the pastors took positions at his feet. I'm sure Wendy wasn't pleased that so many people had crammed into these tight quarters and were getting in her way, but at that point, we had more important business to attend to.

I began to pace the length of the glass sliding doors of his room and pray. Inside, Pastor Jason leaned over John and whispered into his ear, loud enough that the others could hear and agree.

"Lord, put the breath back in John's lungs. Just as what raised Adam out of the ground, just as with the creative power You used when You created the heavens and the earth..." He continued to pray about John's lungs, because we knew he was on a life-support mechanical ventilator, and with all the lake water and the bacteria in his body, he needed a miracle.

Then Jason turned toward the second thing that we knew was essential: that God would rewire, or reset, John's brain. John needed to recover completely, so Jason prayed that no neurological impairment would appear— nothing—and that John would not be a vegetable, but would in fact return to his full strength and abilities.

They were big prayers! But we serve an infinitely bigger and greater God!

Not long into our prayers, a nurse came to me, looking apologetic. "All our rooms are full and we really try to keep this hallway as cleared as possible. Would you mind going back into the room?"

"Of course." My goal wasn't to disrupt the other patients and their families, so I quietly entered the room as the pastors continued to raise John up to God. Since the room was cramped, I squeezed behind the pastors and took a seat on the day-bed couch against the far wall, and joined them in their prayers.

Not long after, while everyone was still praying, I felt a gentle touch on my shoulder. Nurse Wendy was standing over me, wearing a concerned expression.

"John's numbers are really fluctuating, and I'm struggling to get them into an acceptable range," she whispered to me. "He really needs to rest, so I think it would be best for everyone to clear out of the room. Maybe two people can stay, but other than that, we need to limit the number of people here."

Jason and Brad volunteered to remain to keep praying, and so with that assurance, I offered to go back to the waiting room with the other pastors. I took another look at my son. He was just so swollen! "Look at his eyes," I said to Jason. "Why are his eyes that swollen? That seems so odd to me." I exhaled deeply, then the pastors and I retraced our steps back down the hallway and passed the conference room where I'd had my run-in with Dr. Garrett.

I was still angry, but I did wonder if he'd ever had an experience like that before. *I bet I shocked the socks off of him*, I thought as I pushed open the door to the waiting room.

Only a little more than an hour had passed since I'd last been in this place. Where I'd left twenty-five people, now I could barely squeeze in. Teenagers and senior citizens, families and small groups were tucked into every crevice or seat. Many stood. The door to the outside hallway was opened and the overflow crowds were lined down the hall! Everywhere I looked people were gathered in small huddles praying or talking quietly. There must have been seventy-five to eighty people there. I breathed a heavy sigh of relief when I spotted my sister, Janice, and my brother-in-law, Don, and threw my arms around them. They'd gotten word, grabbed their dog, threw some clothes into a suitcase, hopped in their car, and drove four hundred miles from Xenia, Ohio. My son Tom and his wife, Jennifer, also made the long trip from Ohio and were there. After dropping off their dog at our house, they drove straight to the hospital.

The crowd looked at me expectantly and waited. Brian worked his way to my side. He looked pleadingly into my face for any news, any hope. I mustered up a smile to encourage him.

"Well, the doctor said...No," I told the group, "I am not going to say what the doctor said, because I'm not going to give Satan one more ounce of glory in this. I know that my God has raised my son from the dead, and he's going to be fine. And that's what we're going to go with."

Then I slowly made my way through the crowd, hugging and thanking as many people as I could. Many wanted more details, but all I would say is, "Our God is a big God, and He is at work. Now we need to do our part and pray, believing that God is who He says He is and that He will do what He says He *can* do."

I found myself becoming more and more frustrated, however. *First the doctor, and then these people?* I thought. They meant well. They had sacrificed their time to be with us and to offer comfort and support. But I kept overhearing the same conversation in hushed tones—especially parents to their children: "We'll pray, but let's not get our hopes up."

Finally, I could take it no more. Loudly, making sure the entire group could hear, I stated, "We are only going to speak life." And I meant it. I didn't want to hear one more negative word. Either we believed, or we didn't. It was that simple.

CHAPTER 9

Angels Standing Guard

As the evening wore on, the crowd in the waiting room dwindled back to about twenty-five people who opted to stay.

My sweet friend Melissa Fischer, a veterinarian who worked about fifteen minutes from Cardinal Glennon and a member of my Bible study group, had arrived and stuck close to me. As Janice, Melissa, and I were talking, I mentioned how swollen John's face was. "Even his eyes are swollen," I said.

Melissa scrunched up her face in thought. "Does he still have his contacts in?" she asked.

My jaw dropped. His contacts! I'd completely forgotten about those. And with everything else going on in John's body, I can't imagine anyone even stopped to consider that he might be wearing them. They might have frozen to his eyeballs. I shuddered to think about it.

"If they're still in, that could explain some of the swelling," she said.

I jumped up and grabbed the hospital phone to call Casey, the head PICU nurse. "I think part of the reason John's eyes are so swollen is that he's still got his contacts in."

"Oh, all that dirty lake water on those eyes!" she said. "We'll take care of that right away. Thanks for letting me know."

I sat in the waiting room for the next several hours while Jason and Brad remained with John. Later in the evening, I went back in to check on my son. I asked Brian if he was going to join me, but after a moment's hesitation, he declined. I think it was just too much for him to see his son in that condition. His pain was too overwhelming, so by remaining with others in the waiting room, he could pull strength from them to help him handle the grief.

I know, though, just because he wasn't in that room didn't mean he wasn't as invested in John's recovery as I was. Brian adores our son. They're buddies, and I think Brian simply felt lost. And afraid.

So I headed back. Brad was getting ready to leave, but Jason informed me, "I'm here with you, and we're going to keep praying." I needed to hear that, because even with the prayers—even with my firm belief that John was going to live—my son was still struggling. John's PICU night nurse, technicians, doctors, and a host of other medical staff were continually checking on his progress and trying to get him stabilized, something his body kept fighting against. Every fifteen minutes someone entered the room and adjusted or readjusted a tube, an IV bag, a monitor. His temperature was still in a controlled-hypothermia level. The monitor that measured his brain activity showed a line that still hugged the bottom of the screen.

I dragged a chair next to John's bed and stationed myself. I lifted his hand into mine and gently massaged, being careful not to put too much pressure where the ice had stabbed and scratched him.

"John, I'm here," I told him. "You're going to be okay. Your dad and I love you very much." I'd often heard that people in comas can still hear, so I wanted to make sure that John knew I was there and I wasn't going to leave him.

At one point, the nurse came in to take blood from the tube in John's groin, so she asked us to step out of the room. As soon as we cleared the doors, Jason turned to me. It was the first opportunity that we'd had for just the two of us to talk.

"Joyce, John *is* going to be all right."

"Yes, I know," I told him.

He shook his head as though I didn't fully understand. "When you were in the waiting room, and Brad and I stayed behind to pray, we started praying that the Holy Spirit would fill John's lungs."

I nodded. That was similar to what the group of pastors had been praying earlier.

"While we were praying that, something compelled me to look around the room." His eyes were bright with wonder and excitement. "I saw two angels next to each other standing guard. They were huge." He described them in detail—in a back corner were two angels in battle armor, carrying a sword and a shield and surrounded by faint white light. They stood floor to ceiling and, although he couldn't see their faces, he could tell they were looking at John. "I feel like the Lord is saying, *I've got this. These guys are going to be here. They're here to walk John to life.*"

For the second time this day, just as in St. Joseph West's ER, my legs began to give out. God was listening to the cries of His people and answering. If I'd been determined before, I was a thousand times more so now.

"When I turned back to John," he continued, "all of a sudden he took a breath—a *deep* breath—and opened his eyes! He breathed over the ventilator! Even the nurse noticed it and said, 'Whoa!' She told us that's typical with head trauma, that we'll see them open their eyes like that, but I'm telling you, I saw life in those eyes. I *saw* it!"

His words filled me with joy.

"The thing is, I've seen those angels once before."

"Really?" I was even more intrigued now.

"Yes, about two years ago, when I was pastoring in Port Angeles, Washington, I got a call from a lady whose eighty-five-year-old mom was in the hospital in a coma and dying. She had never known the Lord and only had a little time left to live. So this woman asked me to go and pray for her mother."

When Jason had arrived, he explained, the mom was completely gray, as if her body had already begun to shut down. So he leaned in and whispered to her, "You are standing on the edge of eternity. This is your last chance. Jesus loves you, and it's your time. You've got to make that decision. If you want to accept Jesus into your life right now, squeeze my hand." He felt a faint squeeze.

"When I turned around, those angels were standing in that room," he said.

"Angels like the ones you just saw?"

"Yes, exactly. And within several minutes, her toes grew pink, and then after another several minutes, her knees changed to pink."

"Life was coming back to her?" I asked, already knowing the answer.

"From the feet up. Within fifteen or so minutes, she was wide awake. All her vitals were back to normal. The nurses couldn't believe it. Within an hour, she was sitting up. She told me, 'I gave my life to the Lord. I love Jesus!' The next day she was well enough to go home with her daughter."

I smiled.

"God's got this."

"Oh yes, He does," I answered.

"But there's more," he continued, as though we were on a TV shopping network. "Then Brad and I started to pray over John, 'Lord, rewire that brain. Re-create it.' I was right by John's head, and I saw all these lights, thousands of them, rainbow colored, coming down through the ceiling and hovering over John's head, like a halo."

My eyes grew wide. I knew what he was going to say next.

"The best way I can explain it is that God was going *zzt-zzt-zzt*, just putting his brain back together. At that moment, John's eyes opened again and he kind of came off the bed."

"What do you mean, he came off the bed?"

"He lifted his shoulders completely off the bed," Jason said. "Again the nurse claimed that was involuntary, common for brain trauma. But it wasn't that. That was God."

I swallowed hard and told him that he definitely had seen those lights from

God. I knew this because, although Jason had no way of knowing, I'd seen those thousand points of rainbow lights several years before. A guy who had attended our church had throat cancer. We all prayed for him, and when he went for his checkup, the cancerous lump was gone. We all rejoiced, but his doctors wanted to go ahead and do radiation, just to be sure. So we started praying again. Well, one night while I was praying, I was envisioning him lying on the table during his radiation treatments and asking God to remove any and all trace of cancer. All of a sudden I saw all these little different-colored lights hovering over the top and around his head. I'd never had a vision like that before, but I was sure God had allowed me to see Him working through our prayers.

So I sent him a message and told him that I knew the Lord had healed him. That Sunday morning, he was in church and singing in the choir. He'd just been in the hospital with his throat devastated and he was back singing! When he walked off the platform to join his wife for the sermon, she was sobbing.

"What's wrong?" he asked her.

"When you were up in the choir," she said, "the Lord healed you. I saw all of these lights going off over your head, all these little shots of light."

She was right. The man had been healed. Now John had those lights over him, and angels standing guard. He was going to be okay.

But John's long, hard battle was far from over.

CHAPTER 10

The Longest Night

Even with the ventilator on high settings and with other special therapies John received, the PICU medical team were locked in an intense battle to get John's oxygen to a normal level in his blood, and they were not winning. His lungs were just that inflamed. At times the nurse or some other medical person would comment that the ventilator was giving all that it could give. "We're at the edge of what we can do," I overheard them say.

His blood pressure and pulse still weren't cooperating to get anywhere approximating a normal—or even workable—range. And they kept him as cool as they could in what's called a controlled-hypothermia level, which is at about ninety-four degrees Fahrenheit, for fear that his brain would swell—which would be unbelievably bad.

His heart was doing okay, but that was because they had drugs regulating it. He was 100 percent on life support. And the life support was barely keeping him alive.

Dr. Garrett had said that the first sixteen hours were crucial. So I was aware that to the medical team, based on everything they knew, everything they'd learned, everything they'd seen before, John wasn't going to make it. But they didn't know that we had the Great Physician working on him. I knew God had everything in His control—but that didn't make my anguish any less deep or dire. A mother should never have to watch her child suffer as I watched John hurt.

Then John began to have coughing spasms. One of the tubes was continually draining the fluid out of his lungs, but it seemed as though as quickly as it drained, it filled again.

John's body was even fighting the simplest things. That day he had been given sugar water and minerals, the standard IV fluids, but the minerals decided to play havoc on his system and caused his electrolytes to fluctuate so high and so low that the imbalances were causing critical issues. His body just did not want to catch up.

As people in the waiting room started to leave for the night, Brian worked up the courage to visit John. Unfortunately, it was during one of John's coughing spells. Brian stood glued to the side of the room, posed like a deer caught in the headlights, and took it all in. John was coughing so hard and flailing and the nurses were trying to get him under control. He stayed as long as he could before he looked pleadingly at me. His face was covered in anguish.

"I'm sorry," he whispered. "I just...don't think I can...right now."

"It's okay, Brian," I told him. "I understand."

He took one more look at our son and then fled the room.

The nurses continued their ceaseless work. Finally, one nurse told me, "We're struggling to get his levels under control. I know you have been praying; I'd encourage you to keep doing that."

That was something we could do.

Here's what I've learned about prayer. Desperate prayer isn't a one-off kind of thing. Jesus talked about it in this way: "Ask, and it will be given to you; seek, and you will find; knock, and it will be opened to you" (Matt. 7:7). But what many of us fail to understand is that when we pray, we enter a spiritual battlefield. Jesus wasn't telling us simply to pray once and then He'd answer. He was saying this: Ask—and *keep on* asking; seek—and *keep on* seeking; knock—and *keep on* knocking. It's hard and exhausting work. *But* while we're asking and seeking and knocking, He sends us answers along the way. I call them mini-miracles. Too often we miss them because we're looking for the big prayer answers. If we want to see God really at work, we need to look for even the smallest response.

Granted, a heartbeat, angels, lights—those are all big responses. But even if Jason hadn't experienced the angels and lights, that didn't mean that God wasn't working. God is always working—even when we don't see the signs. That's what I had to cling to this first night, because if I hadn't, I would have been just like those well-meaning people who said, "Yes, we pray, but let's not get our hopes up." I would have focused on everything that was going wrong, without lifting my eyes to everything that God was doing right.

So everyone continued to pray. I knew the waiting room group was still praying, too—in small huddles, in a large group, individually. Time was of the essence, and we couldn't afford to become lax. The medical team had their work to do; we had ours. And God, sovereignly, had His.

That entire night, John's numbers never stabilized, his coughing didn't ease up, and his brain function didn't return. But still we prayed.

Then we had something new to pray about.

Late into the evening, Jason, my sister Janice, and I were together in John's room, while the others remained in the waiting room. We were sitting on the sleeping couch and chair, quietly talking about the day's events, when the oddest smell slammed into our nostrils and just about knocked us out. It was so pungent and overwhelming that it brought tears to our eyes and began to choke us.

It was John.

Immediately, I rang the button to alert the nurse, and within moments she arrived and stopped in her tracks momentarily. Her face scrunched up in disgust—a normal response to the smell!

"He's got diarrhea," she stated, moving into full-speed-ahead action. When she asked us to leave so she could attend to him, we were already halfway out of the room. We didn't need to be asked twice!

It wasn't just normal diarrhea; this was much worse. It was the most acrid-smelling odor I'd ever experienced. The medical term for it is ischemic bowel necrosis. When John's organs went into catastrophic failure and the blood flow stopped, the lining of his intestines began to slough off. Normally, that lining turns over every three to four days, but a person doesn't notice it because it doesn't happen all at once. Sort of like how we lose dead skin cells all the time. It happens gradually and imperceptibly. But with John, his gut's lining was falling off all at once because all the tissue was dead. And that produced the worst-smelling, nastiest, foulest diarrhea you could ever imagine. A whiff was making our eyes sting. It caused us to choke and gag, and threatened to induce vomiting. I didn't know how the nurse was in there and able to work. But I was certainly grateful that she was.

I knew this was a bad sign. It made me wonder, *If that's happened to his gut, what's happened to his other organs?*

You've got this, Lord, I said under my breath. *No negative talk. Only life.* We'd had too many answers to prayer and too many good signs to lose hope, no matter what we saw—or smelled—happening to his body.

The diarrhea was bad enough, but he had so many tubes down in that area, the concern rose greater. The nurse worked to keep him clean and to move those tubes, to ensure that no bacteria from the dead tissue got accidentally introduced into any of them, which could then go directly into his heart.

Janice returned to the waiting room to update our group on how to pray now, and Jason and I walked not far down the hall to a small room that had a coffee machine, a refrigerator, and some chairs.

"This has been an intense night," he said.

"This has been the longest night of my life," I said. "I can't imagine what John is aware of or feeling." I'd been telling my son over and over that he was going to be okay and that he didn't have to be afraid. "This is such a horrible experience, I hope he doesn't remember any of it."

"Then that's how we're going to pray," Jason told me. And so we added that to our growing list of prayer requests: "Lord, don't let him remember anything that he has experienced. Don't let him recall the horror of this day."

When we finished praying, Jason pulled out his iPhone and started thumbing through his iTunes library. "Listen to this song," he told me. "I think this needs to be our song for John."

He showed me the title, "When You Walk into the Room" by Bryan and Katie Torwalt, then he hit the Play button and powerful lyrics sang out.

When You walk into the room
Sickness starts to vanish
Every hopeless situation ceases to exist
And when You walk into the room,
The dead begin to rise
'Cause there is resurrection life
In all You do.

Part of prayer is worship, and so we agreed that we would fill his room with worship music. As soon as we returned, Jason placed his phone next to John's ear and played "When You Walk into the Room."

"Hey, buddy," he told John, "this is going to be our song."

By this point, it was getting close to 2:00 a.m. I barely sleep anyway, so I planned to stay awake in John's room all night. Janice offered to remain as well. I was immensely grateful that Jason had stayed as long as he had, but he had a family, too, and he needed to get sleep! So with our blessing, he left for the night.

"I'll be back in the morning," he said. "Well, I guess *this* morning." He looked at his phone's clock. "No negative talk. Only life." He smiled.

"No negative talk. Only life," I responded and smiled back.

The night dragged on, with no other medical signs of health or stability in John's body. Brian and my other sons had entered John's room briefly, but the sight of him swollen and surrounded with tubes and monitors was too much to bear, so they didn't stay long. Janice and I stayed close by, checking in every once in a while with Brian and the others nearby in the waiting room, but mostly sitting with John and watching the nurses and the others continuously and intensely work. We were only (gladly) chased out when the nurse needed to clean up the ongoing diarrhea.

Eventually, glimpses of dawn peeked through John's window. Morning had broken. More than sixteen hours had passed.

The staff still worked to stabilize him. But John was alive. He had crossed over that critical time frame, and he was still alive.

CHAPTER 11

"I Was Wrong"

Tuesday, January 20, 2015

What a difference a day makes. Twenty-four hours before I'd been enjoying the morning, texting my healthy son, reading a devotional, feeling good about the world. Now our lives had altered. Within a split second, everything had flipped on its head, and the world had changed forever.

But I knew one thing had not changed: God.

He was still sovereign. He was still in control. And He was still working. That I knew as surely as I knew the sun was going to rise in the east that day and every day.

Janice had stayed with me, but she'd had a long drive the day before and then stayed up all night, so I encouraged her to go to our house to clean up and get some rest. However, I would stay. I hadn't slept, but I didn't want to. I wanted to be awake and in the room when John woke up! He needed to know that his mama was there. So Janice promised to return with some clean clothes and a cosmetic bag filled with hygienic items—toothbrush, hairbrush, deodorant.

Alone with my son, I talked to him and sang worship songs over him and just generally let him hear my voice. He knows I'm never at a loss for words— so if my voice would nudge him awake, then so be it and praise God.

When the staff shift change occurred around 6:30 a.m., the night nurse brought in Wendy. Even though she had officially ended her shift earlier the previous evening, she'd stuck around to help until late into the night. I was so glad to see her. I noticed that they were careful about what information they passed to each other in my presence. Clearly, news of my confrontation with Dr. Garrett had spread!

Around 8:30, a group of four or five medical students ganged up outside the room, along with the nurses, some technicians, and some residents. The leader, a mustached, bespectacled man with hair on the sides of his head but a clean path along the top, stepped inside, glanced at John, and then looked at me.

"I'm Dr. Robert Ream," he told me. "I'm Dr. Garrett's partner here." He explained that he worked the night shift on the PICU, but that he, just like Dr. Garrett, was also a professor with the St. Louis University School of Medicine. Since the school was connected with Cardinal Glennon (their teaching hospital), every morning he would make the rounds with this group to discuss any updates and what they were going to do that day with the patient.

He walked over to John and examined all the tubes and monitors, then walked back out to the group where he stood and debriefed them for several minutes. Not that I was eavesdropping, but since they were standing right outside of John's door, it was impossible not to overhear them. Even though John had survived, they still considered him at critical risk *not* to survive—or to be brain damaged. So they were focused on keeping his body temperature low to keep the brain from swelling—the critical period for this issue was the first seventy-two hours—keeping him medicated, monitoring his vitals, handling the diarrhea, and still working to get—and keep—him stabilized.

Finally they moved on to the next patient, leaving John and me alone again. "You're going to be okay, John," I said, grabbing his hand. He lightly squeezed back.

Jason had told me that John had squeezed his hand the night before. And

I had experienced it, too. But every time we announced that good news to anyone on staff, they excused it away. It was an involuntary reflex, they said. He couldn't move, he's paralyzed, they insisted. He doesn't know anything is going on, he doesn't have that level of brain stem function, they pronounced.

Well, they were wrong. They just didn't know it yet.

Shortly after nine o'clock, I was surprised but pleased to see Jason stroll into the room. He offered a cheerful "Good morning," then stopped dead in his tracks, his eyes wide.

Oh no! What's wrong? What's happening? I wondered, fear rising within me again.

"Okay, he's a fourteen-year-old boy. If he knew . . . he would be mortified."

What is he talking about?

"We're going to keep him covered. We've got to leave him some dignity."

I looked at John, bewildered, and then I saw. That boy was buck naked.

Between trying to keep his body cooled and having to keep changing him because of the diarrhea, the team was so busy and concerned over everything else that they'd just left him uncovered. And I hadn't even noticed! What kind of a mother was I?

"Yep, you're right," I told him and quickly pulled the blanket over the lower half of John's body.

After we got that taken care of, Jason leaned over to greet John. He got right up to his ear and said, "How's it going, buddy?"

All of a sudden, giant tears started rolling down my son's cheeks.

Jason looked at me, wide-eyed, with his mouth forming an O. "Joyce, he's crying."

I nodded. I saw those tears, too. This kid who, according to the medical world, was barely alive and with only the basest amount of brain stem function was responding to Jason. Even through the constant drip of propofol they were giving him to keep him in a medically induced coma, he was responding. And it wasn't just a few tears. He was flat-out crying.

"Do you want me to stay with you today?" Jason leaned back in and asked.

John gave a slight movement of his head up and down. Jason looked at me again. This kid's brain was healed.

"Okay, I'm here," Jason said. He squeezed John's hand—and John lightly squeezed back. "He squeezed my hand," he told me and smiled.

I wanted to get up and do a cha-cha-cha around the room to celebrate what we'd just seen, but my achy joints wouldn't let me.

Jason grabbed a chair next to me and sat down. "When I left here last night, I spent the rest of the night praying. I really feel like the Lord is telling me that I need to be here for the long haul. That I need to stay and support you and your family in whatever way you need until God releases me. I've talked it over with Paula and she agrees."

Paula, Jason's wife, had been at the hospital almost from the time we'd arrived the day before. She's spunky, outspoken, compassionate, wise, and wonderful. And I wanted to hug her right then. I knew what a big commitment this was—and what a huge sacrifice he and his family were stepping up to take. He had four kids at home who needed a dad. But there he sat, telling me that he was ready to stay and encourage and strengthen us.

"So from this point forward," he continued before I could even reply, "it looks like you're stuck with me." Then he smiled. "Is that okay with you?"

I thought about my husband. Brian had stayed in the waiting room, only leaving to go home to care for our dog, Cuddles, and Don and Janice's dog. Then he returned to the waiting room, unwilling—or unable—to venture in to see John. Although it made me sad, I also understood that we all process our grief differently. It wouldn't be fair for me to get angry at Brian because he wasn't responding to the situation as I was. Neither of us were right while the other was wrong. Our choices were just different. I needed to give him the space for God to comfort and speak to him in a way that Brian needed. My piling guilt on him or nagging him that he *should* be in John's room with me would only serve to create more pain. I'd been married to the man for more than thirty years, and I had learned that he feels things very deeply and that he responds to life's situations very differently from how I do, that he carries a sensitive side to him that I wasn't about to wound.

I guess God understood that, too, and perhaps that was why He called on Pastor Jason to show up and stand in the gap for our family. Regardless of the reason, I was glad.

"That's okay with me," I told him. "I want you to have a front-row seat to see this miracle play out. So when you speak about it someday, you will have firsthand knowledge of what God did for John. I believe many lives are going to be changed because of this miracle."

Mine already had been.

As we rejoiced together over how God had healed John's brain function and was allowing him to respond to us, Dr. Garrett had arrived at the PICU and was looking over the overnight reports on John's progress and consulting with his partner, Dr. Ream, as well as with the rest of the PICU staff. The reports were only slightly better than when he'd left the night before. John was still on life support, he was still full of bacteria, his organs were barely working, he was still under heavy medication to combat all of that, and he was still in a medically induced coma so he wouldn't wake up before he was ready.

His lungs were still in terrible shape. Though the team had gotten a few things going better in those organs, nothing was where it needed to be yet. And it still wasn't clear how or if they'd be able to get his lungs stabilized and working or cleaned out completely.

Although he had decided against it the day before, this day Dr. Garrett was reconsidering whether the ECMO bypass—in which they would remove John's blood, filter it to get rid of the carbon dioxide, and then oxygenate his red blood cells—might be a viable option. Since John had survived the sixteen-hour window, perhaps he could manage the risk and survive the procedure. But something within Dr. Garrett gave him pause. He knew that of the patients they put on ECMO for lung disease, only about a third were able to survive. He decided against it.

The numbers still weren't that good over John's blood pressure or blood sugar levels. He'd had a prolonged high-blood-sugar, hypoglycemic response, so they'd put him on an insulin drip. But as a staunch believer in nutrition being one of the best ways to heal and sustain a body, Dr. Garrett decided it was time to force some glucose into his cells. They needed to get some solid nutrition into him, because his pancreas was struggling to regulate itself as well.

The reports also showed that the brain activity hadn't really changed. Even though John had made it sixteen hours, they still had a seventy-two-hour window to watch for brain edema, or swelling. It was imperative that not happen—or he was done for. And Dr. Garrett wasn't sure how John's brain *wasn't* going to swell after everything he was dealing with.

And yet, word was filtering to him that John was responding to outside stimuli. He was squeezing hands, he was opening his eyes, he had taken a full breath over the ventilator. Dr. Garrett had medical explanations for all of those things—they were all typical involuntary reflexes in trauma patients. And yet... this boy had experienced a heartbeat after being dead for an hour. He had survived through the critical period, when none of the medical team had expected him to. Frankly, there was no way he should still be alive! Was it possible that these other things, then, were true? Dr. Garrett had to concede the possibility that perhaps John was actually responding of his own free will.

He had seen the CAT scan and the other reports. But he knew those were just tests of brain structure and brain electrical activity. They don't really tell IQ or who somebody is. He often joked with his residents that if that were true, no one would need ACTs and SATs to get into college. They could simply get their EEG and their MRI and they'd be set.

He paused to consider the reality that John was willfully and consciously responding. He'd had plenty of experiences in which a patient's family member or close friend thought they saw something, but it wasn't what they believed it to be. Was this the case with John? He knew that I had been firm in my conviction only to speak life—but if he went along with this new revelation, would he be participating in offering us false hope? Was there really another miracle to be had?

And what about the rest of John's body? he thought. What if they were able to save the brain, but still lost because they couldn't keep the heart and lungs going? What if they lost him from clinical sepsis (a blood infection that kills many sick patients)? Or what if John still ended up dying from medical complications because of all the devices they'd put into him?

Well, there was one way to find out if the rumors were true. He needed to do a neurological test on John.

Between10:00 and 10:30, Dr. Garrett appeared in John's doorway. This was the first time we had seen each other after our encounter in the conference room the night before.

I could feel myself tensing up as he entered the room.

"Okay. I was wrong," he said, and then gave a hint of a smile.

I burst out laughing.

"John made it through the night, but—" As soon as he said *but*, he stopped abruptly and just stood there. I could see him editing everything he was going to say, because I'm certain he didn't want another encounter! Finally he said, "—there are criteria that need to be met." He stopped again.

I knew instinctively what he was now trying to figure out how to say. He was trying to come up with anything positive without saying, "Hey, listen, if these certain things don't happen, this boy's going to die." He wasn't going to say those words, though. He was *not*.

So I made it easier for him. "John cried this morning," I told him. "When Pastor Jason walked in and talked to him, he cried. And it wasn't from the lubricating drops the nurse has been putting in. They were actual tears. *Huge* tears. Then he nodded when we asked him a question. He's responding. That's brain stem function, right?"

"Well, a lot of that can happen through involuntary reflexes, *but*"—he quickly interjected, I'm sure, to keep me from refuting his explanation—"let's check it out."

He stepped to the end of John's bed. "Hi, John," he said. "I'm Dr. Garrett. I want to ask you a couple questions and you can answer by moving your thumbs, okay?"

John didn't move. No nod, no breath, no opened eyes, no thumb twitch. Nothing.

Come on, John, I pleaded silently. *Show him you can hear him. Give him some sign that you're alive and okay.* But just like a typical teenager, he didn't want to do what he was told.

Dr. Garrett's lips pursed slightly. Maybe he was hoping for a sign of that miracle, too? He walked to the head of the bed. "John, I'm going to check your eyes, okay?"

No response.

Dr. Garrett gently lifted one of John's eyelids and examined the pupils. "They're less dilated and look to be coming back to normal size, so that's good." He paused again and looked back over at me. "We're doing everything we can. We still have a long road ahead of us. You just keep praying."

He had admitted he was wrong, and that had earned my respect. Now I could hardly wait to hear those words from him again. Because I was certain that he was going to see more miracles take place.

"How's John doing today?" people asked Brian as soon as they entered the waiting room.

Brian would give the updated status and then say, "He isn't out of the woods yet, so thank you for your prayers. Keep them coming."

Many people accepted the report and agreed. And pray they did. Brian watched over and over as groups sat together and talked and then spontaneously grasped hands and began to pray. Those sights were exactly what he needed to build his strength.

God, You see these people—all here for John, he prayed silently. *Answer their prayers! Save my son. Grow his strength. Bring him back to complete recovery.*

Some people, however, just wanted the scoop. And some would agree to pray for John's complete recovery, but then, as soon as they thought Brian was out of earshot, they would reveal their true feelings. On several occasions Brian overheard, "It's good that we pray for John, but let's not get our hopes up. He's in pretty bad shape."

To hear those statements crushed Brian. He worked hard not to let the words penetrate his mind or heart. *My son has to live. God, don't let me focus on what those people are saying. Let them be wrong!*

While Brian worked to help everyone outside keep the focus on John's complete recovery, our goal in John's room was to create an atmosphere of peace, one where God would be free to work and where John could have calm and peace to rest and recover. We prayed and battled to keep that atmosphere, because we felt strongly about that. During the day, we repeatedly played our theme song, "When You Walk into the Room," and we filled the room with praise and worship. The pastors returned to pray over John, and Brian and I would try to connect as much as possible to keep everyone updated.

Soon Wendy, John's day nurse, came in to adjust his levels and check his vitals. She looked a little hesitant before she said, "I have some specific things for you to pray for...if you want them?"

This was like music to my ears. Both Jason and I laughed. *If we wanted them?* This may have been her way to get us information without being negative. Or she may really have understood the power of prayer. Either way, I didn't care! The more focused and strategic we could be in our prayers, the better.

"Yes!" Jason and I blurted out at the same time.

She smiled and explained that at noon they were going to do a lung test to see how bad the bacteria was. "With all that lake water, and then with all the other fluid that keeps building up there, that might be some of the reason that we can't get his breathing under control."

We went onto Facebook to spread the word. We let the waiting room group know, I texted, and we alerted a phone chain.

Noon came, they took the test and sent it off to the lab. We wouldn't know the results for a while. But we had covered the test and that time with a blanket of prayers.

Within an hour or so, someone came in to swab John's mouth to check pH levels.

"Just so you know," he explained. "If John responds, that's a normal reflex reaction, so it's nothing to get excited about."

Okay, buddy, I hear you, I thought. *You don't believe he's responding, either.*

As soon as the man placed the swab in John's mouth, John started to flail his arms and thrash about the bed. He kept turning his head away from the swab, as if to say, *Leave me alone! Knock it off!*

Just a reflex, huh? I thought.

"That's definitely not a reflex," the man said—as if we didn't already know. "That's brain function!"

Finally! Someone saw what we had seen all along. We were sure that would change the staff's minds now. They would have to listen to us and know we were speaking truth. John's brain was healed.

Where's Dr. Garrett now when we need him? I thought. *Where are the neurologists?*

Soon a pediatric neurologist did show up. It was time for John to showcase his abilities! To prepare for the neurologist's arrival, the nurse lowered John's dosage of propofol, which would bring him back into semiconsciousness so the doctor could better gauge his responses.

In she walked and introduced herself. She was extremely difficult to understand because of her thick foreign accent. She asked John to move his fingers at her command. Of course, he didn't. To be fair, I could barely understand what she was asking, so I can't imagine that a drugged-up kid would comprehend her request any better.

He had failed her test. It didn't matter that Jason and I both explained that he had been responding all morning—that he had even flailed around during the swab test. Because she hadn't experienced it, as far as she was concerned, it hadn't happened at all.

I felt frustrated. Not because John hadn't responded. I felt frustrated at the neurologist. John hadn't jumped like a trained monkey at her command, he hadn't replicated his actions in her presence, and so therefore, she upped his dosage of propofol again and made notes on his medical chart that he was unresponsive.

I dug in my heels. *You are going to have to admit that you're wrong. Just wait.*

And just to add more frustration to the mix, some of the hospital public relations people showed up.

"Hi, Joyce," Jamie Sherman said. "We've received requests from the local media; they want to do a story."

I could understand the media's interest. Three boys fell through the ice and were rescued. Of course, that would make the local news. I doubted they wanted to bring a camera in this room to tell every viewer to pray, and I wasn't interested in the media learning anything else. Keeping a tight wrap on it would ensure it would be only a quick two-minute news story and it would blow over soon enough.

"Not going to happen," I told her. If they wanted a story, it would be after John had fully recovered. Besides, this place was enough of a circus, just trying to stabilize John. The last thing we needed was the media added to it.

Later that evening, I took a break and went out to the waiting room to check in with Brian and talk with people who were there. Again, just as the previous night, the waiting room was jam-packed with people.

Pam Watson approached me, holding a sheet of paper. Pam's son Blake had gone to school with John since they were both in kindergarten. "I think you'll want to see this," she said smiling.

I took the paper and looked at the handwritten letter. At the bottom was Kent Sutterer's name. I looked up at Pam. "This is from Dr. Sutterer?"

She nodded. "You know his daughter Anna is a student with John at the school?"

I glanced back down. My eyes filled with tears, making it blurry to read. He was talking about John's miracle. That we serve a mighty and powerful God.

"I know that God can do more than we ever imagined. I know that God has given us a gift, even if it is only for a few days," the letter read. "I was privileged to witness a miracle. I was preparing myself to give a mother the final bad news that her son was gone from this world. She had more faith in God than I did. She called on God and God brought him back."

I inhaled sharply and reread the paragraph. He had been ready to call time of death? I felt my knees grow weak. *Oh, God, You are so good to us. You are so faithful!*

Again I looked at Pam, whose eyes were sparkling with tears to match mine. "We've been passing it around. He sent it to school today to tell the students how miraculous John's life is."

I couldn't have agreed more.

Late into the night as Melissa and I sat encouraging each other with Scripture and talking about life's twists and turns, I heard a sound that made my stomach retch. John's room overlooked the helicopter pad. The thunderous whipping of helicopter blades announced a deathly ill *little one*. I prayed.

A few hours later, I watched the PICU team wheel that child past John's door, followed by a pale and distraught mom and dad. All the raw memories from the day before rushed back to me, and I said another prayer for the child and his parents.

What a rough, crazy day. And John's flailing had turned out to be the best part. The rest of it was stressful, as I helplessly watched my son lie on that bed and fight for his life. The staff was using the highest levels of the most sophisticated medical equipment they had, and John's body still refused to stabilize. All day the battle was heavy for the medical team, and especially for John's nurse. With each person's visit into the room, I could tell they were worn out, exhausted from the work they were doing to help him. And we still had another day until we got past the worst fears of the brain swelling. How much more could everyone take?

★　　★　　★

Early that morning, Pastor Jason had put out an alert on Facebook and through other sources that they were going to have a special prayer vigil for John that night at the church.

One thing I know about prayer. We can never pray too much. We can never wear down or annoy God with our requests. We can never outpray our welcome with God. And so I rejoiced at the thought that people were going to gather together and lift up my son to the Great Physician and Healer.

Jason left around five, feeling a little discouraged that John's numbers and levels weren't regulated and better yet. When he pulled into the church's parking lot, he was stunned by the number of cars already there. Word had spread like wildfire, and by seven o'clock, when the vigil started, around 350 people were in First Assembly Church's sanctuary, ready to go to battle.

Even people who knew John but who had no connection to our church or to John's school showed up. Josh Rieger, his sister, Jamie, and their parents, Cindy and Kurt Rieger, were there. Josh Sander and his parents, Mary and Bob, were there. Both of the Joshes had been briefly hospitalized, but were released within two to three hours.

The vigil started with everyone singing a few songs. Pastor Jason played "When You Walk into the Room"—our theme song—and the room became electric. It was time to get down to business and pray. For more than an hour, person after person walked up to a microphone and lifted their voice to God on behalf of John. And then Josh Sander stood and walked to the mike. He had been there, on the ice with his friends. He had fallen in, but he had been able to pull himself out and get to the safety of the dock. He'd suffered from minor hypothermia. And now he placed himself squarely before God and laid bare his soul.

In one of the most anointed, powerful, sincere, and heartfelt prayers, this fourteen-year-old thanked God that he and his friends were safe, and then asked God to heal his friend.

The vigil encouraged everyone, and they felt as though God had made His presence known, that He'd heard their prayers, and that He was going to answer them.

As Jason got back into his car after the vigil and headed back to Cardinal Glennon, he had his own heart-to-heart talk with God.

"God, You've got to do this. You can't let him die. You can't let him not recover fully. You cannot let this happen. We need this. Be who You say You are. Be the God we read about in the Old Testament and the New Testament and heal this boy. You've done this before. You've saved people. You've healed them. We need You to do it again. Raise up John."

We knew God could do it; we knew God had done it in the past. We believed it. Now we needed to see the complete proof. Better yet, we needed the medical community to witness it.

CHAPTER 12

A Thumbs-Up Day

Wednesday, January 21, 2015

We'd struggled through another long and difficult night. Dr. Ream had spent an hour trying to adjust John's ventilator, because my son was coughing so much. John's poor body had begun flailing as he coughed and choked, so finally Dr. Ream stepped in and went to work on him. But even that took time to get John settled back down.

Melissa and I had spent most of the night praying for him and encouraging each other. But one of the sweetest encouragements came from two of John's friends. Fourteen-year-olds who felt God nudge them to encourage me, and so throughout the night they sent Scripture passages.

"'When you pass through the waters, I will be with you; and when you pass through the rivers, they will not sweep over you. When you walk through the fire, you will not be burned; the flames will not set you ablaze' (Isa. 43:2 NIV). I found this verse and thought it might be encouraging. Praying for y'all tonight," wrote Emma Riley, John's best friend.

"'The mind governed by the flesh is death, but the mind governed by the Spirit is life and peace' (Romans 8:6 NIV). This is so hard for me, because it's so easy to be focused on the bad things, because that's just what our sinful nature does. Specifically prayed for a supernatural overwhelming sense of peace," wrote Chayla Gilky, another close friend of John's.

I particularly appreciated their prayers and the Scriptures, because a new issue had arisen with John. The medical staff had been pushing extreme levels of oxygen into his lungs to force out the liquid, as well as to revive all of his systems. In fact, they were forcing so much oxygen into him that it was seeping out of his lungs and into his tissues, up his neck, and collecting under his skin. It looked like they'd crammed those Styrofoam packing peanuts under there, and everywhere I touched it felt crispy, like pressing my fingers on a handful of dry Rice Krispies cereal.

Meanwhile, John continued to respond to us, but he refused to respond to anybody else. We tried to show the staff that he could respond, but because he was so heavily medicated, his reactions were too fleeting and random. So the neurologist decided to incorporate an hourly test into the nurse's schedule. That test was simple—and simply infuriating. Every hour the nurse would stick her fingers in the sensitive part of John's pectoral muscle, right by his armpit, and twist hard. That was supposedly to see if he would respond to pain. Although he didn't react, I sure did. With each tenderizing, torturous twist I wanted to come out of my chair and clock her one. But then I had to remind myself that the nurse was not a cruel, heartless fiend. The neurologist might have been one, but the nurse was only following her orders.

If they'd only listen to me, I thought, *we could avoid all of this nonsense.* But I was only his mother; what did I know?

Jason had again stayed with us until around 2:00 a.m., and then my friend Melissa Fischer came to stay the rest of the time so I wouldn't be alone. We spent hours talking about what we'd been studying in our Bible study group, and how amazingly appropriate the timing of our study was to what we were going through. She was exactly the person I needed during those long, dark hours.

Janice and Don arrived around 6:00 a.m and came into the room to stay with me. Brian and my sons Charles and Tom were still camped out in the PICU waiting room, not leaving the hospital except to take care of the dogs and to change clothes. They went back and forth in shifts between John's room and the waiting room, since they couldn't stay for long with John—it was too emotionally draining, especially for Brian.

At around 6:30 a.m. on our third day, the shift changed again, and my heart leaped to see our little blonde nurse Wendy step into the room for the shift-change updates. I'm not sure why she needed any updates, since she'd stayed until eleven o'clock the night before. She looked tired, but not as weary as she had earlier.

The previous night, not long after Jason had arrived back from the prayer vigil, we'd spotted Wendy, still there after her shift had ended hours before.

"What are you still doing here?" I asked her, concerned because she looked so exhausted and frayed. That whole day, she had gone above and beyond her job, checking on John constantly. Adjusting and readjusting. Cleaning him, changing him, making sure his meds were correct and his IV bag was filled. But her work had taken a toll on her, and I think she was worried about John. She had invested in my son. Not just in his care, but I think her heart wanted to see this boy survive and thrive just as much as we did.

"I'm still working on reports and helping out," she'd explained.

My heart went out to her. She looked like she was on the verge of breaking down.

"Can we pray for you?" Jason asked her.

"Please do!" Her voice trembled.

Jason prayed for God to renew her strength, he blessed her work and praised how she'd given her all. He prayed for her family, and he asked God to give her a strong, clear sense of His presence in her life. When he said amen, I saw tears sparkle on her eyelashes.

"Go home and get some rest," I said to encourage her. She nodded her agreement and her thanks.

Now here she stood this morning, back for more intense work. She smiled and wished me a good morning.

I hoped it would be.

At 7:00 a.m. Nancy Benes, John's middle school principal, called to check on John's status. Every morning at this time she called and then gave the report to the school so they could pray.

"We still don't have any change," I told her. "He's pretty much like he was." That wasn't the news I wanted to pass along, and I know that wasn't the news she wanted to receive.

"Well, we're still praying."

Jason showed up at nine, and then Mark Shepard, John's former children's pastor, arrived shortly after that. Between the bed, all the medical equipment, the chairs, and the people, the room was jam-packed. We had to squeeze just to get around anything.

The previous night the nurse had begun to slowly lower John's dosage of propofol and raise his temperature. The doctors wanted to see if John could possibly wake up. They didn't expect him to actually wake up, and if he did, they didn't anticipate anything more than perhaps his eyes opening—which was something they let us know not to get too excited about.

I was eager to have John awake. We all were. And Janice and Don wanted to be there when he did finally open his eyes.

My sister and brother-in-law adored that kid. Janice's office cubicle was a shrine to him, with all of his basketball and school photos placed every-where. They'd never had children of their own, and so they doted on him and took every opportunity to spoil him rotten. They loved my three other boys, Joe, Tom, and Charles, too, but those kids were no longer kids! They were grown men. So from the time John was a baby, Janice and Don showered him with affection and gifts galore. One Christmas, when he was three or four, they showed up in their Chevy Tahoe SUV with the whole back end filled with Fisher-Price toys. As he grew older, their Tahoe continued to be filled, but with each year, the presents became more sophisticated. You'd have thought Brian and I neglected the kid with everything they brought him. They genuinely and wholeheartedly agreed with Brian and me that John hung the moon. Even several states away, they stayed in constant contact with him. The feeling was mutual. John thought they were the best people in the world. Whenever they visited or when he got to stay with them in Ohio, he acted as though he had won the lottery.

Around 10:30 that morning, Janice stepped out of the room, leaving Don, Jason, Charles, Mark Shepard, and me talking and reminiscing. I looked over at John.

His eyelids fluttered, as though he was trying to open his eyes.

"Look! He's waking up!" I nearly shouted from the sleeper couch to his right.

"He did that earlier this morning when Ari and I were in here with him," said Charles. My friend Melissa's daughter and John's good friend Ari had come in the middle of the night and sat with John and Charles while I tried to rest briefly in the PICU waiting room.

"What are you talking about?" This was the first I'd heard of it.

"Yeah!" Charles said, getting excited. "He was fluttering his eyes just like that. Ari and I both saw it and when we spoke to him, he turned his head toward us and looked right at her. But the nurse said that he wasn't waking up—that it was just an involuntary response. But it was just like what he's doing now!"

I looked back at John. His eyes fluttered, then opened wide! He blinked and then he closed them. Then he opened them again, but this time they went really wide and he started looking around the room. When his eyes landed on Don, he stopped and stared intently.

"Look, Don, he's staring at you," I said, wishing Janice and Brian were in the room to see this.

Immediately Don's eyes filled with tears and he was on his feet, walking to John's bedside. John's eyes followed him the whole way, locked on him. And then tears began to trickle out of John's eyes.

When the nurses had started to raise John's temperature in preparation of trying to get him to wake up, they'd told us, "Don't get emotional because he's not going to understand." At the time, we'd all agreed and acknowledged that we understood.

But that instruction fled our minds! How could we *not* be emotional? He was the child whom the entire medical community had told us over and over had no brain function and would be a vegetable, *if* he lived. Even though I had not accepted their diagnosis, I felt overwhelmed to actually see my son recognize someone—that definitely took high-brain-functioning ability.

I knew enough to know that the medical people would try to explain away what was happening by suggesting that John's eyes merely followed Don because he had been moving. But we saw recognition and then confusion in those eyes. I could tell by that look of confusion on his face that his brain was processing everything and going, *Why is Uncle Don here?*

The entire room exploded with tears and noise. All at once, we were talking to John and praising God and laughing and whooping.

The noise got Wendy's attention, and within a flash, she was in the room, ready to attend to what had gone wrong. But nothing had gone wrong; it had all gone wonderfully, providentially, amazingly right.

She looked at us, looked at John, saw his tear-filled eyes locked on Don, and she joined the rest of us as we sobbed our joy. "He's awake!" she said, not bothering to wipe her own tears that came fast and furious. She grabbed her work phone from her uniform pocket and immediately dialed Dr. Garrett's number. "Dr. Garrett needs to see this!" She was so excited I thought she might take off running up and down the hallway, shouting and crying over what she'd just witnessed. And I was all too ready to join her.

Everyone started texting and getting the word out. A few people rushed to the waiting room to tell Brian and the others, while I made calls, including to John's principal on her cell phone. Nancy normally doesn't answer during school hours, so I figured I'd just leave a message.

After the first ring, she picked up. "When I saw your number come up I knew I had to answer." She sounded hesitant, almost as if she was afraid of what news I may be giving her.

"Nancy, he's awake!"

I had to jerk the phone from my ear because she started screaming. Next I heard her chair push back from her desk. Then the fast clippity of her shoes echoed as she raced across the tiled floor. I could visualize where she was headed. Her office was connected to a long hallway that overlooked the gymnasium. When you walk and talk through that hall, the sound reverberates. I heard her screams of "He's awake! He's awake!" punctuated by her footsteps. Then as her announcement sunk in, my ears were filled with the screams and cheers of students—some at full volume, others muffled behind classroom doors. The entire Christian Middle School and Christian High School of a combined four hundred students had been praying for John's recovery. After school let out, John's friends had their parents carpool them to the hospital, where they'd hung out in the waiting room until late into the evening. Now they were rejoicing along with us.

If John only knew… I thought and then laughed. I wanted to tell him, but when I looked back at him, his eyes had closed again, and he drifted back into unconsciousness.

That was okay. *We knew.* God had provided another miracle. He had healed my son's brain.

After John woke up, I took a quick break and headed to the waiting room to celebrate the good news with Brian, Charles, Tom, and the others. They already knew, but I wanted to share the experience with them. We laughed and hugged and talked about what miracles God had performed. We couldn't wait to see what miracles he had planned next.

When God opened John's eyes, it filled the room with such peace and confidence in Him—that's the best feeling when we go through troubles and trials, to have that peace and confidence that God is going to work things out. And it overflows.

I had no idea how *much* it was about to overflow.

I headed back to the PICU, and as I rounded the corner toward John's room, I ran into Chris and Leann Suhling, the parents of another boy, Jackson, who was lying in the room next to my son's. I didn't know the Suhlings, but I'd seen Jackson's name on the post outside his door, and wondered what had brought him in.

Now his parents stood in the hallway, holding each other and crying. Three days ago, I would have walked by and given them their privacy. Three days ago, I wouldn't have been so bold to approach an unknown couple who were clearly distressed. But three days ago, God had rolled the tombstone away from my boy's deathbed—and John and I were both changed.

I approached them and stood until the mother quietly acknowledged my presence. She wiped her eyes and moved slightly away from her husband. They both looked as if they hadn't slept or eaten in days. Their eyes were sunken in and surrounded by dark circles, showing many sleepless nights. Clearly they were at the end of their ability to cope.

"Can I pray with you?" I didn't know what was wrong. I didn't even ask them what was wrong. I didn't have to know; God knew.

"Yes, please do!" The desperation in their voices broke my heart.

I had no idea that three-year-old Jackson had been in the PICU for three weeks because of a rare freak side effect from the flu, which had left him paralyzed. Whatever it was, the virus had slowly moved through his body, leaving each part paralyzed as it went, and no one in the medical community could figure out how to stop it. That morning, it had moved up to his neck and started to affect his ability to breathe. Chris and Leann thought they were losing him. As Jackson was being prepped by the nurses for emergency surgery with the hope that they could open his air passageway, his parents were being prepped for a funeral.

But I didn't know any of that there in the hallway. I just stepped in closer, put my hand on that mother's arm, and prayed for God to take care of whatever the situation was. "Lord, this doesn't take You by surprise. You know what this is. So I'm asking the Holy Spirit to come and do for Jackson what He did for John."

God had taken my son who was hopelessly dead and gave him life, opened his eyes, and healed his brain. If he could do that in John's dire situation, he could work a miracle in Jackson's, too.

I promised that I would check on them down in the surgery waiting area, that I would bring my pastor, and that we would pray. A glimmer of hope seemed to rise in those sunken eyes. It was time for God to show up for them as He had for us. We just needed to have faith and wait.

It took more than forty-five minutes for Dr. Garrett to appear in John's room. I had returned by then, and as soon as he arrived, the room exploded again with everyone telling him the news. "He's awake!" we all said. "He woke up. He looked at people. He recognized us!"

"That's great!" Dr. Garrett said and smiled politely. It wasn't that I thought he didn't believe us—I know he did. But I'm not sure he believed that John had actually recognized us. "Let's see if we can get an encore performance."

He stepped close to John's side. "John, this is Dr. Garrett. Can you open your eyes for me?"

Nothing.

That kid! *Don't do this again*, I silently told him. His unresponsiveness was not the kind of repeat performance Dr. Garrett was going for.

"John," Dr. Garrett tried again. "Open your eyes. Can you do that for me?"

Nothing.

Dr. Garrett looked at me. "Mom, come over here and talk to him."

I couldn't move fast enough! I got off the couch, wiggled around all the chairs, and took John's hand. "Hey, John. This is Mom. Can you wake up for me, please? Can you open your eyes? I need you to open your eyes for me."

His eyelids fluttered briefly, and then I saw the darkest, most beautiful deep brown eyes I'd ever seen in my life. His gaze locked with mine. "Dr. Garrett's here, and he wants to see that you're awake and that you recognize people.

Can you look at him?" I glanced to the opposite side of the bed to show John where Dr. Garrett was.

John slowly turned his head and found Dr. Garrett.

Dr. Garrett swallowed and nodded his surprise and approval.

Ha! I told you so! I thought.

"Hi John, I'm Dr. Garrett. Do you know where you are?" When John didn't respond, Dr. Garrett tried again. "Do you recognize any of the people in this room with you?"

And of course, John gave him nothing. Nothing at all. He just stared at him. To be fair, he didn't know who this stranger was! I thought, *You try waking up, disoriented, and have some stranger talk to you, and you respond like everything is perfectly normal! He doesn't have a clue who you are!*

"Ask him about basketball," Jason chimed in. "Basketball's his favorite sport. He likes Michael Jordan and LeBron James."

Dr. Garrett smiled. "John, do you like basketball?"

John slowly nodded, since with the ventilator and all the tubes, he couldn't speak—not that anyone expected him to.

"Why don't you give me thumbs-up and thumbs-down. Thumbs-up for yes, thumbs-down for no."

John nodded his okay.

"Do you like basketball?"

John gave him the thumbs-up. Since his fingers were still stiff and turned inward toward his palms from when the blood left his extremities, he had to fidget his hand around to bring his thumb up toward the ceiling.

"Who's your favorite player? LeBron James?"

Thumbs went down.

"Michael Jordan?"

Thumbs-up.

"He's good enough that he knows who those people are, but let's see if he can tell the difference," Dr. Garrett said to us. "Let's do this. Since he doesn't have fine motor skills"—something he'd lost from the cold water—"John, I want you to lift your left hand if the answer is LeBron James, and raise your right hand if it's Michael Jordan, okay?"

John nodded.

"Who won six MBA titles?"

John lifted his right hand for Michael Jordan.

Dr. Garrett smiled slightly. "Who was from Cleveland?"

John raised his left hand: LeBron James.

"Good! Who moved to Miami?"

Again, the left hand went up.

"Which player played for Chicago?"

The right hand raised.

After several more questions that John answered correctly, Dr. Garrett's face registered shock and then a smile broke out. He knew—just as we all did—that a lot of eighth graders wouldn't get these questions correct because they wouldn't know that level of detail about LeBron James and Michael Jordan. But a good basketball fan who liked both would know. John got them all right. Every single one.

"John, you did an excellent job," he said. "You got them all right. I'll tell you what. I'm going to wear my Michael Jordan tie for you, and if you will get better and get out of here, I'll give you my tie. Deal?"

John's eyes sparkled as he nodded.

This kid was so sick that you'd think that if he were going to cooperate at all, he might just give one response, but then think, *I'm not going to talk to this doctor. I don't have the strength.* But no, John did. He did everything Dr. Garrett asked him to do.

"Do you realize that you're a miracle?" Dr. Garrett said.

John slightly moved his hands, but didn't answer. He was drugged, he had no idea where he was or why, and this stranger was telling him he was a miracle. I'm not sure I would have known what to do with my hands, either!

But Dr. Garrett had verified what we already knew: This boy *was* a miracle. That a medical professional—an expert in hypothermia and drowning, who had no doubt believed my son wasn't going to make it—had just uttered what must have seemed foreign to his lips. After confessing that he was wrong, and now testifying to John's miracle, we were on a roll!

He shook his head in wonder again. "His encephalon—his brain—is so sick from his body being sick," Dr. Garrett uttered, as though he were speaking to himself. "I don't know how it can function as well as it is, but it sure is."

"That's God," I said.

All he could do was smile and nod.

Later, after Dr. Garrett left, Mark Shepard decided to perform his own neurological test. He held John's hand and said, "Do you know who I am?"

John nodded.

"Am I Pastor Mark?"

Again, John nodded.

"Can you squeeze my hand?"

John did.

"Oh, you can do better than that!"

John lifted his arm and squeezed tightly.

"Were you just at my house not too long ago?"

Another nod.

"Am I still the best-looking man you ever saw in your life?"

John's head shook from side to side, and then the corners of his mouth lifted. *No.*

We all laughed. "That's John," Mark said. "That's *all* John. He's there. There's no doubt that he's there."

"I don't think the doctors need to worry about brain function!" Don said.

By the afternoon, Dr. Carter, another pediatric neurologist, showed up carrying a large notepad. He looked at Janice, who's three years younger than me and who was holding John's hand, and said, "Are you John's mom?"

Without missing a beat, she said, "Yes, I am, but I do let my sister borrow him from time to time."

Everybody laughed.

"I'm John's mom," I said.

He laughed along at the joke. "I hear your son is full of surprises today."

"Today and every day."

He turned to John, whose eyes were still open and now watching him. "I know that you can hear, but I'm going to write something down for you so you can see. I'm going to write on this piece of paper and show it to you, and I want you to do what it says. Okay?"

John nodded.

In big letters, Dr. Carter wrote, "Blink your eyes twice." He held it up in front of John.

Without any hesitation, John responded: Blink. Blink.

Dr. Carter faltered back a step and his mouth fell open. "That's amazing!" He looked at our group. "I saw his brain scan from when he came in here. There's no way that he should be able to do that. He shouldn't be able to respond. He shouldn't be able to read! As long as he was without oxygen, he should have so much brain damage that none of this stuff works."

John wasn't just responding; he was responding as if his brain hadn't experienced any trauma at all.

CHAPTER 13

Protecting Peace

Even though John remained in critical condition, our hearts continued to soar with the thrill of what we'd seen this day. And the miraculous news of what God had done was gathering chatter all over the PICU.

Around 4:30 Wednesday afternoon, my sons Tom and Charles were in with John, so I stepped out to the PICU waiting room to visit with friends and family. Earlier Pastor Jason and I had gone to the surgery waiting room to pray with the Suhlings during Jackson's operation, so while I was visiting, I was also wondering how Jackson was doing. I didn't have to wait long! Leann, Jackson's mom, burst through the door. She looked around the room until she found me and then rushed over, holding her iPhone in the air.

"Look! Look! You've got to see this," she told me, shoving the phone into my hands. Her eyes appeared as though they'd had an extreme makeover. Even though she still seemed tired and worn down, her eyes glowed with tears and a huge smile covered her face.

She tapped the Play button on the screen and up popped Jackson, her toddler son, who had just hours earlier been paralyzed up to the neck, and who had been potentially hours, if not minutes, from death. I couldn't believe my eyes. Less than four hours after his surgery, Jackson was sitting up in bed, strumming his Lightning McQueen guitar, and singing "Rooftops"!

"I shout out Your name," he sang. "From the rooftops I proclaim that I am Yours."

"The staff is stunned!" Leann said. "They'd hoped that Jackson would be able to breathe, but they never imagined he'd be in this kind of shape—sitting up and singing. God is good!"

God had performed another miracle on the PICU. Laughter rolled up from the depths and burst out of everyone sitting at our table. The surgical team did their part—but *this*? For three weeks, this poor boy had been in a hopeless state, and within mere hours, God had touched his body and healed him. God was at work. And the coolest part? A lot of people were starting to take notice. Something amazing was happening in the PICU.

Everyone celebrated Jackson's remarkable recovery, as though we were all family and hanging around especially for him. It was amazing and wonderful.

What if God starts moving all over this PICU? I wondered and felt a tingle of excitement flow through me. We'd been worried about John being infected by some contagious virus or bug, but I wondered, *What if miracles could become contagious?*

Later I walked back to John's room, feeling reenergized. I knew what had happened with Jackson was because of God stepping in. Did I do that? Was my prayer that powerful? No, I don't have the power to do that, but God honored my request. When God nudged me to step out of my comfort zone and offer to pray with Jackson's mom and dad, I had said yes—and God had responded with a yes.

As we talked about how God was working, Casey, the head PICU nurse, walked in the room and made a beeline for me. "Last night we brought a little boy in—"

"Yes, I know. He's on the other side of John. I heard the chopper when they brought him in."

Casey nodded. "He has a lot of the same things that happened to John. He drowned, and his parents are in the hallway."

A groan escaped my lips. I knew what those parents were going through.

And then the most beautiful words came from Casey's lips. "Would you pray with them?"

I couldn't get out of my chair fast enough.

Remington—Remie—Davis was three years old. The day before, he had been outside playing with his siblings and went missing. When his parents, Paul and Ciera, began their search, Paul noticed the gate to the pond was ajar. They purposely kept that gate closed so the kids wouldn't wander in that area and get into trouble in the water. But little Remie had somehow maneuvered the latch. Paul ran to the water's edge, and there under the dock, he saw the tiniest pair of feet floating. In one distressed, frantic move, he pulled Remi's limp body out of the water, called 911, and began CPR on his son.

By the time they reached the hospital, just as with John, their dark-haired boy with the liquid brown eyes and plump cherry cheeks had no pulse. Doctors at that hospital worked hard, but for three hours they couldn't get him to keep a heartbeat.

Just as I had desperately called out to God, this gentle, sweet Christian woman had done the same. "Jesus, save my baby!" she cried out over and over.

Finally, by Tuesday night the medical team had him stabilized enough to airlift him to Cardinal Glennon. And wonder of wonders, the PICU had one room open—the one on the other side of John.

Okay, God, You've shown up twice now—for John and for Jackson, I prayed as we walked the hallway. *Now show up for this precious boy and his family.*

As soon as I saw them, my heart tore into a thousand pieces. It felt as if I had been transported back in time three days.

I put my arms around Remie's mom. "I'm so sorry," I said.

Her tears flowed onto my blouse. "We've already lost a child. I can't bear to lose Remie, too." Their young daughter had been killed in a car accident five years before, and as one could imagine, they were still reeling from that devastation. "Now they're asking us if they can harvest his organs." Another rush of tears burst from her eyes.

"We're not going to let that happen," I said, feeling just as determined as I had been with John. "We're going to pray. And we're going to keep praying until Remie is healed."

I knew John was still considered in critical condition, but God had not abandoned us. Jackson was going to live. And I was absolutely certain that Remie was going to live. Why? Because it had been that kind of miraculous day. Because we had all needed a miracle. Because I felt as though God was parading up and down that floor and saying, *Hey, listen, I'm still here. And the truth is that I do miracles. Still do. Still can. Always will.*

Even though John had awakened and his brain stem function was miraculously intact, the medical team was still concerned about losing him. His lungs remained, to quote Dr. Garrett, "very sick," the potential for brain swelling was still high, and we had until Thursday before he passed that seventy-two-hour benchmark. All the devices and tubes and any other number of things could still fatally affect his weakened immune system. And he was still battling an unexplained fever that would come and go. Even though they didn't know what was causing it, they knew something was going on in his body, some infection somewhere.

To battle the fever, they lowered his body temperature and upped the dosage of propofol again, and back into the induced coma John went.

"Yes, John's brain functioning level is amazing, *but* don't get too excited yet," they told us.

Dr. Garrett had admitted that for John to exhibit that kind of high-detailed neurologic function was indeed miraculous—he'd even admitted that he'd never given a neurological test in quite that fashion before! But I could tell he wasn't ready to look us in the eyes and say, "He's going to make it. We'll get him through this. You don't have to worry about any of this breathing stuff and all these problems and alarms. Don't worry."

I'd had enough experience in hospitals to know that you can enter for one problem and pick up some serious infections while you're there, so I knew Dr. Garrett and the others were also concerned about that possibility. Hospital-borne infections can be deadly in and of themselves because when you enter the hospital, your immune system is already weakened. With all the conditions John had as a result of his drowning, I'd say he was full to overflowing on the complication front. And the longer he remained in the PICU, the higher the chance of getting an infection. It was as though John's body was wearing a neon sign welcoming any and all infections to "come on in and make yourself at home!"

But we also clung to God's promises. And one of them that we prayed over John often was Jeremiah 29:11–13: "I know the plans I have for you, declares the LORD, plans for welfare and not for evil, to give you a future and a hope. Then you will call upon me and come and pray to me, and I will hear you. You will seek me and find me, when you seek me with all your heart."

We were committed to seeking God with all our hearts, and yet we had to be on guard against becoming lax in our prayers. It's human nature that when we start to see glimpses of good news and good signs, our desperation level can soften and our resolve to "pray without ceasing" (1 Thessalonians 5:17) can become lighter.

So as each nurse, technician, or doctor showed up and warned us not to start planning any trips to Disneyland any time soon, they actually did a great job of reminding us that our work wasn't done. Every morning when Dr. Ream and his medical students made their rounds, Jason would act as our spy and listen to their reports about John. (Mostly they were concerned that even if his brain did get better, they would lose him because of his lungs and other issues.) After the report, Jason would come back in and pass along the information so we knew how to pray. I still doggedly believed that God didn't start John's heart to let him die—I didn't care what the medical community said or what anyone else believed. And with each troublesome report, I dug in my heels and said, "We're going to pray until we see the answer we're asking for."

While John was sleeping, we got back on social media and texts and presented that day's prayer list, based on what Wendy and the others encouraged us to pray:

1. that there would continue to be no brain swelling;
2. that even though his lungs were now drained, they would continue to steer clear of any infection; and
3. that his digestive system would begin working as it should, because they were gearing up to begin more substantial nutrition.

Within an hour of sending out our prayer list, news came back: John's lung culture, which we had been waiting for, came back sterile. We rejoiced with that news. And again, the staff was stunned by that test result. To have lungs that had been filled with lake water be completely cleared of any bacteria was almost unheard of. But there was another fun fact. As Dr. Garrett explained to us, almost everyone who lives in the Midwest shows some kind of issue with their lungs because of the air we breathe here. No one ever has sterile lungs in the Midwest. But John did. It was another miracle!

With that good report, however, came more mystery: If the lungs weren't the cause of John's fever, what was? The team wanted to be certain that this wasn't a fluke result, so they ordered another lung culture.

When John was awake, we were able to gather that he wanted his hand held as much as possible, so we promised him we would. While I focused on John's health and sat holding his hand, Jason began to focus on someone else's potential health crisis: mine. I had given little notice or concern to my own needs. My diabetes requires me to eat on a regular schedule, usually every two hours. From Monday when I got the news, I'd eaten very little. And I'd slept even less. People would bring food to the room so that I didn't have to leave, but I barely gave it notice. I was fighting for John, not for myself.

During a quiet moment when the visitor shift change was happening, leaving Jason and me alone with John, he took up an uncomfortable subject. "I'm concerned about you," he told me. "I know you haven't slept since Sunday night—and it's Wednesday. You need to take a break and get some rest. You need to take care of yourself, because this could be a long haul. And you'll be no good to him if you're so worn down."

I told him I understood, but he wouldn't let it go—probably because he knew that I had no intention of taking his well-meaning advice. I would manage; John needed me here.

"I'm serious," he said, his voice insistent. And as though reading my mind, he said, "John needs you healthy. You'll do him no good if you end up in a hospital bed, too. If you don't get some rest, you're going to crash."

"I know," I told him, appeasing him. "I'll rest. I just want to get past this critical period and then I'll—"

"Don't wait. I mean it."

I told him I would, and he shook his head in frustration. I was going to brush him off—he knew me too well.

He didn't understand, though. I couldn't leave John. Part of my job was to safeguard the room and my son's ears from hearing any negative chatter. Like a dog with a bone, I remained vicious about not letting anyone speak anything other than words of life.

But some people refused to get with the program. As new visitors entered John's room, they would often look at him and show shock and pity, but then step up and show compassion and optimism. But one visitor insisted on informing me that John wasn't going to make it.

"He's going to die. It's bad."

Multiple times the pronouncement came that he was going to die and it didn't matter what miraculous signs we saw. The truth was the truth, and we needed to step up and embrace it. Killing that person in a hospital room—especially when I'd informed the group that we were only to speak life—would be wrong, I knew . Throttling was not an option, either. Nor was kicking this person in the shins, poking my fingers in the eye sockets, or just generally causing harm. But don't think it didn't flit through my mind.

I thought about what John and I would often say to each other when we'd quote the movie *Rush Hour*. (We loved quoting movie lines to each other.) I wanted to get up in this person's face and say, "Do you understand the words that are coming out of my mouth?" That too, however, would not be a Christlike way to appropriately handle my frustration and anger.

"You know, we're sticking firmly to our decision to only speak life in this room," I finally announced.

The death pronouncements stopped, but I could see that the thoughts hadn't.

And soon John took a downward turn.

Around 2:30, after Pastor Jason left for the midweek church service, my son Tom and his wife, Jennifer, came to sit with me and John. John adores his brothers, so when Tom greeted John and held his hand, John returned the hold.

Later that afternoon, the night nurse came on duty. We'd not had this particular nurse before, and I didn't think anything about her, because all of our nurses had been excellent.

But something about the way she entered the room and went over John's vitals and monitors caught Jennifer's attention. Jennifer, who is a telemetry nurse—someone who works with electrocardiogram and other medical devices on patients with acute health issues—scowled as she watched the scene.

As soon as the nurse left, Jennifer said, "She doesn't know what she's doing."

And every time the nurse entered the room, Jennifer responded with a glare.

John must have felt something change in the room's atmosphere, because he slowly started to get agitated. Now his face also wore a scowl, and his arms and legs started to move around, as though he was uncomfortable and unsettled.

Sometime between 8:30 and 9:00 p.m., my friend Melissa showed up to cover night duty with me, something she informed me she would handle for the rest of the time John was in the PICU.

As Tom and Jennifer gathered up their coats, Jennifer looked intensely at me. "Keep an eye on that nurse. I don't trust her."

"Okay."

"*Watch her.*"

I thought Jennifer was being melodramatic. I hadn't noticed anything off or worrisome about the nurse. But since Jennifer knew what to look for, I gave her the benefit of the doubt and promised that I would. This nurse would be the primary person on the staff who would be monitoring John all through the night.

Soon we had another visitor. A short, heavyset woman with reddish hair, who looked to be in her late fifties, showed up in the doorway. She had the sweetest voice. "Hello, I'm a chaplain here. May I come in?"

"Sure!" I said, always grateful for any new people who showed a desire to pray over my son, which I assumed she would, being a chaplain and all.

She was pleasant and asked how I was holding up, and how John was doing.

We made some small talk, and then I asked her, "What's your religious background?" I was interested to know where she fell on the prayer spectrum.

"I practice Native American healing methods."

Uh-oh, I thought.

"I find that when we get in touch with our roots and send out good energy," she continued, "we get that good energy back."

I don't like where I think this is headed.

All of a sudden she extended her arms over John's body and started humming. "Hummmmmmmm. Hummmmmmmmm. Hummmmmmmmm."

It was the oddest thing, and it made me uncomfortable.

John's body went crazy.

All the monitor alarms started screaming. His arms flapped and his legs restlessly kicked as he tossed from side to side.

I stood stunned and helpless as I watched the numbers on the monitors go out of whack. His blood pressure and heart rate went up, while his oxygen levels dropped.

"Oh!" the shaman cried out.

Immediately I pushed the Call button for the nurse to come.

"John, calm down," I told him, trying to grab his hand unsuccessfully. "It's okay. You're okay. Just calm down."

But he wouldn't. His agitation had exploded and his thrashing grew worse.

It took several minutes for our night nurse to arrive, and when she did, she immediately set to work. "We need to hold him down or he'll pull out his IVs," she told us.

So Melissa, the shaman, the nurse, and I each grabbed a limb and tried to keep him stationary. But he was fighting us hard.

With perfect timing, Jason arrived. "What happened?"

"I don't know!" I said. "He's been a little agitated this evening, but just a few minutes ago, he went crazy." *Exactly the time the shaman started her "energy send."*

The nurse indicated that Jason should take her place, while she went to grab some belts to tie my son down.

"John," Jason said. "You're okay, John. We're here. Can you calm down for us?"

John continued to battle us, pushing his arms and legs and fighting to get free.

The nurse returned with the ties and secured him down. But even then, he wouldn't settle himself.

There was no explanation for what was happening. I could tell, though, whatever it was, it was dark. In the spiritual realm, the room had erupted into chaos.

"I just don't know what to do with this boy," the nurse said, as though he were specifically causing her trouble. "He just won't settle down." Then she hit the propofol pump multiple times.

Is she overdosing him? But he's not struggling against the tubes or the ventilator.

The propofol was there in case he would wake up and start fighting the tubes attached to the ventilator and trying to pull them out. Now she flipped it on even though he wasn't struggling against that. He was flailing around, but that wasn't going to pull a tube from his lungs. So why turn it up?

I shrugged off the thought and exhaled my relief when both the nurse and the shaman took their leave. But the damage was already done. The peace we had worked so hard to protect had totally left the room.

I told Jason everything that had happened. He kept his eyes focused on my still-struggling son and the monitors that were continuing to beep and whine.

"Our job is to keep peace in this room," he told me and Melissa. "We've got to, at all costs, keep peace in this room." That became our new assignment and battle cry.

"This really feels like a spiritual attack, because he's been so good today," I said.

We prayed over John and played worship songs for him, but nothing seemed to change the atmosphere. And strangely enough, the nurse disappeared.

It took two hours for John to finally calm down. Jason left shortly afterward and Melissa and I settled in for the night, thinking that everything was back to "normal critical." But by 11:30, John had started to cough. Each cough grew worse until they turned into horrible coughing convulsions that shook his whole body.

I pushed the Call button for our nurse, whom we had not seen since she'd tied John up and turned up the propofol. Though she should have been checking in about every fifteen minutes, it had now been two hours and no sign of her.

The minutes ticked by as John continued to force loud and treacherous coughs. Still no nurse.

I pushed the Call button again. And again.

Finally Melissa headed out to find the nurse. In frustration, I tried to think back to what Dr. Ream had done the night before when John had struggled with the coughing fit. I'd watched him pull out the nostril tube, which cleared the passage and had helped some. I put my hand on the tube, but couldn't remember what the special trick was.

"Uuuh!"

"I can't find her anywhere," Melissa said as she walked back in.

Helpless and more angry than I could control, Mama Grizzly went into action. I stuck my head out in the hall and looked both ways. Nothing. I felt my blood pressure rise and my face fire up with heat. I squinted across the hall at the nurses' station, but it was empty, too.

John's coughing was growing louder and scarier.

When I get a hold of her...

Stepping into the middle of the hallway, I shouted, "WHERE THE HELL IS MY NURSE!"

Four nurses stuck their heads out from their patients' rooms to see what the commotion was about.

"What's wrong?" Jackson's nurse said as she came out of his room and met me in the hall.

"He's coughing terribly. And I haven't seen our nurse since *nine.*"

Into our room she went. "Let's get you taken care of," she told John. Her voice was quiet and kind. She adjusted his ventilator and cleared out his tubes. "I know you're uncomfortable, but hopefully this will ease that a bit." His coughing gradually subsided, with a few coughing spasms coming over him every few minutes, but he eventually calmed down. He moved his head slowly from side to side in a way that suggested he was worn out and uncomfortable.

"She's done," I told Melissa once we got settled back down. "She is so done."

Around 3:00 a.m., our nurse finally waltzed in. She looked over his monitors and vitals, turned down his propofol, and acted as though she'd been there and checking on him all night long.

"Where have you been?" I asked her, not bothering to hide my annoyance.

"I had other things to do."

Wow.

I started to come off the couch, but Melissa gently touched my arm and shook her head. She was right. I couldn't preach to everyone that we would speak only life and that we would protect the peace, and then be a source of disruption in the room myself.

I took a deep breath and stated as evenly as I could, "We needed you, and you weren't here."

She ignored me. She didn't even try to make an excuse for herself. She simply finished doing whatever she was doing to John's monitors and then left without another word.

CHAPTER 14

A Bad, No-Good, Rotten, Lousy Day

Thursday, January 22, 2015

After her reappearance at 3:00 a.m., the night nurse showed up for the remaining three hours of the shift she had left. And she continued to act as though I wasn't in the room. My daughter-in-law Jennifer had been right. And now I watched this nurse like a hawk.

Throughout the early-morning hours, Melissa and I did our best to restore the calm and peace—actually, it was more Melissa, because I was so upset by the earlier events, I wasn't sure I wanted to calm down. Especially when I saw the state the nurse had left my son in. He had been overmedicated and was now totally out of it. No responses from him, no hand squeezing, no acknowledging our questions. Nothing. It was as if he had reverted back to how he was on Monday. I wasn't happy about it. At all.

To make everything worse, our beloved day nurse, Wendy, wasn't working this day, so we had a new day nurse. I cringed at the thought of potentially getting the night nurse's twin, but fortunately, this one was another excellent and caring worker.

At around 8:00, Dr. Ream and his team of medical students arrived.

"Good morning!" Dr. Ream said cheerfully. "How are you doing, John?"

He waited for my son to offer some response, but instead he got John 1.0.

"John?" he walked over to the monitors and studied them. His furrowed brow showed his confusion and concern. The numbers were low and out of whack. Then he turned to the day nurse. "I don't understand it. He was so responsive yesterday, and now he's not. Why are we having this setback?"

While he and the day nurse conferred over what might have caused the setback, I finally spoke up. "This is what I think happened," I told him. "I think that night nurse overmedicated him. She turned up the propofol levels so she could leave and not have to mess with him. And then she didn't come back till three a.m." My anger level was rising again as I spoke. "I don't want her back in here *under any circumstances.*"

Dr. Ream listened. He looked at Melissa, who verified my story with a nod. Two witnesses and a doped-up, nonresponsive kid who should not be in this condition. That was proof enough. He told me that as soon as his rounds were complete, he'd talk with Casey, the head nurse, and have her stop by to get the story directly from me.

Oh, she'll get the story all right.

Just giving voice to my complaint renewed my fury.

"How about I spend the day with you today?" Melissa asked. "It's my regular day off."

Even though she'd spent the night, I appreciated her proposal—and I had a feeling her offer was more to keep me calm and sane than for any other reason.

At around 9:15 a.m., Jason entered the room, and oh, he was just the audience I needed! Since he had been there the previous night to see what had happened, I knew he would understand my anger and agree with me. I walked him outside of John's room and then let it all out. I wanted that nurse's head on a platter. I wanted her fired. I wanted to make sure that no other child had to suffer from this woman's utter lack of ability or care.

"She is not going to be his nurse tonight—or ever again."

Jason's body tensed up. I knew he understood and I knew he could tell that

John wasn't right this morning. He let me get out all of my frustration and then assured me that she wouldn't get near my son.

"Let me go find Dr. Ream and reiterate your concerns, and then make sure *he* makes sure that nurse doesn't return."

"Thank you."

I reentered the room and sat next to Melissa. I wanted to calm down and regain some control, but every time I revisited in my mind what that nurse had done, my anger boiled to the surface.

John had to deal with enough health issues without adding too much medicine to the list. It wasn't just the fact that John had been overdosed that was the problem. The fever wasn't going away—no matter what they tried. So they placed him on antibiotics—which, of course, caused a new bout of diarrhea. His oxygen levels weren't staying up. And he continued to cough. This poor kid! It was breaking my heart to watch him suffer so much.

As John started becoming more aware, he became more uncomfortable. The more he woke up, the more he thrashed and struggled. Several times Jason and I had to hold down his arms and legs.

"John, calm down," we'd tell him. "You're okay. I know this isn't comfortable, but you need to relax."

It seemed that we'd get him calmed down finally, and then someone would come in and adjust some tube or take his vitals or jiggle something around, and off he'd go again, thrashing and flailing and fighting us. It was exhausting work. But the last thing I wanted was for him to get doped up again on the propofol to force him to calm down.

Brad Riley showed up at around 10:00, and he and Jason stood around John's bedside to pray. Just as they started, though, Dr. Garrett entered the room, so they edged away for him to work.

"No, no," he told them. "What you're doing is working much better than what I'm doing. Actually, we need you to pray for John's lungs. The breathing is the issue. If these lungs don't get fixed, even though he's coming back brain-wise—" He stopped himself so he wouldn't say anything negative. Finally, he said, "We need a miracle with the lungs."

Later in the morning, amid all the visitors and the nurse and the technicians constantly coming in and out, the female neurologist with the thick accent showed up (we'll call her "Dr. Johnson").

"Good morning," she said, lifting her clipboard and looking it over. "How are you this morning, John?" At least I think that's what she said.

John didn't respond.

She asked him a few other hard-to-understand questions with no results, so she marked it on her clipboard.

"I'm going to order an EEG for him for tomorrow, because I'm worried that he is having underlying brain seizures," she said.

What? They had warned us that part of that seventy-two-hour window was going to be John's brain swelling and then he would start having seizures. His brain still hadn't swollen, though, so he shouldn't experience any seizures. But Dr. Johnson seemed certain that he was supposed to have them, and so he *was* having them.

"I'm concerned that we cannot get him to respond."

Well, maybe if that nurse hadn't pumped so much propofol into his system, we wouldn't have this problem, I thought and took a deep breath to steel myself against going down that anger road again. I couldn't figure out why she didn't think John could respond. *Hasn't she heard from Dr. Garrett about how John woke up yesterday and answered all the basketball questions?* I wondered. *What other response does she need?*

I just wanted this woman out of John's room. It was as though as wonderful as yesterday had been with John waking up and communicating with us, today the pendulum swung all the way to the other side and chaos was everywhere.

Lord, we need this boy stabilized and we need peace in this room, I prayed.

Toward noon, John finally calmed down enough that he was able to rest. But just as we breathed a sigh of relief, more trouble ensued. Apparently, chaos was today's order of the day.

Monica Sullivan from Cardinal Glennon's public relations team walked in. "Good morning."

We'd let the PR folks know that we didn't want to deal with the media or give any interviews, so I wasn't sure why she was here.

"We have a situation," she said, getting right to the point.

Uh-oh, a "situation" is never good.

"It appears that someone from John's school posted Dr. Sutterer's letter on Facebook. It went viral."

Dr. Sutterer's letter to the students at John's and his daughter's school, talking about the miracle that had happened in his ER room, was powerful and moving. But it was private, meant only for those who knew John personally—students, family, and friends. It certainly wasn't for public reading.

"What do you mean someone posted it on Facebook?" I asked her.

She shrugged. "I don't know, but it's out and it's everywhere. The media is all over it. And we need to get ahead of the story."

Up to this point no one had made any statements to the media about the specifics of John's situation—even though we knew the local media had been trolling the school's and our church's Facebook pages to see what information they could glean. Now thanks to this letter going public, they knew John's name and other information that, as a minor, they had no business knowing.

"I can't deal with this, too, today," I told Jason. I was still reeling from wanting to scalp the nurse and the neurologist. I couldn't take on the media, too.

While I called Brian, Jason called the school's superintendent to figure out what was happening and ask the school to remove it from their page immediately. They agreed and apologized, but unfortunately, the mess was already done.

I was frustrated that we had to deal with this situation. I knew people were excited about what God was doing, and I knew they shared the letter out of that excitement. But we had worked hard to protect John from what we knew would become a media circus, and now we would have to deal with it. This added another layer of stress, and I didn't know if I could take on one more

thing. Ready or not, here came the media—and now it was left to us to perform cleanup duty.

"I think you're going to have to respond to this," Jason told me. "Otherwise,
who knows what kind of story they'll tell?"

He was right. We had to get a hold of the story and make sure the media
told the truth. I didn't want John to become the latest gossip in the frenzy that
I knew was about to break loose. But that didn't mean I had to like it.

I was so wiped out—despite Jason's advice, I still hadn't gotten any rest—
the thought of facing anyone was just too overwhelming for me. I couldn't
handle that and focus on my son. "I just can't deal with this, too. Would
you...?"

"Of course," Jason said, as if reading my mind. "I'm here for you and Brian.
However you need me, in whatever capacity."

"Actually, do you mind running point on all the media stuff?" I knew I
couldn't handle it all. If I couldn't carry it, I was certain Brian couldn't. And
if Jason was willing to shield us from the media and handle the arrangements
for interviews, then in my book, he had just risen from wonderful pastor to
glorious saint.

"Absolutely," he said and then looked at Monica. "I think we should set up
a meeting with your team to put together a game plan on how we want to
move forward."

She agreed. "How about meeting tomorrow?"

"That's fine," I said. Monica was a lovely and kind woman. She was efficient
at her job. But to be honest, I wished I had no need to interact with her—or
with any public relations person. I just wanted to be with my son, to focus on
his care and his healing, to make sure he had what he needed and that he knew
I was there for him. Basically, I just wanted to be a mom.

I felt wiped out. *How much more to this day?* I wondered.

"Joyce," Jason said with a dad kind of tone to his voice. "It's time for you to
go and rest."

"I'm fine."

His eyebrows rose, as if he didn't believe me.

"Really," I assured him.

His face didn't change.

"I can rest fine here. I'll just lie down on this couch."

A smirk passed over his lips and then his face went tight. He knew exactly what I knew. The room could have been Grand Central Station with everything that was going on, and I was looking him in the eyes and with a straight face trying to convince him that I could actually get rest.

"No, and you need to eat something, too."

"I'm not that hungry," I insisted.

"*Joyce,*" Jason said again. This time I really did feel as though I were a teenager who'd just been grounded. "I'm here. I can cover this. I'll stay by John's side and make sure he's well cared for."

"You're kicking me out?"

"I'm kicking you out."

What is this? I thought of this onslaught against me. My *friend* was kicking me out of my son's room!

"There's the Ronald McDonald Family Room upstairs," he reminded me. "You can get some food up there and then rest in the nice lounge chairs. It will be quiet and no one will bother you."

Very much against my will, I slowly rose from the sleeping couch and dragged my feet out of the room. I could tell if I didn't move, he was probably going to physically pull me up and escort me out.

I exited the elevator on the fifth floor and easily found the Ronald McDonald Family Room. It had a cheerful entrance, with smiling, happy children's faces greeting me and multicolored handprints covering the wall. I was surprised to find the room empty when I entered. It had a fully functioning kitchen, with a refrigerator, microwave, and stove. I steered clear of it, though, even though I knew it held plenty of snacks and drinks. I just didn't want to eat.

The rest of the room had lots of oversized lounge chairs and sofas that looked inviting. I chose one of the recliners by a window, plopped myself down, and lifted the foot rest. I sighed. *I don't need to be up here. I should be down in John's room. He's had a rough day today. What if something happens and I'm not there?*

My eyelids grew heavy. And soon I drifted into unconsciousness.

While I was up in la-la land, a friend of Brian's arrived at the PICU waiting room.

"Why aren't you in there with John?" he boldly asked Brian.

"I—"

"It must be difficult to see your son like that," the friend said. "If he were my son, I don't know that I could see him that way, either. Especially when the outlook seems so bad." He shook his head sympathetically.

"We're praying for complete healing," Brian finally responded, feeling tense and fearful.

"Of course! But...well, no one has ever recovered from something like this, have they? Not that God *can't* heal him, but it's tough to hold out that hope, isn't it?"

The friend's words sent shock waves and pain through Brian. *I don't want to hear this*, he told himself. "Well," he said shakily, "we're trying to keep focused on a positive outcome."

"Yes, of course. I just think—"

"Let's go back," Brian offered. "John can't have a lot of visitors at one time, so I usually stay in the waiting room to allow others that opportunity. Then when things slow down out here, I go in and check in on him."

Unfortunately, they picked a bad time to visit, as John's numbers were still down from where they had been and needed to be.

"Oh, he looks bad," Brian's friend blurted out as soon as he walked in and saw John with all the tubes and with the monitors beeping. "Look, I know you're trying to think positively. I get that, but...I really think you need to prepare for the worst. The odds are just stacked too much against him. I would just hate for you to get your hopes up and then have John not make it."

Brian swallowed hard as tears filled his eyes, but he said nothing.

John responded by thrashing and coughing. His condition grew so bad that the alarms on multiple monitors and machines started going off.

"See, this is what I'm talking about," his friend continued. "I don't think he's going to make it. Such a shame."

Jason pulled out his phone and texted my sister, who was in the waiting room, and asked her to come back to the room ASAP. He needed help to keep the peace in the room. Within seconds Janice was there and grabbed John's nurse, who went right to work on John. John's breathing numbers went crazy, his temperature spiked, and the nurse was having a hard time stabilizing him. His thrashing became more intense. His legs kicked around violently and then he forcefully dropped them down on the bed. He lifted his arms and flailed them and grabbed for the tubes in his throat and his nose.

"I need you to get this person out of this room," Jason told Janice quietly. "I also need you to keep anyone away from this room who isn't going to speak life." They looked at Brian, who now appeared pale and deflated. They quickly decided that Jason would stay with John and take care of him, while Janice would take care of our family and friends in the waiting room.

Janice turned to Brian and the guest. "John needs to get some rest, so I think it's best if we all leave him alone right now."

Jason reached over and touched Brian's arm. "John's going to be okay," he whispered. "Don't let anyone tell you otherwise. God's got this."

Brian nodded weakly, took another look at our son, and then he and his friend left the room.

In the meantime, Melissa was hanging out in the waiting room when some people from our church arrived. On my way up to rest, I'd texted her and asked her to keep an eye out for them. When they arrived she was to come up and get me. Now they had arrived, but Melissa wasn't sure about bothering me. So she went to Janice, who had returned to the waiting room, to get her opinion.

"If she's actually resting, I don't want to wake her, since this is really the first time she's slept in, what, four days now?" Melissa said.

"You're right," Janice said. "We should probably let her sleep a little longer."

They waited for a while, but then Melissa brought up the subject again. "I'm not sure what to do," she said. "She really needs to eat, too. I don't think she's had more than a nibble of something this whole week."

"Yeah, maybe we should wake her."

Melissa rose. "I'll just go and check on her."

She entered the Ronald McDonald Family Room and found me still alone there. "Joyce?" she said softly. "Joyce, hon, your friends are here."

Melissa's voice slid into my brain, but I couldn't wake up. I could hear her talking. I tried to answer, but my vocal cords wouldn't work. I told my body to react, but it was as though it had gone on strike.

Yes, I'm awake, I was telling her. Or at least I thought I was telling her. I wasn't sure I was saying anything. I was in a dense fog and was unable to pull myself out of it.

When I didn't respond, Melissa figured I was finally deep in sleep, so she returned to the PICU waiting room.

"I don't know," she told Janice. "She didn't respond, so she must really be sleeping. That's good." But something nagged at Melissa. "On the other hand, she is diabetic. She really needs to eat, and I wonder what her blood sugar level is." She decided to check my level without waking me, just to see my numbers.

"Brian, does Joyce carry a glucose tester or anything?" she asked my husband, who was seated nearby.

"No," Brian admitted. "Although I suppose she should. Do you think something's wrong?"

Melissa didn't want to concern Brian if I was just sleeping. He had so much to deal with already, so she quickly said, "Nothing to worry about. I was just wondering about it."

Back up to the fifth floor she went.

"Joyce?" She tried again to wake me, but I wouldn't respond. So she figured she'd just ask one of the nurses if she could borrow a blood glucose machine. No big deal, she thought.

Only, it was a big deal.

"Do you have a glucose measuring tool? I want to check my friend's sugar levels and then give her some sugar or something to eat to bring them up if they're too low. She isn't responding right now, but I think she's sleeping," she explained.

That simple request was like a major emergency alert. The nurse grew concerned and told her that if someone was not responding, the hospital had to step in. Melissa tried to explain again that it wasn't necessary for them to do that. But the nurse remained adamant. Melissa knew I wouldn't be happy about that. She knew the hospital was probably overreacting, but she also knew the last thing our family needed was for me to end up hospitalized as well.

"Code Blue, floor five, Ronald McDonald Room. Code Blue."

The alert blared throughout the hospital, and within moments, eight hospital personnel were there, with a gurney.

Melissa was still trying to wake me, but I could only look at her. I felt so dazed.

"What day is it, Joyce?"

I knew that answer—I'm sure it was on the tip of my tongue—but it just wouldn't come to me. "Uhhh," was the best I could get out. I thought harder. *Come on, Joyce. You know this one.* Nope, I had nothing.

"Are you hungry?" she asked. I didn't know the answer to that one, either. When a diabetic hasn't eaten and goes into a slump or a crash, that person typically won't want to eat. I didn't know if I was hungry or not. I couldn't think of when I'd last eaten. *It wasn't that long ago, was it?*

"Let's get her on the gurney. We need to take her down to the ER." The voice came from somewhere beyond Melissa. My mind screamed, *No!* But I could only look dazedly at my friend.

Strong hands reached under my arms and legs and hoisted me on the gurney. All the while, I was mentally, groggily, protesting, but I was unable to utter any words. I knew I should have stayed in John's room. I shouldn't have come up here. Now how was I going to get back to my son? He needed me, and I wasn't going to be there for him.

I was finally able to utter a moan, as they pushed me through the elevator doors and punched a button on the wall. This was turning out to be a horrible day.

CHAPTER 15

A Surprise Visit to the ER

No. Absolutely not."

I jostled around on the shortest and most uncomfortable gurney in the world, feeling much more sober and alert after having received some orange juice and a hefty dose of glucose to rev up my insulin. Apparently, my body's sugar level had taken a nosedive when I'd decided that I was above the need to eat.

But now the medical team in the ER thought that giving me juice and sugar somehow entitled them to tell me where I needed to be for the next eight hours. They'd just informed me that they were admitting me to the adult hospital across the street.

Clearly they did not know who they were dealing with.

"No, no, no. That's not happening," I told them. "There's no way you're taking me away from my son. No way. I shouldn't even be down here!"

"We're not only concerned about your insulin levels," they said. "We've diagnosed you with exhaustion. That means you *must* rest. This is a serious issue, Mrs. Smith."

"Don't care. I'm not becoming a patient."

Melissa, who had come down to the ER with me, chimed in. "Maybe you should consider it, Joyce."

"*No.*"

The doctor left me alone in the room, and within about ten minutes, my sister appeared.

"How are you feeling?" she asked, her voice filled with concern.

"Better. They gave me some stiff stuff to get me going again. But now they're trying to admit me as a patient to the hospital. Can you believe this? They want to ship me across the street!"

Her lips drew into a thin line, and I knew something was about to go down. "Joyce," she started hesitantly, "I think you *should* go ahead and let them admit you."

What? I couldn't believe it; the one person they could actually find to make me do something was my sister. They were brutal.

I steeled myself, took a deep breath, and then shook my head. Even *she* wasn't going to get me to budge. "Uh-uh, I'm not going. No way."

"But you aren't in any shape to go back up there," Janice argued. "You'll be no good to John like this."

"There is no way. I'm not doing it."

"But—"

"No. Period."

With a heavy sigh, she finally agreed to back off. "Okay, let me go tell the doctor…"

You've got that right, sister. Tell the doctor that he might as well give up on that idea.

She disappeared and then not long later, she reappeared with the ER physician.

"So your sister couldn't talk you into it, huh?" he said. He didn't sound pleased or accommodating.

Yeah, yeah, you've got a job to do, buddy—and so do I.

"Well, I'm willing to release you—"

"Good."

"*Under one circumstance*," he said, cutting me off. "You have to take your medicine. You have to eat—regularly. And you have to stay down here and sleep for at least eight hours."

Eight hours? Was he crazy?

Looking at the set of his jaw, I knew he was ready to be just as stubborn and strong willed as I was. *Grrr.* "Okay, fine. Yes, I promise I'll do those things."

"I mean it. Eight hours down here. We have a room you can use to sleep. Otherwise, we're going to have security escort you across the street."

What was I, five years old?

"Understood," I said through clenched teeth.

Janice gave me a hug and promised that she and Jason would handle everything while I rested. "Don't worry about it, and don't give it another thought. We've got it taken care of. You know I love that boy and I'm not going to let anything happen to him on my watch. Okay?"

"Okay. Where's Brian?"

"He's on his way down. He stopped in John's room first to pray with Jason."

I was glad to hear that.

Sure enough, not long after, Brian showed up.

"How are you feeling, hon?" He looked as worn-out as I felt. His eyes had dark circles and a glazed-over look about them. I thought maybe he was going to need to join me in the ER rest area. He closed his eyes tight and then opened them and fixed them on me. They were filled with concern. "I can't lose you, too, Joyce. I need you. Please get some rest and take care of yourself, okay? Promise me you're going to do that."

I didn't want to be down there, but I finally realized that my son needed a mom who was at full strength. And my husband needed a wife who could help carry his burden. It was time for me to rest.

A nurse escorted me down the hall to a room with several sterile-looking bunk beds lined up around the perimeter. I took the one farthest from the

The very first picture we got of John from Guatemala that captured our hearts.

Joyce and John

Aunt Janice and John

Aunt Miriam and John

John, age three

Uncle Don and John

Brian, Joyce, Charles, and Tom, 1984

Charles, Tom, Joe, and John, 2003

Grandpa Smith and John

John, age four

Cousins Jan and
Tom with John

Brian and John at
Busch Stadium, 2006

Chayla, John, and
Emma

Josh Rieger, Josh Sander,
and John on the ice the night
before the accident

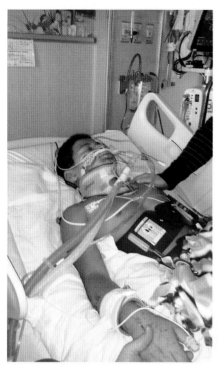

John's first night at
the hospital

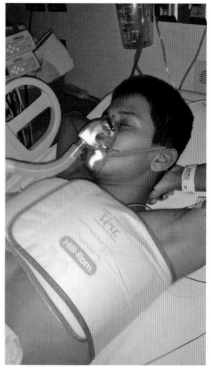

John after removing
his vent

John's basketball team visits on day twelve of his stay

John walking out
of the hospital
completely healed

John, 2016

John and Dad doing
their Friday night bas-
ketball games

John, 2016

Uncle Don and John before the homecoming dance, 2015

Pastor Brad Riley and John

Tommy Shine,
Pastor Jason
Noble, John, and
Chief Marlo

Pastor Jason,
John, Joyce, and
Brian, 2016

door and lay down. Only the bed was so short compared to my five-foot-ten-inch height that I had to pull myself into a fetal position just to stay on it.

"I'll come and check on you, but try to get some sleep," she said, as she turned off the light and shut the door.

Sure, no problem. Let me just turn off my brain and sleep while my sick son is up-stairs battling who knows what.

I shut my eyes, but sleep wouldn't come. Not because I wasn't sleepy; the walls were so thin, I could hear every passerby. Every bit of conversation, every footstep, every PA announcement. It seemed that all of it passed through the walls, echoing and magnifying itself in its volume.

Great. Eight hours in this room, in this cramped position. A sigh escaped my lips.

I concentrated on my breathing. Maybe that would relax me enough.

But my thoughts soon turned back to my boy on the floor above me. My precious son who had come into my and Brian's lives unexpectedly when most parents were entering the empty-nest stage.

God had delighted us with this child. And God had redeemed a terrible choice I had made more than three decades before.

★ ★ ★

I'd always been a hardheaded gal, and when I was seventeen years old, I fell in love with Charlie, a man six years my senior. He was divorced and a father to two children. But that didn't concern me. He made me feel alive and free and wonderful. It didn't matter that he didn't share my faith. It didn't matter that my parents saw trouble and warned me to steer clear of him. They didn't know him as I did. As far as I was concerned, they were wrong and I was right, and I was going to prove it to them. I was going to marry this man and have a family and enjoy life happily ever after.

So when I became pregnant right after my high school graduation, I was thrilled.

Charlie wasn't. "Get rid of it," he told me.

He didn't know what he was saying, I believed. I would help him see what a great thing this pregnancy was.

I might have been delighted to share my news with Charlie, but I wasn't about to tell my parents. I didn't need the hassle of them preaching at me, so I didn't tell them. It wasn't that difficult, actually. I was somehow able to hide my pregnancy through the entire thing wearing baggy clothes so it just looked as though I'd gained weight. Which, of course, I had.

As my ninth month grew closer, I started to get scared. Charlie hadn't proposed, and he'd suggested several times that I should give up the baby for adoption. I kept putting off that decision, thinking that he was just dragging his feet but that he'd see the wisdom in marrying me and us starting a family. In the back of my mind, however, I began to wonder, *If he doesn't marry me, how can I possibly support this baby by myself?* I was just out of high school and had a scholarship to go to college for music, which I'd turned down because I thought I was getting married. I had no skills, no way to live.

Finally, I agreed to give up my baby for adoption. I signed the papers and tried not to think about it. Instead I started to create this dream that once the baby was gone, Charlie would marry me, see the error of his ways, and insist that we get our baby back.

My due date came. My parents still didn't know the truth, and I told them I was going out of town for a few days to help care for some family friends' children, since the wife had recently had a baby. Instead Charlie picked me up and we went to the hospital where my doctor induced labor. I was in the delivery room, scared, alone, and far from God. What should have been a time for celebration with family all around was instead a cold, sterile reality with a man who already had children and who wasn't interested in having any more.

I gave birth to a beautiful boy with a round, chubby face, huge blue eyes, and a light covering of blond hair on his head. He had long fingers and toes and long, skinny legs. He was perfect. For two days while I was in the hospital, I held and cuddled him. I couldn't get enough of this precious baby, and I was completely in love. How could I possibly give him up? How could Charlie not want this child—his child?

During one of the times I was holding my newborn son, Charlie came in to visit me. This was the first time I had seen him since he dropped me off to give birth. His tight face and tense body language clearly communicated that he was not happy that I was holding the baby.

"Do you want to hold him?" I asked.

Reluctantly he gave in. I could see this child affecting him. He smiled and played with his baby's little fingers.

I was right. He's going to change his mind! But all too soon he lifted the baby and placed him back in my arms. "When are they taking him?" was all he said.

On the third day, I awoke excited to hold my baby again, but the nurse entered alone. She sat on the edge of my bed and took my hand. "The agency came this morning," she whispered kindly. "They took him."

A pain as I'd never felt before ripped through my body and tore at my heart. I begged for death to take me, as I sobbed into my pillow.

With an empty heart and empty arms, I left the hospital and tried to continue on with my life—but the hole that had pierced my heart wouldn't close. I still held out with the faintest hope that Charlie would reconsider everything and go after our child. But as the days passed and he acted as though nothing had happened, I slowly realized he had no intention of doing anything other than leaving the past in the past.

I returned home after four days, thirty pounds lighter and naïve enough to believe my parents wouldn't figure out something had happened. This was the late 1960s, when people—including the hospital—didn't offer details, and my parents never talked about sex or anything with me, so I didn't know the changes that take place in a woman's body after she gives birth. The next Sunday I put on my favorite dress, which I could now wear again, and headed downstairs. But halfway down, I felt moisture from my chest seep onto the dress. I ran to the kitchen to try to mop it up with a towel, but I couldn't get the flow to stop. I did not realize I was lactating.

My mother walked in, took one look at my dress, and froze. Her eyes pierced mine with shock and terror.

"What did you do with that baby?"

I crumpled against the counter and sobbed. I had lost a baby, I'd disappointed and angered my parents—to the point that my father didn't speak to me for a year—and I was still unmarried.

Despite all the pain of giving up our child, I stayed with Charlie and I got pregnant again less than a year later. And again, hope rose. But just as with our first child, Charlie wasn't interested in marriage and a family. At least not until he received a draft notice. The Vietnam War was in full force, and I think he thought that if he married me and we had this baby, he would get out of serving in the military. So on October 25, 1969, with my mother as a witness, Charlie and I stood in front of a justice of the peace in Liberty, Indiana, and said our vows.

Unfortunately, Uncle Sam didn't seem interested that he had a wife and dependents to care for. A month after our wedding, into the army Charlie went, and I moved back in with my parents.

One afternoon eight weeks into my pregnancy, while Charlie was away at boot camp, terrible cramps suddenly began to slice through my womb, and blood started to pour from the lower region of my body.

"Please, God, don't take my child," I begged, terrified that I was suffering a miscarriage. "I've already lost a baby. Please don't let me lose this one, too!"

I called out to my mother, and my parents rushed me to the hospital. On the drive over, I called out to God. I hadn't talked to Him in months. I still went through the motions of going to church with my parents and acting as though I believed. But really, now that I was married and pregnant, I thought my life was good, so I hadn't really needed Him up to that point. Now I couldn't stop praying. I pleaded, I begged, I bargained with God. If He would just save my baby, I would do anything for Him.

The doctor at the hospital put me on strict bed rest, and God answered my prayer. At nineteen, I gave birth to another son, Tom. I was ecstatic. I had a child I could hold and love and cuddle. Although he didn't take the place of the son I had given up for adoption, he was his own boy—and I adored him.

Then two years later, on Mother's Day, we were blessed again with another precious boy, Charles. Our family was complete—or almost. My heart still ached with the emptiness from losing my firstborn son. To make matters worse, my marriage, which wasn't the strongest to begin with, began to crack.

With my strong-willed, controlling personality, I was sure that I could fix it. I could make my husband love me and our children. I could woo him into wanting to be a family man. But the harder I tried, the worse things became, until finally I knew I needed a savior to rescue me and my family.

After He'd answered my prayer and saved me from miscarrying Tom, I'd thanked God and then sent Him back outside of my life. *I've got it handled now, but thanks, God*, I essentially told Him. Now I'd failed at making my marriage solid. I'd struggled and worked and forged ahead, but with results that devastated rather than blessed us. It was time to find God—and this time, I knew I had either to commit or completely walk away. There was no halfway vow with God.

I started by going back to church. I loved it; it felt good and familiar. But even though my spiritual life was getting back in order, my marriage wasn't. Many nights, while Charlie was out of the house working or doing *other* things that I later found out about, I lay on our bedroom floor after the kids went to sleep and begged God for a Christian home. It was not to be, and after eight and a half years of marriage, Charlie and I finally divorced, leaving me as a single mom to two growing and active boys.

But now I had matured. I recognized that my need for God wasn't just in the desperate times—it was all the time. If I clung to Him in the good and easy parts of life, and witnessed His faithfulness to me, then when the difficult parts came, I knew I could count on a faithful companion and rescuer whom I didn't have to try to find and bargain with.

Life certainly didn't get easier after I made an all-out commitment to God and worked on my relationship with Him, but I did feel more satisfied and complete. I felt an underlying contentment I'd never experienced when I'd worked so hard to control everything.

Almost six years after my divorce, another man entered my life. Brian loved God and was kind and compassionate and sensitive. He listened to me and respected me. He loved my boys and opened his arms to them fully—being the kind of man they needed in their lives.

We fell in love. Although life seemed good, and we got engaged, I kept a secret from him that began to gnaw at me. Before our wedding, I sought advice from a well-meaning, but terribly wrong, friend.

"Brian doesn't know that I gave up my first child for adoption," I told her. "I've wanted to tell him, but the timing has never seemed right. And then, the words haven't been there. What should I do? What if I tell him, and he calls off the wedding?"

My friend listened compassionately and then spoke ill-fated words. "Joyce, the chance of you ever finding that child—or that child finding you—is slim to none. Why go back and dig up all that stuff? Anyway, there aren't too many people who know about it and who would let it slip to Brian, so don't worry about it. Let the past stay in the past."

In my heart I knew her advice wasn't sound. I'd been around the proverbial block enough to know that when we think there's no way for a secret to come out, *it always does*. But she was offering me an easy way out, so I took it. I married Brian without him having a clue that I was actually the mother of three boys, not two.

Brian adored my boys, but they were getting older, and he wanted us to have children of our own. I wanted that, too. I wanted to have a family that stuck together and loved one another. I wanted a Christian family where together we attended church and followed God. It seemed that God was finally answering my prayers from years before.

Only, God wasn't answering them the way I anticipated. One miscarriage followed another. And my birthing days were over.

Brian and I settled into our life, both of us brokenhearted, but still committed to each other and to making our family as happy and wonderful as we could. My boys graduated from high school and set out to start life on their own as adults. The house, which we'd hoped would still echo with the sounds of children's laughter, felt empty and hollow.

I was inching up toward fifty and contemplating what I wanted to do with the next stage of my life. We were involved in church and our work. Everything seemed settled. But God remembered my prayers and Brian's heart's desire, and He chose the most unusual time and way to redeem what we'd lost.

Brian had started going with our church on short-term mission work trips to Central America. As a professional videographer, he would take his equipment and film the work our group was doing, then share the stories and video with our church upon their return. While Brian was there, his heart broke with compassion over the orphaned and hurting children of the villages he visited.

After several trips to Central America, he returned and quietly began researching adoption possibilities. Over the years we'd talked briefly on and off about that possibility, but the financial piece of it had always proved too much of a challenge for us. Now our age was "upward of ideal," so we were denied domestic adoptions. But international adoptions were still open to older couples.

One night in February 2000, armed with his research, paperwork, and applications, he came into the kitchen where I was cleaning up after dinner.

"What would you think about adopting a child?"

Here Brian stood, with his heart on his sleeve, aching for one last opportunity to be a dad. I was forty-nine years old! Brian was forty-six. Could we handle all the midnight feedings, sleepless nights, teething, diapers, and everything else that comes with a baby?

I looked at my sweet husband who had been so kind and giving to me. How could I possibly deny him this request? Plus, to be honest, the thought of having another baby did thrill me.

"I'm fine with it," I told him. "But just one thing." I watched his body tense up as he braced himself for some sort of bad condition I might place on it. "If we adopt, I'm not working again. I've already done that scenario of working and having kids. I'm going to stay home and enjoy this child."

Immediately his body relaxed and he smiled brightly. "Okay!"

"All right. Where do I sign?"

We started the process to adopt a baby. The finances were still an issue, so we took out a second mortgage on our house and trusted God to help us stay financially afloat. We hadn't intended to choose a baby from Latin America, where Brian had gone and had such a soft spot for the people there, but God knew what He was doing when He sent Brian to that area and opened his eyes to their plight. So when a baby in Guatemala became available, Brian was thrilled, and we jumped at the opportunity to make this child ours. Almost nine months to the day that Brian had first approached me about the adoption, on November 15, 2000, we held five-and-a-half-month-old John in our arms.

He was extremely underweight when we got him—still in newborn clothes and diapers—but we took him home, plumped him up, and smothered him with affection. And we *may* have spoiled him, too.

I praised God for His goodness to us and thought our family was now complete. But God wasn't finished redeeming my past.

My heart never stopped aching over my firstborn child and my choice to give him up for adoption, but adopting a child brought my past up with a tsunami force. I thought about how John's birth mother must have cried and ached over her decision. I wondered where my firstborn was. *Is he okay? Are his adoptive parents taking good care of him? Do they love him? Are they spoiling him and showering him with affection?*

One morning when John was three years old, I put him down for his nap and sat to do my daily devotions with God. I picked up *My Utmost for His Highest* by Oswald Chambers and opened to a random day's reading (being a strong-willed gal, I never liked to actually follow what day I was supposed to read!). The page opened to June 30 and the title jumped out at me: "Do It

Now!" It was about making amends, and the reading ended with, "Be reconciled to that person—*do it now!*"

I didn't think much about it—until I opened my next devotional book, *Experiencing God* by Henry Blackaby. Again, I opened to a random page and started reading. And again, I got the same message: *You need to take care of your past.*

Wow, that's really strange, I thought. *God, what are You trying to say to me? What is it You want me to do?*

The answer came fast and loud. Almost as if it were audible, I heard in my heart God respond: *I want you to find your son.*

"Are You kidding me?" I said out loud. "You know what all I went through. And *this* is what You're asking me to do?"

I want you to find your son.

I was certain I wasn't hearing God correctly. He clearly didn't understand what this meant. The trouble I might be bringing on myself. Brian still didn't know what I'd done all those years ago. "Where do I begin? I don't even know where to start!" I told God, hoping that would end it.

On the computer.

I probably won't find anything anyway, I thought. I turned on the computer, brought up Google, and typed in "Ohio adoptions."

Within seconds a list of options popped up. In big red letters at the top of the page, the description of the first site, "Searching to Reunite: Kenna Peterson" read, "Special to Ohio birth mothers, $175."

I just about fell off my chair, I felt so dumbfounded.

With a click of the mouse, I knew I could potentially change my life forever. *Nah, it's a scam*, I thought. *They won't be able to find him....But...what harm would it do? It's not like I'm going to pay that money if they don't offer some proof.*

I clicked on the site's link, and up popped a form to fill in. It asked the gender of the baby and the day and year of the baby's birth. I typed it in—although I couldn't remember the official birthdate, since he was born sometime during the night and I'd been doped up during the long, hard delivery, so I wasn't completely certain.

I typed in "Baby boy, born May twenty-first or twenty-second, 1969." Then I gave my name and phone number and hit the Send button.

I leaned back in the chair and stared at the screen for a few moments. I'd done it; I'd tried. A heavy sigh escaped my lips. Hope had returned, but so had fear. What if they didn't find anything? But what if they did? What would I do either way?

"Okay, Lord, I did what You asked," I said aloud, pushing myself from the computer. I tried not to think about it as I went about the day's work. I did a couple loads of laundry, I washed the dishes, I played with John.

About three hours later my phone rang.

"Hi, this is Kenna Peterson," said a pleasant, female voice. "I'm from Searching to Reunite. Is this Joyce Smith?"

Never at a loss for words, I now strangely found myself without a voice.

"Hello?" Kenna said.

I cleared my throat and then uttered that yes, she was speaking with Joyce Smith.

"Finding your son is going to be easy," she said, "because I've just done all the transcripts from microfiche to the computers from mothers to babies, but not from babies to mothers yet. I checked and in 1969, during the month of May on those two dates there were only three children put up for adoption in Ohio. Only one of them was a boy."

I blinked hard. Not only was I speechless, now apparently, I'd also gone dumb. I couldn't process what she'd just told me.

She continued as though my lack of response were the most normal thing in the world. "I'm going to the bureau of vital statistics on Friday, and I'll have more information then. I'll call you back on Saturday, okay?"

I grunted my approval and then managed to squeak out a "Fine."

When Brian got home that night, he asked how my day had gone. "Anything interesting happen?"

I paused. *Should I tell him?* I bit my lip, and then decided that Kenna would probably not call back on Saturday with any news. "No, just a pretty normal day."

Only, she did call back on Saturday. She'd located his parents. "If your son has filed for an Ohio driver's license, I'll have his information on Monday."

Brian! This was all too real, and I had to confess to my husband.

For the next twenty-four hours my stomach was in a continual state of nausea.

Tell him. Tell him. Tell him! my brain kept nagging me. And then another part of my brain said, *No, no, NO!* It was as if I had a little devil on one shoulder and a little angel on the other shoulder pulling me back and forth—like the '70s comedian Flip Wilson used to joke about. How was I going to break this kind of surprise to him? Only this wasn't a surprise, this was a bomb.

Finally on Sunday morning, while we were still lying in bed, I rolled over and touched Brian's shoulder to wake him. "I have something I need to tell you." And then I spilled the whole story, from giving up my child for adoption to Kenna Peterson's phone call. When I was finished, he said simply, "Okay. What's our next step?"

If I thought I'd loved him before that, it was nothing compared to how overwhelmed with love I felt for him at that moment.

While we were at church that morning, our pastor, Jerry Harris, gave the usual altar call at the end of the service, in which he invited people to the front of the room who needed special prayer. As if God placed a cherry on the top of a sundae to really make His point, Jerry said, "Someone here this morning had a baby in their past. God wants you to know that He is taking care of everything."

After my knees buckled and I shook myself out of my stunned state, I couldn't run fast enough to that altar.

That Monday Kenna contacted Joe first to see if he even knew he had been adopted and if he wanted to speak with me. The answer was yes to both, and that same day, she put me in touch with my son. It was only ten days after I did the computer search. Interestingly enough, as is so delightful with God and how He works, my first conversation with Joe was on June 30—the very same day written on the page of the "random" devotional reading that started me on this whole journey. We had several phone conversations and explanations and tears after that. And less than two weeks later, I met my sweet son Joe for the second time in my life. And he was everything I'd hoped and prayed he would be.

Now, I lay curled up on the hard cot in the ER area and thought about everything I'd experienced in my life. I'd lost a child—and God brought him back to me. He redeemed my past. Then out of God's great kindness and compassion, He gave me another child, whom I'd lost, and whom God had given back to me just four days prior to this moment.

"God," I whispered in that dark room. "You gave me back Joe and You gave me back John. I know You didn't bring us this far—with all these miracles—to let anything happen to John now. Show Yourself to be faithful again. Healer, come, and be who I know You to be. I believe."

Slowly, peace began to flow up over my body like a blanket covering me from my feet to my head. And for the first time in almost a week, I slept.

CHAPTER 16

Exchanging Fear for Faith

Brian stood in the doorway to John's room, shaky and feeling the weight of the world. He'd been down to see me and now he stood in our son's room. *First John and now Joyce*, he thought. *I'm not sure I can take much more. I need Pastor Jason to pray for me, to help me regain some sense of hope.*

"Hey, Brian," Jason greeted him.

Tentatively Brian walked into the room and carefully looked around at everything except John. His shoulders were slightly stooped over.

"How are you doing?" Jason asked when Brian didn't answer.

Finally he turned and looked at Jason, with huge tears welling up in his eyes. "I can't do this without Joyce," he said. "I can't even imagine taking care of all this without Joyce."

"Come and sit down. Let's talk."

Brian walked to a chair close to Jason and fell into it. "I just saw Joyce down in the ER. I'm scared. I can't imagine losing Joyce *and* John." He paused, closed his eyes, and thought about all of the stress he'd been under for the past year, even before all this. "I'm struggling with work, and I'm not feeling all that well. I just don't think I can do this."

"First of all, you're not going to have to do this without Joyce. Don't let the enemy lie to you and bring fear into your heart. Second, you're not going to lose John. It's not going to happen. We are speaking life over John and now over Joyce. She just has to take care of herself."

Brian shifted in his chair, unconvinced. *I know Pastor Jason is right*, he thought. *But I'm tired of constantly fighting to keep everything together.*

"John needs his dad right now. You're his hero, and he loves you so much. He *needs* you to be strong."

Brian processed Jason's words for a few moments, still feeling unsure and lost. His mind knew the truth, but in his weariness, his struggle not to listen to the enemy's whispers of fear seemed too much for him to handle. In some sense Brian felt caught between a spiritual rock and hard place. He desperately wanted to be with me and our son, but emotionally, it was just too much for him to bear. He looked at John with all the tubes and listened to the rhythm of the life-support machines, and then his mind flitted back to the earlier scene with his friend when John was thrashing and in obvious pain. He didn't want that for his son, but he fought the dark thoughts of, *What if my friend is right?*

No. I won't let my mind go there. Pastor Jason can help me to not go down that path.

"It's hard to be in this room," he finally confessed.

"I know," Jason said.

"If I stay in the waiting room, I'm still close to John, but being out there sometimes..."

While Pastor Jason and I demanded that we would not allow any words of death spoken over John, Brian was encountering some people who were not as vigilant. He was forced to listen to or overhear words of doubt, fear, hopelessness, and death—all spoken by well-meaning people who probably thought they were bringing comfort by preparing him "for the worst." *Anybody* would struggle to maintain a life-giving perspective in that environment. But Brian had another dimension to his emotional struggles. He'd had some health problems the year before that had left his sixty-one-year-old body worn down. Plus all the hours he put in at his job left him teetering on the edge of burnout—*and* he was feeling extra stressed because Boeing was in the midst of layoffs and that possibility was hanging over his head. All of that *combined* would be a sure recipe for emotional overload for anybody.

He would often pull Jason or another pastor aside to pray for him, because he felt that the enemy was using others' words and all of the year's struggles to fill him with fear. "I feel like I'm battling nonstop spiritual attacks," he would often confess to me.

So while we were speaking life over John, Brian was battling the negative talk and was worried over not getting his hopes up, because what if he did and then he lost John? The pain of that thought was too great for him to bear. But now the reality of having the two people who meant the most to him both ending up in the hospital shook him to his core. He needed to surround himself with a life-giving atmosphere.

"Pastor, I don't know if I have the strength in me. I'm tired. It's been a long year. I'm afraid."

"You're right. You *don't* have the strength to handle this. God does, though. When Scripture tells us that 'the joy of the Lord is our strength,' the Bible really means it." He went on to explain that joy doesn't come from what we see around us, or even from what the doctor says or doesn't say. True joy is a supernatural transaction that happens when we go to the Lord and honestly say, "I can't do this on my own."

Brian sat a little straighter in his chair, taking in our pastor's words.

"Listen," Jason continued. "Don't buy into fear. You can't have faith if you're buying into fear. When we give fear a place in our hearts and minds, it opens the door for the enemy to attack us. Everything that we are hearing right now from the doctors and even other people is false evidence that the enemy is trying to convince us is real. God told us that John was going to live, and *that's* the real evidence. The angels in the room, the colors over John's head, his heartbeat, the other miracles. We have to hold on to *that.*"

"How do you do that? I just feel like I'm under constant attack. My mind keeps telling me to listen to those other voices, that they're right, that we shouldn't get our hopes up." Brian likes things laid out very practically. "I think that most people who enter a church building on a Sunday would agree that God has the potential to put the worlds into being, to start from a blank canvas. I don't think that's too hard for most people to believe. It's the specific stuff where we need the miracle. God putting the universe together, okay, that was His big plan. Whether He can do it for my family, give me the miracle turnaround that we need, I struggle with that because I've never seen it before up close and personal."

"Over and over Jesus performed miracles for everyday, regular people," Jason reminded him. "When the enemy tries to come after you with false evidence, ask God what the truth is. You can be honest with God. He understands fear. But He wants you to exchange fear with faith. Tell God how you're feeling, and then right away go back to the promises that God gave in His Word."

"I get that. I'm just so overwhelmed right now."

"I completely understand," Jason told him. "Here's what I want you to do. Scripture tells us not to worry about tomorrow. Let's go a minute at a time. Don't worry about an hour from now or even a day from now. God's already there taking care of the details. Let's go moment by moment. Every day is a new day. Be on guard and take every thought captive, just as it says in 2 Corinthians 10:5. Don't let the enemy convince you of anything different."

Then he challenged Brian to make sure he was reading his Bible and praying. Often in the midst of trauma, that's the first thing to go—and it's the very thing we need! "If you aren't filling your mind with God's Word, the enemy will try to fill it with his lies," Jason said. "Bottom line, don't let your mind wander. When those fearful and lying thoughts come, don't give them any space to take hold and grow."

"That makes sense. I'm going to use that strategy." Brian took a deep breath and then looked at John. "I really love him. I'm so thankful he's my son. I can't imagine life without him." Tears filled his eyes again. "He's my buddy."

Brian got up, went to John's bedside, and took John's hand. "Hey, buddy."

Brian's voice trembled slightly. "John, I'm so proud of you and I'm thankful to be your dad. You're going to be okay. I'm here with you. You're going to make it. Keep fighting." Tears trickled down his face, and with each sentence, his voice grew stronger, more certain. "I miss my basketball partner. I'm so thankful that God gave you to us. From the moment we got the call to adopt you, you were my son, and I was so proud to be your dad. I love you. You're going to make it."

The stooped shoulders that Brian had carried when he entered were now straight, and Brian continued to hold his son's hand. *We're not going to lose you, son.*

* * *

I was an obedient gal and stayed as long as I could down in the guest family sleeping room. I did get some sleep and I willed myself to rest as long as I could, but all the noise through the paper-thin walls finally got the best of me. I found a nurse and promised "on my honor" that I would rest if they would release me to go back upstairs. Which by that point was late in the evening.

I checked on Brian first, to let him know I was okay and then I headed to John's room. The room was peaceful. Sounds of worship music danced in the air and brought with it a calmness and serenity. Jason, who was sitting next to John, looked up and smiled. He looked tired.

"So you crashed," he said.

I knew what was coming: the old *I told you so*. I might be bullheaded, but I knew when I was beat. "Yeah," I admitted and sighed. "Okay, I've got to take care of myself. I'm not a spring chicken anymore, and I just don't bounce back from this stuff like I used to when I was *your age*. You've been saying this could be a long haul. You were right. I'm going to do better."

It's tough to grow old! My brain kept telling me that I had the energy and stamina of a thirty-year-old, but my sixty-four-year-old body was telling me,

Nah-uh, not so fast, Miss Thing. I knew that I had to take care of myself. A hard lesson learned.

"I'm glad you got some rest. When we heard that Code Blue announcement and that it was for the Ronald McDonald room, my heart sank. I had a feeling it was you."

"Hey, Cupcake," I said, leaning over John's bed, wanting to change the topic. I often called him "cupcake" when I wanted to get a rise out of John. We picked it up from the new *Star Trek*, in which Captain Kirk calls the police cadets "cupcake," and then later when those same cadets arrest Kirk, they return the term of endearment. I hoped calling John this would make him feel more at ease. "Mom is here." I looked at Jason. "How is he? What did I miss?"

Jason filled me in on the visitor speaking death over John, John's violent reaction, Jason and Janice kicking everyone out, Janice stepping up to help, and Brian coming in and sitting with his son.

"He stayed for quite a while and held John's hand and talked to him," Jason said.

"Really?" Brian had briefly visited John off and on every day, but he would become so emotionally burdened and broken down that he would have to leave. "He stayed?"

"Yes, and we had a really good conversation."

I was thrilled to hear that Brian spent time with John—even though I knew the sight of his boy in this mess would distress him.

"Dr. Garrett also came in," Jason continued.

"Again? Why?"

Jason explained that Dr. Garrett had visited the room for a second time out of concern for John's numbers. "He said that, just as the neurologist had feared, they were worried that John was having miniseizures."

"Wait," I interrupted Jason. "How can that be? John passed the seventy-two-hour mark for his brain swelling, right? While I was downstairs, that time frame expired. Are they saying that his brain actually is swelling?"

"No, his brain isn't swelling. Praise God for that. But that's what they can't figure out. The monitors are showing signs that something is going on, but they don't know what. And they think it's miniseizures."

Jason told me that Dr. Garrett was concerned because John's neurological function, which had brightened, had now gone south as his body got so sick. They couldn't be sure that he was still where he had been. "They're also concerned that John's fever isn't going away, and they're afraid it might be because of an infection—but they can't find that, either. And his breathing still isn't where it needs to be, even though they have him on the maximum amount of oxygen."

As much as I hated being absent through all of that news, I realized that being forced to rest probably was the best thing at that time. The day had already been so chaotic that I don't think I could have handled having all of the afternoon stuff piled on me, too.

"They're doing an EEG test for seizures in the morning."

I nodded, since I knew the neurologist had ordered it while I was in the room earlier that day. I grabbed my phone and put out a notice on Facebook that we needed people to pray for John. Our list kept growing. We prayed for John's health, we prayed for life and strength, we prayed for rest and calm, and we prayed for protection and peace. Now we prayed against chaos and the disruption that it could cause.

"I think we should concentrate on praying for *shalom* to envelop this room," Jason said. The word *shalom*, "peace," actually means the power to break the authority of chaos in our lives. That was a perfect addition to our prayer list.

Dr. Ream was true to his word; that dreadful night nurse was nowhere to be found that evening. John had another rough night with the coughing issues, but the new nurse worked hard to help him get things under control.

Jason stayed until about 2:00 a.m. When he got up to leave, he smiled. "Get some rest. Remember, this could be a long haul."

"I will. I promise." *A long haul*, I thought. The doctors had suggested that we should expect John to be in the PICU for another two weeks—and we were only four days in. Would every day be like this?

CHAPTER 17

Letting Vengeance Go

Friday, January 23, 2015

Every morning around 7:00 a.m., John's principal, Nancy Benes, called me to get the update on John. This morning, however, she had an update to give me.

"We've had the most amazing thing happen," she told me excitedly. "You know how the school has a chapel service every Thursday?"

"Yes, you mentioned you were going to have a special prayer time for John."

"We did, but something else happened."

"Oh?"

"A pastor came to speak. He'd already been scheduled months ago to come and talk, so he didn't know about John or mention him during his message, but his words were perfect for the situation." She told me that he talked about the fact that people never know what tomorrow will bring and that the important thing is to have a solid relationship with Christ. At the end of his message, the pastor invited any students to the front of the room who wanted to commit or rededicate their lives to God. "More than a hundred people came forward!"

I did a quick mental calculation. The school had four hundred students—and it was a *Christian* school. "You mean to tell me that more than a quarter of the school's students got saved or recommitted their lives?"

"Yes! And even adults were going forward! Some teachers recommitted their lives and a lady who works in the cafeteria gave her life to God."

"Praise the Lord!" I nearly shouted. *That's just like God!* I thought and laughed. Even in the midst of the chaos and craziness, even when it looks as though God isn't working or answering our prayers, even when it seems as if all hope is gone, God shows up and does something spectacular, reminding us that He is always working. He never sleeps, He never forgets, He never lets a single moment go to waste. God was already redeeming what had happened to my son.

I was still riding the wave of that great news when Casey, the head nurse, popped in.

"Hi, Joyce, I stopped by yesterday but you were resting. Is now a good time to talk?"

All of a sudden, the joy I'd just felt disappeared as the pent-up frustration I'd harbored toward that awful night nurse came seething back to the surface. Even though I hadn't seen her since two nights before, I couldn't let go of my anger over all the unnecessary harm she had caused my child. There was no way I was letting this one go. Casey needed to understand the kind of nurse she had in this department. And that nurse needed to find a new occupation ASAP.

"As you know, John had a horrible day yesterday," I began. "His numbers were way out of range. He was unresponsive. He had a major setback."

She nodded. I could tell she was listening and concerned. So I forged ahead with my complaint. I told her how the nurse had spiked John's propofol levels and then disappeared, how she'd been rude to me and didn't appear to know what she was doing. I told her that I was concerned for other patients who were under her care. But most of all, I let her know in no uncertain terms, "She will not be his nurse again. At all. *Ever.*" I didn't care if she were the last nurse on the face of the earth, I meant what I said. "I want to file an official complaint against her." Then to make sure Casey truly understood how serious I was, I reiterated my demand: "I don't want him near her or her near him ever again. I don't want her back in here."

"Absolutely," she said, reassuring me. "We'll make sure that doesn't happen. You'll have a different nurse. You don't need to worry about that."

That better be true, I thought. Because if it wasn't, the PICU was going to witness an all-out women's wrestling match: Joyce Smith versus Nurse Ratched. And I was going to win it. Nobody was going to do this to my son and get away with it.

Not long after my conversation with Casey, Jason entered, accompanied this time by his wife, Paula. Because of her work schedule, this had been the first opportunity she'd had to come to the hospital since that first night. I was so glad to see her.

And I was so riled up again from thinking about what that night nurse had done, I welcomed a friendly audience to share my grief and frustration with!

"You know, some of John's setback and challenges didn't have to happen, but *that nurse...*" I said. On my tirade went. I brought up every little frustration I'd had with the night nurse. "I filed a complaint this morning. I want her fired." More ranting. Finally, I stated loud and firm, "God has done all of this amazing work, and she was trying to undo it? Oh, no, no, no, she isn't! I'll take her down!"

The day nurse walked in and asked us to step into the hallway so she could change John's bedding.

As we stepped into the hall, Paula turned to face me.

"Joyce, listen to me," she said. "That nurse, whatever she did, she can't undo what God did. You know that. The Lord has just raised your son from the dead. Now, we're not going to partner with this controlling spirit. We're just not going to do it. Your son's still here. God's still going to take care of it. Let's not be vindictive about this."

I felt as if an arrow had just punctured the space in my brain between my eyes. As soon as she spoke the words, I knew she was right. I needed to let it go and calm down and let God take care of things. I'm a strong-willed, control-the-situation kind of person, and so I wanted to help God handle this situation! But I knew the truth in my heart *before* Paula said it, I just needed somebody to check me and say, "Okay, we're not going to do that."

Her challenging words penetrated my anger and helped ease me off the ledge of being vengeful. She was brave to confront me. It's scary to challenge someone who is ready to fight. But she loved me and our family enough that she was willing to let me potentially turn my anger toward her. God used her to help me realize that the situation with the nurse was over.

"Joyce, God saw that nurse. He'll take care of it—in His time and His way."

She was right. I would still file the report, I would still refuse to allow that woman to have access to my son, but I would no longer allow her to control my emotions. I would no longer allow myself to become a force of chaos in my son's room. It was time to get things back under control and to let my anger go.

I sighed heavily. "You're right. This is not who I want to be. And that nurse isn't worth us losing sight of what we've gained and of what God is doing." I chuckled at the thought. Did I really believe that some night nurse was going to be able to thwart God's work and plans for my son? How little *was* my faith even to entertain that?

And so still standing out in the hallway, Paula and I prayed about it. With that prayer, I felt a peace and calm return. If I was going to fight over anything, I needed to focus my fight on making sure peace and calm remained in that room—and in us.

Riding high from that conversation, I supposed I shouldn't have been surprised to see that when we returned to the room my son was struggling again. I had to remind myself that this boy had drowned. He had literally been submerged in cold water for more than twenty minutes. Recovering from an average cold takes at least ten days! So this poor kid's body—which had been dead!—hadn't caught up yet with the healing that was coming his way.

The fever John had been fighting on and off throughout the week now raged. Upward his temperature rose, past the 100-degree mark, past the 102-degree mark, past 104. Once again a flurry of activity surrounded John.

"We need to cool his body down. We're afraid he's going to get brain damage because he's so hot." The nurse gave him Tylenol and placed the Arctic Sun cooler blue patches over his body to cool him down.

The intense fever, the possibility of miniseizures, his lungs and breathing, and a new possibility for brain damage again, even though we'd only passed the brain swelling concern less than twenty-four hours before. I felt as though the enemy *really* wanted my son dead.

"God, he's in Your hands. Do Your thing," I said helplessly over John's body.

With everything else they were pumping into his body, they didn't want to continue giving him propofol, if they could help it, and propofol isn't meant to be used for more than a twenty-four-hour period, since it can damage the liver, and they'd had to use it for four days now. Without the propofol, he was still out of it, but aware enough to know that he had something unbearable down his throat and he didn't want it there anymore. So he began thrashing and pulling at the ventilator tubes, trying to get them out, and they'd have to give him a dose.

I knew the staff was trying to balance letting him be as awake as much as possible with making sure he wasn't too uncomfortable. It became a question of "Do we just give him no medicine and have him endure everything?" A good side effect (for John) of propofol is that it causes short-term memory loss, so at least he wouldn't remember what had happened. I imagined, *What if he had no pain and was wide awake through all of this? What anxiety might he feel having to undergo all of this treatment while conscious?*

Just as with their earlier work trying to stabilize him those first few days, the staff's balancing act continued. Every time they lightened the medication, John had a severe chilling response where his body would tremble and shake.

My heart ached to watch him, burning up with an intense fever, sweating, then cooling and trembling—fighting the cooling patches and the tubes, and not understanding what was happening to him. Every once in a while, his eyes would flutter open, he would catch sight of me, and then he would glare at me with a death stare, as though I had done this to him.

"John." Jason took John's hand and held it firmly. "You better knock off that glare at your mother." He'd seen it, too.

"It's okay," I told him. "I don't think he understands where he is or what happened."

"Well," he said, still speaking to John, "if you don't stop glaring at your mom, I'm going to pull out your catheter."

"Ha!" We both burst out in laughter. It felt good to let loose and enjoy a moment that had been filled with so much tension.

Every once in a while, during a quiet time Jason or I would gently tell John, "You're in the hospital. You had an accident. You're okay. Everything's fine. But you need to heal now. Do you understand?" He would squeeze our hands, saying that he did. But then the propofol would kick in and he would forget what we'd told him. So I knew he didn't know what was happening or why. All he knew was that he was in pain and discomfort and I was sitting by him not doing anything to ease his condition.

Finally Dr. Vincent Gibbons, one of the neurologists, came in to run an electroencephalogram (EEG) on John. The doctors hoped the EEG would show what was going on in John's body, because they thought he was having brain seizures—in addition to everything else.

It was almost time for our meeting with the hospital's public relations team to try to get a handle on the media frenzy that we knew was on the verge of starting. So we left Dr. Gibbons to his work. I texted Brian to tell him we needed to leave for the meeting, but he didn't respond, so I went to the waiting room to find him. He wasn't there, either. *Where is he?* I tried calling, but nothing. We waited as long as we could, while I continued to text him, but finally, I told Jason that we should just go ahead. I hated not having Brian at the meeting, but without knowing where he was or what he was doing, I wasn't sure what else to do.

*   *   *

"This is a big story, and it's going to have legs. We've already received dozens of interview requests from all over the world," Jamie Sherman, the head of the PR department, explained when we started the meeting. She and Monica sat across from Jason and me.

Oh, that's just great, I thought snarkily. I knew I needed to check my attitude. It wasn't Jamie's or Monica's fault. They were actually kind and understanding, and I knew they were just doing their jobs, but I was frustrated that I had to be there at all.

"John has such an amazing story, so it's understandable that the media wants to cover it," Jamie said. "One of the challenges, though, is that they all want exclusives."

Well, that will be difficult, I thought, but I didn't care so much about that. "I just want to ensure that whoever talks about it treats the story and my son with respect."

"Of course. That's our goal as well," Jamie said.

"Joyce and I talked about it and I'll be the point person for all of this," Jason said.

I breathed a sigh of relief. "I need to stay focused on John, so Jason will handle the media stuff. Brian and I have agreed that you can go through him, because he will speak for our family."

So with everyone on the same page, we drafted a press release that Jamie and her team could send out.

> God has put together a team of people who were selected to save our son's life. John is healing miraculously. Doctors have said countless times that he is a miracle. We are focusing on John and giving time for God to complete what He started. We want to thank all of the people, literally from around the world. Prayers are appreciated, please keep them coming.
>
> We want to thank everyone for their support, from the young lady who called 911, to the first responders in Wentzville and Lake St. Louis

for rescuing him. To Dr. Sutterer, the emergency department doctor at SSM St. Joseph Hospital West, and the critical care team of nurses and doctors at SSM Cardinal Glennon. And especially to our family at First Assembly Church in St. Peters led by Pastor Jason Noble. A team of pastors from various churches—Brad Riley, Mark Shepard, and Al Edney—have been amazing for our family. We want to thank the media for their patience during this incredibly emotional time for our family.

With the media stuff handled, at least for the time being, Jason and I returned to John.

Dr. Gibbons was still doing the EEG on him, so we couldn't go into his room and talk with him or hold his hand. I just felt so helpless.

Sometimes being a mother is the most amazing experience in the world. You care for a child, you love and dote on and delight in seeing him grow and mature and become his own person. Other times being a mother is the most painful experience you can have. I sat next to my sweet boy, a baby I'd nurtured and loved and spoiled—and I could do nothing to take away this pain from him. My heart ached. I would have done anything, given anything, to not have my John go through this misery.

We'd experienced miracles. I knew God was there and working behind the scenes. I'd focused on speaking life and clinging to that faith as small as a mustard seed, that faith that can move mountains, that faith that God loves to see in His children. Somehow I knew if John was to get through this, it would be because of our faith.

In my Bible study group, we'd studied Beth Moore's *The Patriarchs*. While we were learning about the Old Testament patriarchs of the faith, I found myself deeply wanting to know and understand why God so highly favored Abraham and why Abraham's faith was so strong. Abraham had such faith that no matter what God asked him to do he didn't question it. He just did it. When God asked him to leave his homeland of Ur and move to a place that God didn't reveal, Abraham got up and he moved. What was it that Abraham did to be called a friend of God? And why did he trust God so emphatically that he would do anything God asked him to do?

It wasn't that Abraham was perfect. To protect himself against a foreign ruler, he lied about his wife, not once but twice. He let his wife talk him into sleeping with another woman in order to get her pregnant—a decision that still has consequences for us. So it wasn't that God was faithful to him because Abraham never messed up. It simply came down to trust. Abraham trusted God.

I wanted to embrace and practice the kind of faith that Abraham had. That faith was the key to my boldness to pray for John without doubting that God would answer my prayers. I didn't have to know the answers, I didn't have to see the end results. I just had to trust God and believe that He is always faithful, He is always working, and He is always good.

I was grateful for His miracles—but I just wished they were more on my schedule!

By 4:00 p.m. John, who had been restless and uncomfortable all day, finally took another turn and calmed down. No more fighting or flailing or thrashing about. The fever was raging, the breathing was still strained, the other issues were still concerns, and we didn't know the results of the EEG. Nothing within his body had changed. But after Paula's prayer and my release from a need for vengeance and for trying to control the situation, everything had changed.

CHAPTER 18

The Limits of Modern Medicine

Saturday, January 24, 2015

Wₑ think John may have spinal meningitis." Dr. Ream stood against the wall and shoved his hands in his pockets.

The air rushed out of my mouth as though Dr. Ream had punched me in the stomach. *Spinal meningitis.* Just hearing the words struck fear in my heart. I knew it was a serious infection that inflamed the membranes of the brain and spinal cord—and was yet another thing that could ultimately cause brain damage and a number of other health problems.

They'd run every other test they could think of—and all of them had come back negative. We'd received the good news that John's EEG showed no seizures. In fact, it had showed nothing out of the ordinary. No underlying anything. God had answered our prayers about that—but it still didn't explain what was going on in John to cause the intense fevers.

No one could figure it out. They couldn't find any indication of an infection, and his second lung culture again came back sterile, which was great news but didn't get the doctors any closer to figuring out this mystery.

John's body was clearly fighting against *something*.

I didn't cherish the thought that they'd arrived at the possibility of spinal meningitis, nor did I get excited about the test they'd have to run on John to determine if this was what he had. They would do a spinal tap, what they called a lumbar puncture. It can be dangerous and painful because they stick a large needle into the space between the vertebrae in the lower back, puncture the spinal column, and pull out a sample of the cerebrospinal fluid.

I swallowed hard.

"With all that dirty lake water he swallowed, he may have picked up the bacteria there. We don't know. We'll do a CT scan first to see if that shows anything, such as brain swelling or damage to his brain, neck, or spinal cord." If so, and they did the spinal tap, that could potentially cause him to have seizures—something we'd already ruled out and didn't want to have a possibility of again.

"Hang on," I said, picking up my phone. "Let me get Brian in here. This is a decision he needs to be part of."

"Of course," Dr. Ream said and waited as I tried texting Brian. When Brian didn't respond, I called him. Still no response. *Where is he?* I wondered, knowing it wasn't like Brian not to answer.

"Let me run to the waiting room and see if I can find him," said my sister, Janice.

While we waited, Dr. Ream decided to remove John's neck brace. John was still wearing the collar; because of all the life-support equipment that they had on him, they hadn't been able to determine if and to what extent he had neck, head, or spinal injuries. It had been uncomfortable for John and had been one of the things he pulled at when he'd thrashed around.

I knew he didn't need to wear it any longer. I knew he didn't have any brain injuries—or any swelling. Actually after the seventy-two-hour mark, they could have taken it off, but they needed an orthopedic doctor's permission. And that physician was supposed to have arrived on Friday but was a no-show—something that hadn't made Dr. Ream happy when he first entered the room.

Within minutes Janice returned alone. "He isn't there. Not sure where he's gone."

I sighed and wondered what to do. The doctor couldn't wait—especially not if it really was spinal meningitis. But this was serious enough that I didn't feel comfortable making this kind of decision without Brian knowing and agreeing.

I rubbed my forehead to ease the building stress.

We tried reaching Brian several more times, but still no response.

"I'm not going to tell you that this is a simple procedure, because there are potential side effects that are rare but are real possibilities," Dr. Ream explained. Any time they puncture—even that word sounds horrible—there is a chance that something could happen with the fluid, which would put the brain in more stress and could cause a host of other problems.

"I know you want your husband in on this decision, as you should. However, we do need a decision soon, because we don't want to wait on this."

"Of course." I knew if John did have spinal meningitis, they needed to move quickly because it could do serious damage to his body, and it could cause strokes. *I'm sorry, Brian*, I thought. "Yes, let's do it."

Dr. Ream left, and a little while later in came the nurse and a technician. Because John was connected to so many machines—and was still on life support—they had to move slowly and carefully to unhook everything in order to transport him down the hall for the CT scan.

Lord, we don't know what's causing this fever, but You do, I prayed silently. In my heart I wanted it to be some easy find that the medical team had accidentally overlooked. I didn't want it to be spinal meningitis. Wasn't the *drowning* serious enough? Did we have to add this to his health list as well?

Brian walked in and looked curious and confused when he saw the technician unhooking John.

"Brian, where have you been?"

"I took a break up in the Ronald McDonald room. They told me in the waiting room that you were looking for me. What's going on?"

I explained my conversation with Dr. Ream and what he was going to do.

"Spinal meningitis?" It was as though the words didn't compute.

With our son ready to transport, I told John that he would be fine and that we would be back in when the tests were finished. The technician unlocked the bed's wheels and then pulled him away from the wall. I watched them walk down the hallway with my son and disappear around a corner.

I sighed heavily, something I seemed to be doing a lot of lately.

We got back on Facebook to give people the updates on what they needed to pray over. I was so grateful to be in such a large community—a family, really—from all over the world who carried one another's pain and burdens, and who prayed to our Father. We didn't even know all of the people who were praying, but we did know that Mark Shepard's son, who was in the air force and stationed in Germany, had his prayer group on the base praying. We had missionaries in Costa Rica and missionaries in China praying. We had people from the Netherlands we had never met who called the school to find out more specifically how to pray for John. And so many others. I became overwhelmed by the prayer support. It just reinforced the truth: Even when we're at our darkest point, we are never alone.

With John out of the room, another nurse entered and started to wipe down and sterilize the room to prepare for the procedure. Taking that as our cue to exit, we moved to the PICU waiting room to give everyone there the updates. I could barely open the door, however. The waiting room was jammed with people, since it was Saturday and people were off work and school. I thought Monday night, our first night there, had been packed. But this was like a jungle of people. Every space that could have a body had one. Or two.

Apparently, the size of the crowd got the hospital's attention as well, because soon some hospital representatives showed up and informed everyone that they were opening the large banquet room on the next floor down for people to move to. They were also providing food and drinks. I felt so grateful to the hospital for caring for these people. They went above and beyond what anyone expected. The waiting room began to clear out, although my family and I remained.

The CT scan lasted less than a half hour. It actually took them longer to un-hook and transport John than it did to do the scan. Then he was back in the room, getting rehooked, set up, and settled in.

Dr. Ream finally returned to let us know that the CT scan came back clear—no swelling or damage—so they could proceed with the test.

We remained in the waiting room, and I tried my best not to imagine what they were doing to John. I kept myself busy by talking to people and praying. When Jason arrived, I gave him the update. "Wouldn't it be great if the fevers just disappeared on their own?"

He smiled and laughed. "It's amazing with all the technology and medical advances, they still have limits to what they can do and figure out. But God doesn't have any limits, does He?"

"No, He doesn't. Praise Him for that."

Later that afternoon after we'd returned to John's room, the neurologist Dr. Johnson came to check on John. Once again she tried to get him to respond, but he ignored her. She pursed her lips and made notes on her clipboard. I thought she'd be glad that John's EEG came back clear, but she seemed more annoyed by it, as if she didn't believe the test and felt that he was, in fact, hav-ing miniseizures.

She lifted the blanket at the end of his bed and looked at his feet, then she made another note. I caught what she was specifically looking at: John's right foot was turned inward at a severe angle, a condition he'd had since he was a baby.

"That foot is still posturing," she said.

I started to laugh. "If you're waiting for that foot to turn out, you're going to be waiting for eternity, because he was born with it that way." I was certain that the neurologist assumed his foot was an indication that he was experienc-ing seizures.

Her eyes narrowed and a frown crossed her face. "Well, that would have been nice to know a long time ago."

"You should have just asked me. I had no idea that's what you were looking for."

She made another note on her clipboard and left the room.

When Dr. Ream next entered the room, he looked concerned and confused.

Uh-oh, I thought and grabbed my stomach to keep me from throwing up. *It can't be meningitis. No, no, no. We've been praying against that. God, You've got to take care of this!*

"I'm at a loss," he admitted. "John doesn't have spinal meningitis."

Wait, what did he just say? "He doesn't?" I squeaked out.

"No."

"He does not have spinal meningitis." I needed to hear it again.

"No, the test came back negative."

I heaved a sigh of relief so loud, people on the other side of the state must have heard it.

"We've run out of possibilities for what's causing this fever." He scratched his head and looked at his feet. "I'm not sure what else it could possibly be— we've checked everything else out, and it's all come back negative. There is no reason for him to have a fever."

He promised that they'd keep an eye on it and do everything they could, but he didn't sound hopeful.

How could he explain a child who had a fever upward of 104 to 105 degrees for no apparent reason? And with all the knowledge the medical field had at its fingertips, no one could figure it out—even the best and brightest minds were at a loss.

No reason—and no cure. The medications and antibiotics did nothing to alleviate the fever. The Arctic Sun should have been renamed the Desert Sun for all the cooling ability it was offering.

Dr. Ream and his staff were flummoxed. This shouldn't have been happening—and this kid shouldn't be surviving these kinds of temperatures for as long a duration as he had. So we became desperate in our prayers again. "God, the doctors can't figure out what is causing this fever. We believe that when the doctors can't figure it out, that's when You step in and make the impossible possible. We need You to take away this fever in the mighty name of Jesus. Thank You for all You have done!"

At around 6:00 p.m., just as quickly as the fever appeared and raged, it disappeared. Completely. It was as though someone took a rag and wiped it clean away. All of John's numbers returned to a good range, he was calm, and his temperature was exactly where it needed to be—98.6 degrees.

Talk about the staff being flummoxed! We all were! Even though I'd joked that it would be nice to have the fever just disappear, I was still dumbfounded when it did. No explanation, no side effects, no damage, nothing. Just. Gone.

Everything the doctors and staff warned us would happen never did. There was no brain swelling, no seizures, no infection, no more fever.

I'm not a crier. But when John's fever disappeared—and no one could explain how or why—tears flowed from my eyes.

I looked over at Jason and saw him wiping his face with his hands. Then we burst out laughing.

Oh God, how wonderful You are! How full of surprises! You promised You would take care of us—and You do.

"Have you noticed," Jason said, "that everything they're saying, we're praying, and it's as if God is answering with, *No, no, it's not going to be that way.*"

"It's like He keeps showing people, *I can do this, and I can do this, and I can do this.* He works His best when we're at the limits of what we can do."

A couple hours later the new night nurse entered the room and smiled. She looked at his monitors and numbers. Vitals all stable, still no temperature spikes, everything good.

"You know, I think this is a good time for everybody to take a break," she said. "He's fine. He's going to sleep. Let's let him rest. Go home and get some rest, too."

I knew she was right. Whenever new people would come into the room—with all the visitors coming and going, it would raise his intensity—his numbers, his heart rate, and everything would go up. It had been six days since I'd been home. But still, she was asking me to leave my baby. She wasn't just telling me to leave the room—she was suggesting that we all leave the hospital and go home. But home was forty minutes away. What if something happened? What if I couldn't get here in time? What if he woke up and I wasn't here?

Jason placed his hand on my shoulder, and as if reading my mind, he said, "God's got this. Look at the amazing work He's done today. His angels are here. John will be okay tonight. I think the nurse is right. We all should go home and rest."

"If we need anything," the nurse said, "of course we'll call you."

Now was the ultimate test of my faith. I leaned over John and whispered, "Good night, dumplin'. Your dad and I love you. You get some rest, and I'll see you tomorrow."

Then I slowly walked out of the room, trusting that God would continue to be who I believed Him to be: faithful, trustworthy, compassionate, true, honorable, loving, giving. I placed my son in His hands and out of my control. And Brian and I went home.

CHAPTER 19

Clutching a Safe Hand

Sunday, January 25, 2015

As nice and familiar as it was to be home, to sleep in my own bed and shower in my own bathroom, my mind wouldn't let me leave the hospital. All night long sleep refused to come, because all I could think was, *What's happening with John? Is he okay? Are they taking good care of him?*

I lay next to Brian and waited, hoping that the sun would rise and the alarm clock would buzz soon. But the minutes dragged on, and I forced myself to stay in bed, even though I ached to get up and drive back to Cardinal Glennon.

Finally, when I thought I could bear it no longer, the alarm went off, signaling I was now allowed to remove myself from bed and start the day.

My sister, Janice, and brother-in-law, Don, were already up and packing to go back to Ohio. They offered to take our dog, Cuddles, with them, so we didn't have to go back and forth from the hospital to take care of him. "John can come and get him when he's out of the hospital," Janice told me.

They wanted to make one more trip to see John before they left. I offered to stay at the house until they got back, then we could say our good-byes. Then I'd head to the hospital.

Brian was up and getting ready for church—he'd told me the night before that he really felt as if he needed to be there. This morning, though, he was acting odd. He was cool toward me, and when he spoke, his voice had an edge of agitation to it.

"So you aren't going to church?" he said, entering our bathroom where I was fixing my hair.

"No, I really want to get back to John."

No response. He simply picked up a can of shaving cream and began shaking it. Something was up.

I laid my hairbrush down. "All right, what's going on with you?"

"Nothing." He looked unsettled and continued to shake the can.

"Don't 'nothing' me. Something is bothering you, and I want to know what it is."

Slathering the shaving cream onto his face, he said, "I just feel like you're making all these decisions about John on your own without me really being part of it or having any say."

"What are you talking about? I keep you in the loop. I tell you about every decision they need us to make. As soon as I get updates from the doctors, I tell you what they are."

"But I feel like I'm finding out around the same time as everyone else. I just feel like I'm being left out and not informed as much as I could be. I didn't even know about the spinal tap until I walked into John's room, and you told me it was happening. They were already prepping him to go to the CT scan!"

"Whoa!" I said. *Where is this coming from?* "I explained yesterday that I'd tried texting and calling you—and they couldn't wait until you woke up and came back to the waiting room."

"I know that. It's just . . . *Pastor Jason* is in on more of the status reports than I am."

"That's because *he's* staying in the room and you aren't." I paused, trying to keep the conversation nonthreatening and nonaccusatory. "I know you're trying to host friends and family in the waiting room and pray with them. I know that's where you feel you're doing the most good, but that does not mean I am intentionally keeping information from you."

He paused and turned toward me. I could tell he was contemplating something in that analytical mind of his. "Sometimes," he said, his voice quiet. "I just struggle with believing that God is going to completely heal our son."

I wanted to throttle him. I knew that Jason had just talked with him about this topic. I knew that he had been listening to the negative voices and entertaining them in his mind—giving them room to grow and fester. I knew that he was tired, and when he got tired, he struggled more with holding fast to hope. The past year of stress had taken its toll on his spiritual and emotional strength, but I couldn't deal with that today.

"Exactly what else do you want God to do for you to prove who He is?" I said, feeling frustrated. "He's raised your son from the dead. What else do you need before it will be enough for you to stop listening to the voices that lie? You're giving Satan room in your brain to convince you that he's right and God isn't."

"I just don't want us to be too presumptuous in our prayers."

For me to expect him to be on the exact same page I was during this time was unfair on my part, I know, but I also knew that for our son's sake, he needed to deal with what he believed about God now. Either we believe that God is who He says He is—and we embrace and cling to that—or we live powerless lives, not wanting to do as the Bible says and approach the throne boldly to make our requests, believing that God hears them and wants to answer them. Brian needed to close his mind to the enemy—not give him a foothold. Our enemy knows our weakness and does everything he can to prey upon us and make us forget who God really is and who we really are in Christ.

"Brian, you have got to let this go and stop listening to those other voices."

"You've been convinced from the get-go that everything is going to work out well and it's all going to be good. Of course, I'm hopeful and I want it to have that outcome, but—"

"We're not going to do this."

The stress, the lack of sleep, the tension, and the fact that our age wasn't allowing us to bounce back from a week's worth of full-on drama had built up, and the enemy took advantage of it all and decided to do his dirties. He was trying to cause dissension anywhere he could. But I wasn't going to have any of it.

I wasn't trying to be superspiritual or obnoxiously overconfident. But I knew what I knew. I'd stood in a sterile hospital room surrounded by medical experts who see life and death every day and who were ready to call time of death on our son. I'd stood in that room, called on God, and God had jump-started John's heart. To me, this was evidence enough that His will was for John to live. So when I was praying that God's will be done, I knew it would be, because I'd seen God's will at work! That's not being superspiritual, that's being convinced and confident of the truth.

For Brian, he struggled with acting out of that kind of confidence.

"We're not going to do this, Brian," I told him. "We are not going to start this kind of tension between us. This is just Satan coming in and trying to get our focus off where it needs to be." I stepped closer to him. We needed to be on the same team, unified. "I'm sorry for not keeping you in the loop. I'll do better. I know this has been extremely difficult on you. I know you're worried. I love you. We'll get through this." I took his hand. "Why don't we pray about it?"

He looked relieved and agreed.

We took turns praying. We prayed that the enemy wouldn't succeed in his schemes to cause strife between us. We prayed that God would protect our minds and give us the strength to take all of our thoughts captive and make them obedient to God's will. We prayed that God would give us clear thought and keep us from listening to the negative voices that tell us God "won't" do amazing things. And we prayed that God would strengthen our *hope*, that we would remain focused on our son and his total recovery.

When we ended our prayer, Brian smiled and hugged me. I wasn't sure that he was convinced, but I was sure of one thing: There was no way I was going to allow the enemy to drive a wedge in our family.

That morning the church service was electrified. The spirit of the room was alive and excited with what God had done throughout the week. It was exactly the place Brian needed to be. No one there talked about the possibility of John not making it. Everyone praised God for his work and what new things he was going to do.

During the prayer time, Pastor Jason always sets aside a time to pray specifically for healing—for people who are struggling and need a touch from God. Hearing that God had resurrected a dead fourteen-year-old boy, people began swarming the front altars for God to do something spectacular in their lives as well.

After that, Jason spontaneously invited Brian onto the stage to share his thoughts and heart with everyone.

Brian's face grew hot with surprise, but he walked to the front, amid a congregation who had jumped to their feet and applauded to show their outpouring of love and support.

"Thank you," he said simply, swallowing back his emotion. It took several moments for him to gain his composure, and then a boldness came over him. "Don't tell me we don't serve a miracle-working God, because my son was pulled up from the bottom of an icy lake and is alive today." People began to cheer. "It's been amazing to see how much God has done for John. Each time some challenge arises, you all pray and God answers. So please keep praying. We believe he will be completely healed. But he still has a ways to go." He shared about the fever and the spinal tap results. Then he turned to the issues still pressing in, such as John's lungs and breathing. Finally he said, "If you are desperate for a miracle, I want to encourage you to be bold in your requests. God can do anything you ask Him to do. Keep praying! Thank you again. My family and I love you all."

As he stepped down from the platform, once again people were on their feet cheering and applauding him for his boldness, his courage, his faith, and that he had spoken true words about the Great Physician, our God.

Next came Jason's morning message. As Brian listened, he felt as though the Holy Spirit had targeted it at him completely for his benefit. Jason, who had scheduled that week's topic three months before, spoke about the importance of transformation and not allowing old habits and beliefs and our past to hold us back from who God is shaping and calling us to be. When we let go of those things, we can become radically transformed for Christ.

Brian listened to Pastor Jason's words and thought about that morning's conversation with me. They both pierced his heart. Of course, he wanted his son to live and to thrive! What had held him back from completely giving everything over to God and believing that God would come through for him? Fear. Brian realized the best way he could help his son was for him to allow God to radically transform him—how he prayed, what he thought, what he spoke. Now he needed God to deliver supernatural strength to help him follow through. His son depended on it. *He* depended on it.

While Brian was in the service and I was still at home, Janice and Don entered John's room a few minutes before Dr. Ream.

"Good morning," Dr. Ream said. "With John's fever gone and everything calm, I lowered his propofol levels so I can check his responses."

"Yes, he still responds," Janice said.

"One of the neurologists reported that John has been completely unresponsive whenever she comes to test him, so let's see for ourselves."

John was groggy and slowly woke up. He turned his head to look around and spotted Don. Just as the first time, he locked onto Don.

"That's cognitive recognition," Dr. Ream said.

"Yes," said Janice.

"Hey there, buddy," Don said walking to the foot of John's bed. John's eyes followed him the whole way.

"I'd say that's total recognition," Dr. Ream said, this time astonished.

"Yes," repeated Janice, "I would say so."

★　　★　　★

When Janice and Don returned to the house to pick up Cuddles and their dog, I thanked them for coming, saw them off, and then I headed back to the hospital. I knew the staff would have been thrilled to have John completely alone all day to allow him to rest, but that just wasn't going to happen! I wanted—I needed—to get back to him. And because they had essentially banned everyone else from visiting the room, I had him all to myself.

"Hi John, I'm back," I told him. "Did you keep out of trouble while I was gone?" I chuckled. He was still out of it, but he squeezed my hand. He was a different boy from the previous few days. He was calm. His temperature was just right. His numbers were good. I knew, though, that we couldn't let up on praying for him. He was still on the ventilator—he needed to get off of that and start breathing on his own.

I was content simply to look at him and hold his hand.

What a fragile life we have, I thought. Looking at him now reminded me of when we first brought him home.

In November 2000, when we flew to Guatemala to get John, my sons were thirty and twenty-eight. Yet we were committing to do the whole parenting thing all over again. I already had grandchildren!

Brian and I were excited, especially Brian. We left for Guatemala on Wednesday, November 15, and while we sat in the airport waiting to board our plane, Brian pulled out a notepad and began to write a letter to John.

> We're at the airport and have just gotten our seat assignments for the flight from Atlanta to Guatemala City. To say I'm anxious would probably be an understatement. It's been a hectic couple of days trying to get packed and ready.... It seems surreal finally to be ready to travel to get you after all these months. We went to our first meeting at Bethany Christian Services on February 22, 2000, to first talk about adopting. We've now waited almost six months to make the trip to meet you. I

165

remember my trip home from Honduras in March 2000. I cried on the plane knowing the next trip to Latin America would be to get you, not knowing when it would be or who we would see. Writing some of these thoughts down for your eyes in future years helps a lot.

It is odd to be forty-six, almost forty-seven, and not be able to control my nerves. It's a lot to ponder and almost makes it hard to think clearly. I do know that this is definitely an adventure, and your mom and I are both excited and glad to be close to getting you.

I was proud of my husband. We had started this adventure together to bring home our precious John. And what an adventure it was!

We arrived late at night in Guatemala City to discover that we had no luggage. Apparently, it decided to stick around the Atlanta airport when we changed planes. We were also missing Paco, our attorney. He was supposed to meet us when we arrived, but he was nowhere to be found and we had no way to contact him. We'd been warned not to leave the airport without our attorney, since the area was dangerous. But by eleven o'clock, having waited several hours and still no Paco, we were willing to take our chances in the city.

When a teenage boy approached us and in broken English said, "Do you need a taxi?" we said yes.

He got us the smallest car I'd ever seen. I thought it might be from the Matchbox line of cars. It was a teeny blue Toyota that we barely squeezed into. All I could think was that it probably was a good thing that we didn't have our luggage. It would have had to make the trip in a separate taxi.

Off we rolled into the dark Guatemalan night, with no idea if the driver was actually taking us where we needed to go.

I had never been in a Third World country before. So when we pulled up to the Casa Grande Hotel, next to the US Embassy, I wasn't sure if I should be glad that the taxi driver was honest or scared that armed guards with machine guns were standing around the building.

The guards were dressed in camo, each wearing a maroon beret with a thin black band around it. To add to the fashion statement, each wore a belt of bullets crossed over his chest. And of course, they held the machine guns.

Oh my goodness, was all I could think. We sure weren't in Missouri any longer.

We went inside to check in and the desk clerk informed us, "An American who said he was your attorney has been trying to get a hold of you. So glad you're here."

We walked up to our room, which was pleasant enough. It had tile floors and bare walls. Two double beds sat side by side, each covered in a colorful spread. Simple, clean.

No sooner had we gotten settled into our room, which didn't take long since we had no luggage, than the phone rang. It was our stateside attorney, who was frantic because he had heard from Paco that no one knew where we were. While I was talking with him, a knock sounded at our door.

It was almost midnight. *Who in the world could that be?* Originally we were supposed to get John as soon as we arrived in the country, but since it was so late, and since we hadn't found Paco, we figured we wouldn't get our child until the next day.

Brian answered the door, and there stood Paco with his twenty-something-year-old daughter, who was holding the tiniest baby wrapped in a blanket that swallowed him. *Surely, that's not* our *baby*, I thought. This baby was the size of a newborn.

They walked in and his daughter headed straight for me. Before I could even say hello, she unceremoniously handed John to me. I could feel his every vertebra through the blanket.

"We couldn't find you at the airport," Paco explained. I couldn't imagine how they would have missed us, since it was about the size of a 7-Eleven convenience store.

Paco set a bag on the bed closest to him. "Here are a few items to tide you over tonight."

They stayed a total of fifteen minutes.

"I'll be back in the morning to take you to the embassy and they'll handle all the paperwork there," Paco said. Then they left.

Brian and I stared at each other, disbelieving the scene we'd just experienced. It felt as if they waltzed in, said, "Here's your kid for the rest of your life," and then disappeared into the night.

Brian opened the bag to find a box of formula, a diaper, a onesie pajama, a blanket, and a note from the foster mother that said, "Have a good life. He's happy baby."

John was so tiny he seemed to disappear in my arms. "Let's unwrap and see what we've got," I said as I laid him on the bed.

His big brown eyes looked at me, but he didn't make a peep.

I unwrapped his little white blanket that was covered in yellow, pink, and blue rocking horses. He had very little hair. He wore a powder-blue sleeper that was the right size for his age but was still too large for him. He was five and a half months old, but he weighed only ten pounds. I removed the sleeper to look at his body. He looked so tiny and frail, and I could see every vein in his skin. He had spindly little legs and arms that looked like pipe cleaners, and his right foot was turned inward at a severe angle. His head seemed to be the right size, but he looked emaciated.

Oh my goodness, what have we gotten into? What is wrong with this child?

Brian and I just stared at him as he stared back. He was clearly checking us out just as much as we were checking him out. I reached down and took hold of his hand, and immediately he wrapped his little fingers around my thumb.

I was a mom to three children, but I found myself at a loss. *Will he want to sleep in his own bed? Does he want to be held? Is he insecure?* I wasn't sure what to do, so I held him for a while, amazed that we actually now had this child, then I handed him to Brian. "Here you go, Dad," I told him and watched with pride and love as he gently cuddled John against his chest.

Finally we placed John in the other bed where he slept through the night. Never once whimpered, never once cried, never once acted like he was afraid of us.

The next morning I got up, made him a bottle, which he drank without a fuss. Then I changed his diaper and put him in his outfit. I laid him back on his bed so I could get ready for the day. When I returned out of the bathroom, there lay Brian, holding John—both of them fast asleep, both of them looking content, as though they'd been father and son forever.

From the moment that we took him in our arms, John accepted us without hesitation or fear. He seemed content to sit, look at us, and clutch our fingers. But still he didn't cry. Not even a whimper or a gurgle.

I thought he might be mute. In fact, I didn't even know he could cry until a day after we'd returned home to the States with him. He woke up Sunday morning in a fit and screamed with lungs that could have belonged to a town crier.

He was burning up, and when I checked his temperature, I just about fainted to see the thermometer read 105 degrees.

Immediately I called a pediatric nurse practitioner friend. "What do I do?"

"Get him to the ER. You've got a child from the Third World. You have no idea what you're dealing with."

At the hospital, they gave him an IV, which caused its own problems—trying to stick an IV in those tiny arms made him scream even worse. They told us that he had an ear infection. On the flight home, he had sucked fluids back into his ear and it had created an infection. They gave him antibiotics and sent us home. Then the next day we followed up with the pediatrician, who had done his thesis on Third World diseases. Even at five and a half months old, our son received God's amazing protective and miraculous care.

The doctor looked at him. "Oh, he's fine. They just didn't give him enough calories. They fed him, but he was probably a preemie and he just needs more calories. Put him on preemie food and he'll be okay."

A month later, we went back for a checkup. By this time John had gained eight pounds. He went from this little emaciated child to this round, fat-cheeked little chunky child. When the doctor saw him, he said, "Whoa, whoa. Let's back off the preemie food—or we're going to have to go the other way."

Even when he was sick, John was the easiest, most contented child. His foster mother had been right; he was a happy baby.

I smiled at the memories of raising him and looked at him lying peacefully in his hospital bed. I looked down at my hand. His fingers were clutched around mine.

CHAPTER 20

A Stunning Discovery

Monday, January 26, 2015

Monday morning started out peacefully.

Things between Brian and me were much better. He had come to the hospital Sunday night and, as he held John's hand, we talked about the church service and the afternoon basketball game that John's school team had played and that Brian had attended on John's behalf.

"They really miss you, John," Brian told our son. He told us that before the game, the entire team and coaches gathered around Brian in the hallway and prayed. "To hear all these young boys praying for John was so amazing," he said. Then he told me that earlier that morning he'd had a change of attitude. He wanted to live victoriously and not weighed down by worry and fear. To combat it, he decided that the first step was to spend more time reading his Bible to help him safeguard his thinking. "I've been doing that SOAP Bible Plan, to read through the Bible in a year, so I can get caught up on that. You know, it's like if you get a bad golf swing, you go back to the basics and you hone it to where you're doing the simple things right again. Well, I think I need to get back in front of God. Whatever hope there is, it's going to come from Him, so I need to focus more on Him."

"I think that's a great idea," I said. It encouraged me to hear my husband taking that initiative. And I knew that God would honor Brian's step of faith.

I smiled as I thought again of the change I'd seen in Brian. I knew we would need to stay vigilant, but that he recognized it was a giant step forward.

John was relaxed and his numbers seemed okay Monday morning. Jason was with us and was joking with John, asking him why he hadn't made it to the church service the day before, then he began to tell me about how well Brian had done and how people were praying and excited to hear how well John was doing. While he was talking, at around 9:30, the neurologist Dr. Johnson showed up to check John's responsiveness.

That's odd, I thought. I didn't remember seeing our day nurse, Ciera, turn down the propofol level, which the nurses typically did before the neurologists showed up to test him.

I caught something else peculiar. Dr. Ream also arrived, but instead of entering and making his presence known, he stood by the door and behind the privacy curtain. It was as though he were hiding and spying. But why?

"Good morning, John," Dr. Johnson said.

Before she could examine John, Dr. Ream pounced.

"I want you to listen very carefully," he told her firmly. "Quit calling my staff and expecting them to turn down that propofol and then fifteen minutes later you come down here and expect him to perform for you like a circus animal. He's a prepubescent boy—so that propofol is seeping into his cells. It will take him longer than fifteen minutes because he still has to deal with all the leftover in his system."

I had liked Dr. Ream from the get-go. He had a great dry wit—his humor saved my sanity multiple times—and he was compassionate. But after this scene, I could have gotten up from my chair and kissed him. I knew I didn't care for how Dr. Johnson worked—but to know that another doctor had figured out her mistake left me ready to start a ticker tape parade.

After Dr. Johnson left—not at all happy—Dr. Ream turned to me. "John is now at a place where we need to get him off this ventilator and get him breathing on his own. His lungs are still sick. And the longer he stays in the PICU, the greater his chance of picking up an infection, since the department is filled with germs, given all that we're treating here. Obviously, we don't want that to happen. The reality is that people either get out of ICU, or they don't make it out. So pun intended, John's out in the middle of the water, and we need him to swim to shore."

He explained that they needed to start permanently backing him off of the propofol and getting him more alert and awake. I agreed and when Dr. Ream left, I turned to my social media network and, with a renewed desperation, put out that day's prayer list: (1) that John's lungs would become completely clear so the doctor could remove the ventilator; (2) that John wouldn't experience any fear when he awoke. We needed God to intervene once again to get John off the ventilator and out of the PICU. Jason and I prayed over John that the breath of God would once again blow through John's lungs and bring complete healing.

With that excitement behind us, the room returned to the peaceful and calm state that it had had the day and night before. Then Jason was unexpectedly called to two other hospitals for emergencies, so he left, promising to return later in the evening.

Because John was no longer in a life-and-death crisis situation, Brian and I discussed it and decided that Brian would return to work and come back to the hospital in the evenings. And so with Jason, Brian, Janice, and Don gone, I was pretty much the only constant person in John's room.

The rest of the day passed without any incident. Our day nurse, Ciera, kept tabs on John, still checking on him regularly. But his numbers stayed in range and in the afternoon, they began slowly lowering the dosage of his propofol.

Tuesday, January 27, 2015

When things appear to be the calmest, that's when we have to reinforce our guard against the enemy. The apostle Paul wrote that "we do not wrestle against flesh and blood, but against the rulers, against the authorities, against the cosmic powers over this present darkness, against the spiritual forces of evil in the heavenly places" (Eph. 6:12). In other words, when something bad happens, we need to look beyond the physical to consider that perhaps what is really happening is in the spiritual realm, but the enemy is using the physical realm to disrupt, create chaos and confusion, and keep us from focusing on God and His work and will in our lives.

The day passed without any incident. John was doing better. His lungs even started to strengthen—or, to quote Dr. Ream, John had slowly started to swim to shore. So I shouldn't have been surprised when the nursing shift occurred.

Casey, the head nurse, had been true to her word, and Nurse Ratched wasn't John's night nurse anymore. Oh, but she was still on the floor. And she made sure that she walked past John's room and stopped in the doorway just to stare in. At first I was so stunned that she had that kind of audacity! But then I started giving her the mean eye right back. I wanted her to understand that she couldn't intimidate me—especially not where the health of my son was concerned.

Melissa Fischer arrived in the late evening, as she had almost every evening since John was admitted to the hospital, ready to spend the night. We talked briefly, and we rejoiced together over how well John had been doing. His oxygen levels were good, and now we needed his lungs to get to the point that they could manage breathing on their own without the help of the ventilator.

As Melissa and I stood at John's bedside and began to pray over him, I sensed someone enter the room. Then a hand settled lightly on my back. As soon as we said "Amen," a woman's soft chanting began. It was the shaman lady humming over John.

Within seconds, John's body went into chaos. The monitor alarms went crazy, his oxygen levels plummeted, and his arms and legs started to thrash and pound the bed.

"Okay, we're not going to do that anymore," I told the chaplain.

We'd just prayed peace over my boy and her spiritual "influence" had brought disruption.

Instead of leaving, she took a seat and remained quiet, as Melissa and I again covered John with prayer. Slowly, his body calmed and the alarms quieted.

And just outside of John's door during the chaos stood Nurse Ratched, with her arms folded and the darkest half scowl, half-twisted smile covering her face.

Later that night when everything calmed down again and Melissa and I recapped the craziness, Melissa said, "Okay, that's just creepy."

"Yes, it is," I agreed.

"You don't think she'll do anything...do you?"

"Oh, honey, I'd like to see her try."

Wednesday, January 28, 2015

Dr. Ream and his medical students made their early-morning stop in front of John's room. Once John's team of nurses and technicians joined them, Dr. Ream filled them in on John's progress—which was good. So good, in fact, that he wanted to take John off the ventilator.

My ears perked up.

They went through John's blood gas numbers, his respiration, and other issues pertaining to his lung function. As the resident assistant read off John's numbers for the group to hear, Dr. Ream commented after each, "Well, his numbers don't meet the criteria for removing him from the vent." And as if to cement the argument, after the resident assistant finished, Dr. Ream confessed, "He doesn't meet most of the criteria. And we're still dealing with the trouble keeping the lower part of his lungs inflated, which means they may collapse if we remove the vent. He should really be on for at least another two days. But we need to get him off that ventilator before he picks it up and carries it down the hallway."

But they keep saying how sick his lungs are, I thought. And then one word flew through my mind: *God.*

Someone from the group asked a question, which I couldn't hear. But Dr. Ream responded, "If it were any other boy than the boy lying in this room, I would leave him on the vent a few more days, but I'm going to look really bad if John is walking up and down the hall with his vent still in."

The group laughed, while my mind tried to quickly process what I thought I'd heard. *They're going to remove the vent. Today. Wait, this morning?*

I was nervous and excited and grabbed my phone to call Brian. "They want to take him off the ventilator."

"Today?"

"Yes! Now, actually. Pray!" I knew Brian would have dropped everything at work to join us if he could, but his work schedule wouldn't let him with such short notice.

My next call was to Jason. "They're going to take the ventilator out," I said as soon as he answered his phone.

"I'm on my way," he said.

I called my other boys and Janice to give them the news and ask them to pray.

From the time Dr. Ream announced his intentions, it felt like a whirlwind of activity.

First Ciera turned off John's propofol. It was time for John to wake up and start breathing on his own. We knew it would take a while for the drug level to dissipate since he'd been on it for so long and his body had been storing it.

Next a respiratory therapist showed up to give John a misting breathing treatment. "This will help his lungs and airways open and clear up," she explained to me, as she adjusted it to his vent tube.

While the therapist was administering that, she placed a high-frequency chest wall oscillation vest on him—a fancy name for a vest that would shake him up like a rattle in the hands of a hyper baby. Sure enough, when she turned it on, John's chest started to vibrate and jiggle rapidly to remove any mucus or fluid that may try to clog his air passages once he was free of the breathing machine.

While the therapist was still working on John, Dr. Ream showed up again and conferred with her. "Once we proceed, I need two respiratory therapists down here and an anesthesiologist in case we have to re-vent him."

Re-vent him? All the air seemed to leave *my* lungs. What had been a mixture of excitement and anxiety now turned to 100 percent anxiety.

"Dr. Ream," I called out to him. I couldn't help myself. I had to know exactly what that meant. "How likely will it be that you'll have to re-vent him?"

He exhaled as if this was not a conversation he wanted to have right now with the patient's mother. But I knew he would be straight up with me.

"Very likely. We have to re-vent about 90 percent of the time."

"Because he'll…just stop breathing?" I said it more as a comment than a question. We were potentially back at a life-and-death moment.

"Just stop. Yes." But then as if to ease my mind, he said, "That's why we'll have everyone on hand. We'll be prepared for whatever happens." He went on to explain that part of the problem with John was that the bottom section of his lungs were not fully inflating and they kept sticking together, so they were having trouble with the lungs staying open.

That must have been one of the criteria that they needed to meet before removing the ventilator, I realized. So if they pulled it out and those lungs didn't cooperate, they would have to reinsert. It was risky.

Because every teenager knows when to push his mother's anxiety buttons, as if on cue, John started to become crazy. He threw his arms around to hit anything they came into contact with. Then he slapped them up and down, smacking the bed over and over. He kicked his legs around like he was doing karate moves. He grabbed for the ventilator tubes. He shook his head violently from side to side.

No one told me how John would react, and it wasn't pretty. Being on propofol for ten days, his body had gotten used to it. Now that it was depleting, he was in withdrawal. But more than that, the propofol kept him unaware of what was happening to him. Coming off its effects meant that he was becoming more alert to his surroundings, and that brought confusion, panic, and full-on discomfort. That tube down his throat wasn't exactly massaging him.

He'd thrashed around before, but this was different. It was wilder and more intense.

Oh my goodness, I thought in panic. *Does he have brain damage? Is this what he's going to be like?* Even though I knew God had healed him and was going to heal him completely, my human nature took over. A wave of nausea and fear hit me like a tsunami.

I tried to grab his arms because I didn't want him to hurt himself if one of them smashed against his bed rails, but he kept fighting me. Ciera, another nurse, and the respiratory therapist were fully engaged in prepping John, watching over the treatments, and trying to secure his arms and legs, so we all had our hands full.

Fortunately, Jason entered the scene just in time to see John lift his legs and slam them against the bed. "What's going on?" he said, trying to grab John's legs to hold them down.

"They took him off the propofol."

"They're working fast."

"Oh yeah. They're planning to pull the vent out soon."

John's eyes were wild with fear and he laser focused them on me with a death glare.

My face flushed and I lessened my grip on John. I felt terrified. My eyes must have communicated my fears, because Jason asked, "What's going on with you, Joyce?"

"What if…what if this is really how he's going to be?" I looked at Jason. "What if he can't breathe and that affects his brain? What if he ends up with brain damage?"

Now it was Jason's turn to remind me of the spiritual battle to control our thinking, just as earlier that week I had reminded Brian. "Whoa, Joyce, no," he said. "We're holding the line. God didn't bring us this far for this to happen. We're not going to settle for anything less than 100 percent healing."

"Right," I said and swallowed hard, as though willing myself back to the focus we'd maintained. "One hundred percent." But my confident words didn't match what I was feeling. *What if...what if...what if...* kept rushing through my mind.

"Joyce. God isn't going to take us out into the middle of the water and dump us there," he continued. "That isn't who God is. Right?"

"Right."

More of the medical team came in, so we backed away and watched and prayed. Dr. Ream reentered the room and positioned himself against the wall where he could supervise everything before they started the actual removal procedure. The team was able to secure John's arms and legs with straps, even though he still fought hard against them. The vest was still shaking his chest, which made his upper body look like he was in the midst of an earthquake.

While the team was working quickly to prep him, he turned his head and found me. His eyes were pleading and panicked. I swallowed hard again, willing myself not to cry. I knew this was going to hurt him, but he had to endure it if he was going to be at 100 percent again.

"Go comfort him, Mom," Dr. Ream said above the noise.

I was in such a panicked state myself, wide eyed and breathing hard, that I wasn't sure I would be much help in comforting him. In a daze I half-nodded, and then I sat in the chair nearest John's bed. My mind went frazzled, staticky. The room was thick with anticipation and stress. The things Dr. Ream had told me floated through my mind. *Ninety percent of patients have to be re-ventilated. He might not be able to breathe on his own.* I couldn't even muster up a prayer, except for *Oh, God.* Jason walked to the end of the bed, grabbed John's foot, and began to pray.

"Talk to him, Mom. Hold his hand," Dr. Ream said again.

I picked up John's hand and squeezed. His eyes still reflected panic.

I was never at a loss for words, so why were they failing me now? Finally, I blurted out the only thing I could think of. "Don't get used to that vibrating vest. I can't afford to buy you one."

From the back of the room, Dr. Ream piped up, "Oh, buy him one. I have the vibrating pants and I love them."

The room erupted into laughter. I could hardly breathe I was laughing so hard. That one comment broke through my apprehension and stress, and my mind worked again. It was just the thing I needed to help me relax enough to talk John through the moment.

After a few more minutes everything seemed to be in place. The respiratory therapists and anesthesiologist were nestled into one corner of the room, watching and waiting.

"Okay, we're going to move fast," Dr. Ream instructed. "Are we ready?"

Ciera and another technician said yes.

Jason and I stepped away from John to allow everyone to work unimpeded. And silently I prayed hard. It was one of the most intense prayers I've ever prayed. Just as I prayed over John's heartbeat, now I prayed over his lungs. He had to breathe on his own. Other than that first day, I had never felt as anxious as I felt at this moment. It wasn't because of a lack of faith; after all John had gone through, I just did not want them to have to re-vent him in any way.

What I didn't know or understand was that all people react similarly when they come off that drug. Had someone told me that before or during the nightmare, I might not have responded so desperately, but watching John violently slam his legs and arms up and down was horrid.

As soon as Dr. Ream and his team started, they worked methodically and as gently as they could, but we all knew time was of the essence. They had to turn off the ventilator, pull the long tube out of John's throat, and place an oxygen mask on him. Within three to four minutes, the procedure was completed.

The team moved out of the way to allow access to one of the respiratory therapists who gave John his second breathing treatment, essentially to mist his air passages and to make sure they stayed clear.

Now we had to see if John's lungs would do their thing.

One hundred percent healing, I thought. *Ninety percent of patients may need to be re-vented, but 10 percent don't. Okay, God, do Your thing.*

"How much longer is John going to be in the PICU?" I asked Dr. Ream.

"At least ten more days."

Everyone silently and tensely watched and waited to see what would happen next to John.

And then John's lungs woke up and started to work on their own.

Dr. Ream smiled and chuckled, as though astounded. "That kid..."

He'd remained with us throughout the entire procedure—even through the prep work and the second breathing treatment, which all lasted about twenty minutes. He could have told his staff, "You guys do this and call me when you're done." But he camped out until he knew for sure that John was okay.

"We'll keep watching him," he told me. Although John didn't need to be re-ventilated, I think Dr. Ream wasn't convinced that John wouldn't still need to be later in the day.

Around noon, my son Charles arrived. "Hi, bubby," he said, greeting John.

"Hey, bubby," came a quiet, raspy, muffled voice from inside the mask.

The whole room stopped as three jaws hit the floor. Jason, Charles, and I looked from one another to John and back to one another in disbelief. We all broke down into tears. Charles and Jason let out sobs and then turned their heads away, so John wouldn't see them. I figured they wanted to be strong for John. I just let my tears roll. After only about three hours since the medical team removed a ventilator that had been giving John life support for ten days, the kid was talking. That was impossible! He shouldn't have been able even to breathe, let alone speak!

I moved from my chair next to John so that Charles could sit there. And Jason and I sat back on the couch and watched these close-knit brothers chat. It was difficult to hear everything John was saying, but his language skills were intact.

Finally, John got so frustrated with the oxygen mask, he lifted it off his mouth and placed it on his forehead so he could talk better.

About an hour later, at around 1:00 p.m., Dr. Ream came in to check on him and stopped dead in his tracks. He looked at John, wearing his oxygen mask on his forehead, and blinked hard. He readjusted his glasses. "You can breathe?"

John simply nodded.

Dr. Ream looked at us—by that time, we were enjoying the show! He smiled and left the room. Within minutes, Ciera was at John's side with a nasal cannula, the two-pronged tube that sits in your nostrils and delivers oxygen. She got him set up with it, told him how amazing he was doing, and then left.

But after a while, even that irritated John, so he pulled this tube out and once again, placed it on his forehead. I laughed. If that kid could breathe, I wasn't about to reprimand him into putting it back in his nose.

About two hours later, around three o'clock, Dr. Ream reentered to check on John's status. This time when he saw John with the nose tube on his forehead, I thought the good doctor was going to pass out. His eyes grew so big, they covered most of his face!

"You can breathe without that?" he asked.

"Yes," John said.

Now I was certain Dr. Ream was about to have a heart attack. "You can *talk!*"

He called for Ciera. "I want a blood gas work up on him."

Within a half hour, Dr. Ream returned again. "Okay, we're taking him off all the oxygen. He's got 100 percent blood oxygenation." He chuckled again. "I...There's no textbook. We don't know what he's going to do next. We have no idea what he *should* even do next. We're not even going to try to make guesses. We're not going to say, 'It's going to be moment by moment.' We just..." He shook his head and grabbed his forehead.

They moved John out of PICU that night.

CHAPTER 21

Up and Not Quite Running

Thursday, January 29, 2015

The tiny room in the Transitional Care Unit on the fourth floor was a far cry from the PICU. John's PICU nurses hovered over him, checking on him so regularly they could have pitched a tent in the room and camped out. On this floor, we were lucky to see a nurse twice in a day. It was as though we'd gone from the Hilton to a Motel 6. Not that I wanted us to return to the PICU! But I had to remind myself, *This is actually good. He's getting better and doesn't need a lot of attention.*

We were also delighted to hear that they'd moved Jackson—the little boy whom we'd prayed over and who made a remarkable recovery—to this floor at the same time they moved John. Remie was also doing well, but I knew we'd lose touch with them now that we'd moved to a different floor.

As I sat in this new room, watching John sleep—without the aid of a breathing machine—I smiled. Dr. Ream had predicted John would be in the PICU for at least ten more days. In reality, he had been in the PICU for ten more *hours*.

Since I promised I would take better care of myself, I settled in on a small sleeping couch and tried to rest. At around 1:00 a.m., John began to pull at the feeding tube in his nose. He was persistent and yanked it completely out, which woke him up. He then became restless, which woke me up.

There he lay holding the tube in his hand and crying. "Mom, I don't know…" His voice was still raspy and just above a whisper. He lifted the tube to show me. "I pulled this out. I thought it was a booger," he confessed.

I laughed and relaxed. "That's okay, honey. I don't think you're going to need it anymore anyway. But I'll call the nurse just to let her know." I pushed the Call button.

He looked around, taking in his surroundings. With only the help of one small light dimly shining over the room, along with the light from the hallway casting its eerie glow across the floor, he slowly moved his head around. "Why am I here?"

I didn't expect to have this conversation in the middle of the night. Whenever he woke up in the PICU, I'd tried to tell him in the simplest terms—usually just "You've had an accident. You're in the hospital. You're okay. I'm here." But being so drugged, he would quickly forget.

Now, even though he still had some remaining propofol in his system, which made him groggy, he was alert and aware enough to ask and want a better explanation.

I moved to a chair next to his bed and held his hand. "You had an accident," I told him.

"Did I fall into the water?"

"Yes, you did, sweetheart."

Tears began to stream down his cheeks.

"Was it for a long time?"

"Yes, but you are going to be okay!"

He paused, letting this revelation sink in.

"Who knows I'm here? Do my friends know?"

I laughed. Of everything he could have asked, he was more concerned that his friends might not be aware of the situation. "Honey, the *whole world* knows you're here." He had no idea how true that statement was—the media had just run its first longer story on the accident with interviews from both of the Josh boys, the doctors, and Jason. "Yes, John, all your friends have been here checking on you and praying for you."

He squeezed my hand tightly for comfort and we talked for a couple hours about all that had gone on over the past ten days. He wanted to know every detail. It was difficult for me to answer, because I did not want to cause him to have nightmares, so I measured my responses, keeping the details to a limit. It felt so good to sit and listen to his voice and see that his thought process was totally intact—no brain damage, no problems processing information. God had knitted his brain back together as Jason and Brad Riley had prayed over him that very first evening. One hundred percent healing.

Eventually, John lifted his hands and ran them through his hair. His face took on a horrified look and a fresh round of tears sprang to his eyes.

I tried not to laugh. I knew exactly what he was thinking: *I look terrible!* This is my kid who is obsessive about cleanliness. It's nothing for him to take multiple showers in a day. He doesn't like to be sweaty or dirty. If clothes have touched his body for five minutes and then he changes, those clothes get placed in the dirty laundry hamper. As far as he's concerned, the motto "Cleanliness is next to godliness" might not be in the Bible, but it should be! And now he'd gone ten days without a shower.

"Don't worry," I said, hoping to sound comforting. "None of your friends have seen you. We'll make sure you get cleaned up in the morning. Now try to get some rest. We'll talk more then."

He squinted his eyes as though he didn't believe me. "Ari."

"What?"

"Ari saw me."

What is he talking about? And then it hit me: His friend Ari had visited him early in the morning the day he first woke up. Charles had told me that John opened his eyes and saw her, but surely John didn't remember that...did he? "You remember Ari visiting you?"

He nodded, and I sat stunned.

A few hours after I pushed the Call button, a nurse finally showed up to take his vitals and check on him. It had been so long that I almost forgot why I'd called for her in the first place.

"He pulled out his feeding tube while he was sleeping." I pointed at it, which was lying at the side of the bed.

"We're going to have to put that back in."

Wait, what? "I don't think you're going to need to do that. I'm sure the doctor is going to have it pulled out later this morning."

She looked at me as though I'd grown a third eye. "No, he's definitely going to need that reinserted."

I didn't like those *re-* words—*re-ventilate, reinsert.* Having a tube forced through your nose all the way to your stomach is a very painful process, and there was no way I'd let John suffer any more than was absolutely necessary. "Not until you get me a doctor who says they're going to have to put that in, because he's already done the swallowing test and passed. They're doing another one this morning, and I'm sure he'll pass that one, too." Before they moved John up from PICU, they ran a swallowing test on him to see how his throat was doing after they'd taken out the ventilator. He'd done fine, but they scheduled another one for the morning. I assumed that pulling out the tube wasn't that big of a deal, because they were going to remove it in the morning anyway.

She pursed her lips, as though she didn't believe me, and disappeared. About an hour later she returned with another nurse. "We're going to go ahead and put it back in."

I did not like this news—and I was certain the nurse was making a mistake. I looked her straight in the eyes to make sure she understood what I was about to say. "I'm going to tell you this right now. If you put that back in him and the doctor comes in here at nine o'clock this morning and pulls that out, I'm going to come looking for you."

She asked me to leave the room.

"No," I said and planted myself firmly at the end of the bed. I wanted her to know how deeply unhappy I was at what they were about to do. They held him down and shoved that tube back down his sore and raw throat—without anything to numb or ease the discomfort. He fought and cried the entire time. I knew it hurt him—and I wanted to hurt them.

Hours later, in the morning, the neurologist Dr. Carter and his team showed up and had John swallow water through a straw.

"Okay." Dr. Carter seemed pleased. "We're going to go ahead and pull that feeding tube. We probably should have pulled it last night."

I saw red.

"John pulled out the tube last night when he was sleeping and the nurse insisted they reinsert it. I told them last night that you were going to remove it today anyway, but they shoved that tube back down his throat. They hurt him."

The doctor uncomfortably cleared his throat. I could tell he wasn't sure how to respond to my outburst. I didn't care, because all I could think was, *Let me at her!*

And out came the feeding tube for a second time.

About an hour later the nurse came as far as the door—actually several feet from it, planting herself firmly in the middle of the hallway. She looked in and saw me see her. "So does he still have his feeding tube?"

"No, he does not." I spat out each word. Before I could say anything else, she wheeled on her heels and took off down the hallway. If I still had access to that feeding tube, I wasn't sure what I was going to do with it—maybe shove it down *her* throat to see how *she* liked it!

Fortunately for her I had other matters that needed my attention. This was the day we were going to start getting John up and moving around.

The physical therapist came in very perky and upbeat. "Hi, John! Ready to get up and moving?"

John was an agile and coordinated boy—after all, he played basketball where he had to dart in and around oncoming players while dribbling a ball. But even the most agile and coordinated person is going to struggle with atrophy after being bedridden for eleven days.

His fingers were still gnarled and crunched up in a frozen position, because of lack of use and the trauma to his body, so he didn't have dexterity to do things, such as push himself up, tie a knot in a hospital dressing gown, or use the new iPhone that his brother Charles had given him the day before (his old one, along with his favorite pair of shoes, was at the bottom of the lake).

The therapist and I maneuvered him around on the bed until we were able to get him sitting up with his legs swinging over. I had to stop, just to let this moment sink in. Something so simple, and yet miraculous.

"Okay, we're going to put this on you so you won't fall," the therapist told him. She held up a woven netting belt about four inches wide and then wrapped it around his waist. Then with a *heave* and a *ho*, we lifted him onto his feet.

John's eyes did such a huge roll that it could have landed him in the *Guinness Book of World Records*. "Nice dog leash," he said, as she stepped several feet in front of him holding a handle that was attached to the belt. "Let's go."

His right foot—the same one that had been turned since birth—was atrophied at an awkward angle, and his legs were very wobbly, so he moved slowly.

"That's okay, take your time," she told him. "We're just going to the bathroom here, so we don't have very far."

After he got his shower and used the restroom, he was in a better mood. He got settled back into his bed, exhausted, and the therapist concentrated on loosening up his muscles. She worked his legs and feet, then his arms and fingers. "Mom, you can help him by massaging these fingers, rubbing them and straightening them back out," she told me.

I was only too happy to help.

Later, Jason showed up bearing gifts. "Hey, John, I hear you got a shower today. I know how much you like your showers, so I brought you this." Jason plopped down a bag filled with Axe products—shampoo, deodorant—all in Dark Thunder scent. "I thought it appropriate," he said, not trying to hide his laughter. "That's to help you smell purty again."

John rolled his eyes.

Ah, my son had truly returned to me—in all his adolescent glory.

Friday, January 30, 2015

Now that he was awake and alert and could have lots of visitors, as soon as school ended, his room was filled. He was delighted to see so many friends and classmates, but his real excitement came when his basketball team showed up. They were all wearing black arm sweatbands with his number 4 displayed brightly in teal on it to show their support for him. His face broke out into a wide smile. They had even signed a basketball, which they gave him. The room was boisterous as each team member recounted the games he'd missed, what was happening at school, and how their lives had been changed by John's experience.

Now that he finally didn't have the sedatives keeping him asleep and un-aware and with all his visitors, as well as medical people constantly coming in to poke, prod, test, and evaluate him, John had to struggle to rest. He would just start to nod off, and someone would be there shaking him awake.

"I'm so tired!" he cried.

I could feel his pain, but there wasn't much I could do.

By Friday afternoon when Dr. Carter popped in, John was wiped out. "I'm worried that he isn't getting enough sleep," Dr. Carter said. "Maybe we need to start him on a mild sedative."

"Hold on," I spoke up. "Before we jump off the bridge here, let's think about this. He's having trouble sleeping because it's a hospital. He goes to sleep and two minutes later he's got a nurse coming in and checking his temperature, taking blood to test his oxygen levels, giving him breathing treat-ments. I understand what you're trying to do, but you can't talk out of both sides of your mouth. If you want him to sleep, then you've got to *let* him sleep."

By the look on the doctor's face, I wondered if this had been the first time he had ever considered what it was actually like to be a patient in a hospital room. "Yeah, that does make sense," he said.

"Just leave him alone. Let him sleep. If he needs something, I'll get a nurse."

"You're probably right," he said. "Let's see how that goes tonight."

They left him alone that night. And—surprise of a lifetime—he slept soundly and got the rest he needed.

CHAPTER 22

Get Me Out of Here!

Saturday, January 31, 2015

 King John was holding court. A constant flow of well-wishers, his "fan" club, and friends were coming to visit and talking and laughing incessantly. They'd missed their friend—and he'd missed them. They gave him updates on what he'd missed over the past two weeks, showing him the T-shirts they'd had made that said, ASK ME ABOUT JOHN SMITH, and how they'd prayed for him. He also received a large framed photo of all the students sitting in the gymnasium holding a giant sign that said, WE LOVE YOU, JOHN! He ate it up.

All the attention, however, also made him homesick. "How much longer do I have to be here?" he complained one night to his dad and me. "I'm fine! I just want to go home."

"I know, son," Brian told him. "But they still want to make sure you're completely recovered before they let you go."

"But I am! I want to get back to playing basketball and hanging out with my friends."

Brian smiled. "Soon. And just think, you'll be out in no time and we can catch up on all the sports we missed."

I chuckled. These two and their sports. I was just glad to see them reconnecting. Brian had his son back.

"You look too skinny!" Marie Glenville—or Mama G, as John called her—told John Saturday evening when she and her daughter Alyssa, John's friend and classmate, came to visit. "We need to fatten you up. Why are you so skinny?" He'd weighed 130 pounds when he fell into Lake Ste. Louise. Now he weighed 112. He looked like a concentration camp victim.

"I'm *hungry!*" he said, whining as he nodded toward the Ensure sitting unopened on his hospital tray. Getting him to eat had been a big fight for him from the time they removed his feeding tube. They wanted him to drink Ensure, since he hadn't had any solids in a week and weren't sure how his digestive system would handle regular food. But John hated the Ensure and refused to drink it. Jason's wife, Paula, had been the only one to get him to drink an entire can—and that was because she doctored it up and then threatened him. When the doctor finally acquiesced and let him have solid foods, he snubbed his nose at it. "It doesn't taste or smell or even look good," he'd complain and then push it away.

"You're hungry?" Mama G asked. "How come you're not eating?"

"I hate the food here."

"Fine. I'll cook you something and bring it up."

John looked as though he had won the lottery. Mama G and her sister used to own a restaurant and were the best cooks this side of the Mississippi—possibly on both sides. If he had to be stuck in the hospital, at least he could look forward to getting a great meal soon. I just wanted to see him gain a little weight. Mama G was right; he *was* too skinny.

Monday, February 2, 2015

"He's blown through every milestone we've set," Dr. Carter announced while examining John. "We don't even have a road map to figure out where to go next with this kid. I guess we just need to keep following his lead." He laughed. "He's going to end up in medical textbooks."

John wasn't impressed. He was breathing normally, swallowing normally, speaking with a rasp but normally. His vitals were good, his oxygen level remained strong, and although he was still walking slowly and needed to get his strength back, everything else had returned to normal—even his finger dexterity.

Next to the cleanliness issue, not having use of his fingers drove him crazy. He wanted to text his friends and couldn't! So on Friday he'd started his own physical therapy—texting exercises. He doggedly pushed his fingers on the phone's keyboard. His first text had been to his friend Emma, and he hadn't stopped texting since. How anybody understood what he was typing in those first texts is beyond me. Since his fingers still weren't as flexible as they should be, half of his texts made no sense—a lovely gobbledy-gook of words—but that didn't stop him from reaching out to the outside world. Jason really stepped up in this department, too. He and John had text emoji wars, in which they would go to the emoji section of their phones and see who could post the most emojis the fastest. Since they're both competitive, they both fought hard to win. And by Monday, John's fingers were flexible and good—and they flew over his keyboard with texts that were 100 percent readable.

His physical therapist was pleased over his finger work, so she concentrated more on limbering up his legs and feet. She had John stepping up and down on blocks, walking up and down stairs, taking a shower on his own, touching his toes, and doing squats and other things that required balancing abilities. "He's doing really well," she told me. She even mentioned that at the rate he was progressing, he wouldn't need her in a few days, since he was recovering his strength, balance, and flexibility so quickly.

Overall he was doing so well that all the doctors and therapists coming in to examine him annoyed him.

"It's like they're *trying* to find something wrong with me," he told me after one of the neurologists left. The tests were always the same: He had to put his hand out and then bring his finger to touch his nose, which he did perfectly every time. All the while rolling his eyes, of course. I thought the added bonus of doing the finger point *and* the teenaged eye roll simultaneously would impress the neurologists, but apparently, they didn't see it that way.

He was so irritated that by this point whenever a neurologist would walk into the room, his jaw would set and he'd just automatically start performing. Finger to nose. Eye roll. Finger to nose. Eye roll...

They were just doing their jobs—and honestly, I think they were confounded. They'd never had a kid die and then come back to life with absolutely no impairment—not even something minor! So they did the only thing they knew to do—keep examining and testing. But to John, they were keeping him from going home and resuming his fourteen-year-old life.

Starting Monday, John also had to deal with the media. It's one thing to get a hero's hello from your friends and family, it's quite another to receive that kind of attention from strangers. The media had been all over this story, and Jason had done an amazing job keeping Brian and me in the loop of who wanted what and when and helping us figure out how to prioritize everything. From radio interview requests to newspapers to television, reporters all wanted their quotes and the "scoop." But up to this point, all the stories had included the doctors and the two Joshes, but not John. Monday afternoon, just two weeks after John had drowned, Kay Quinn, a news anchor with the local NBC affiliate, showed up with her camera crew to do an interview with John, our family, the first responders, and the PICU nurses and doctors. It was the first interview we had allowed in which the reporter could talk to my son. I trusted Kay. Brian had worked as a technical director for the weekend news for five years and got to know her. He felt that she would respect our wishes and honor John's story by including God and the miracles he had performed.

John wasn't keen on the idea of being interviewed—in fact, the thought of it made him emotionally distraught—but after I explained why people were so interested in this story and how he could share what God had done for him, he finally agreed.

"But only on one condition," he told me. "You and Pastor Jason both have to promise to be with me in this—and in any—interview I do."

"Done," I promised.

We got him settled into a chair in the PICU waiting room, and Kay began to ask him questions about that day and what had happened. All he could remember was that he and his friends had gone onto the ice.

"I remember sliding my feet on the ice, like sitting on the dock and sliding back and forth," he told us. "I remember turning around, putting my hands on the dock, and then pushing my feet under me to stand up. I remember taking videos on our phones of each other doing stupid stuff like running back and forth and standing as close to the open water as we could. We were texting our friends and having a good time. And then I got the call from Mom and everything went dark."

After that, he had no memory.

I smiled as I listened to him say, "I don't remember anything else," because the wonderful thing for us—although I'm sure it wasn't for the media—was that God had answered another of our prayers. We'd asked God for John not to remember the horror of his experience. And John didn't.

Around dinnertime, the most amazing aroma wafted into our room, followed by Alyssa and her mother, Mama G, carrying a large bag of food. Pot roast, mashed potatoes and gravy, green beans with almonds, rolls, and a luscious homemade dessert—all for John. True to her word, here Mama G stood, unloading container after container of the most delicious-smelling food, and placing it on the tray. If he wanted to eat it, then I didn't want to refuse him that, but I was concerned that his body wouldn't handle it well. We'd already dealt with enough diarrhea!

"Now that you're finally getting some real food, I guess you'll live," Brian said, joking with John.

John nodded, smiled, picked up a fork, and dug in. With that first bite, he breathed in deeply, groaned, and closed his eyes in ecstasy as he chewed. Each bite brought the same results.

"This is so good," he kept saying. "This tastes so good!"

His system handled it perfectly—as if he'd been eating that way every day. Another miracle.

Wednesday, February 4, 2015

Around midmorning, Dr. Carter walked into John's room wearing a big smile.

"Well, John, it looks like we don't have reason to keep you here any longer," he said. "We don't know what else to do. You are quite the miracle."

His words were like the sweetest whisperings to my ears.

"Today?" John asked, getting excited.

"Today," Dr. Carter replied, smiling.

We were thrilled. I immediately texted Brian. I knew he would be just as excited as we were. We just had to wait for the release papers, and then John was finally going home!

Only...apparently that wasn't what some people thought would happen. That afternoon, a social services woman informed me that John would leave the hospital and head directly to a full-time, in-house rehabilitation hospital.

"What?" I barked out, wondering how insane she had to be. "On what grounds? He doesn't need it."

"The staff here feel that John needs additional therapy."

Now I knew she was out of her mind. "I'm not putting him in a full-time rehab place. I'm not doing it." I sat up straight and crossed my arms to send her a clear message.

She received it, because she stood and smiled a tight-lipped smile. "I'm sure I'll see you again before John leaves."

Don't count on it, I thought as I watched her exit the room.

Even though John was scheduled to be released, while we waited for Dr. Carter or Dr. Gibbons to officially sign the paperwork, John was still scheduled to go to his final round of physical therapy, so off he went to the physical therapy room, walking well and without any assistance, while I remained in his room. Several people had already shown up, giving me release instructions, and orders about following up with checkups. Not long before John was to return, a squirmy-looking man entered the room and introduced himself as a doctor representing the rehab organization I'd turned down when I spoke with the social services lady.

"John is going to need extra care once he's released from the hospital today," he told me.

"No, no, he isn't," I told him. "He doesn't need any more physical therapy."

John was walking, he was talking, and he was now eating (thanks to a lot of smuggled-in food), so I was trying to figure out what exactly he needed physical therapy for.

"Well, let me be clear about this," he said. "If John doesn't have full-time, in-house therapy, the doctors here aren't going to release him from the hospital."

I felt as though he'd just punched me in the gut. And then, just as quickly, I almost came out of my chair and put *him* in the hospital, because they were telling the control freak that I didn't have any control. Worse, they were telling a parent that I didn't know my kid as well as they—the "experts"—did. Well, I'd proved that theory wrong over and over since we first landed in the emergency room. Now this determined, arrogant man I barely knew rolled into John's room and told me that John was going to be in full-time therapy, and they didn't know how long he was going to be there.

"He's not going into full-time therapy," I told him. Again.

"He needs it."

"Have you even seen him?"

He paused, as though he didn't want to admit his answer. I tilted my head and gave him a sharp look. "No," he said finally.

"Then how do you know he needs full-time therapy? What is it that makes you come to that conclusion?"

"The neurologist said that he was struggling with his responses."

This was news to me. All the neurologists had been stunned by how well he was responding.

"Which neurologist, exactly?"

He paused slightly. "The doctor of record."

"Really? Well, I don't know what they're telling you, but Dr. Carter and Dr. Gibbons both have stated that he's doing so well they don't know what to do with him—that he's basically writing the textbook on this one. So you have no idea what you're talking about."

Apparently I offended him, because he straightened his back, jutted out his chin, and announced, "Well, he's going to have therapy. And it's going to be an in-house program."

"No, it isn't happening."

He turned abruptly on his heel and stormed out of the room. Coincidentally enough, he met John out in the hallway as my son was returning. So John came in the room with this man hot on his trail.

He introduced himself to John and started to explain why he was there. As soon as John heard where the man was from, his temper flared and he glanced at me with a glare that said, *I am so over this—how many times do I have to prove that I can do this stuff?*

"John, I'd like you to follow me and do what I do, okay?" the man said.

John didn't say anything, but his jaw clicked his ire. This was going to be the angriest game of Simon Says ever.

The man touched his nose. John touched his nose.

Every movement the man made, John did it just as quickly—and in most cases more quickly than the man could do it!

With each movement, the doctor's face grew redder. Finally, he turned toward me and said my favorite words to hear: "Okay, you're right." But he was stubborn and refused to completely give in. "He is still going to have to come for therapy."

"And again my question to you is, for what?"

"There are little nuances going on that you don't see."

How stupid do I look? I thought. *You can save all that medical jargon for your-*

self, because he doesn't have any nuances that are going on that need therapy.

He left with a smirk, and I immediately called Brian to give him the news.

About a half hour later, the social services lady reentered the room with a stack of paperwork and wearing what appeared to be the same smirk as the squirmy man. "I have some things for you to sign." Then before I could say anything, she said, "Or we won't release him into your care."

Against my better judgment, I signed.

Now we waited for Dr. Carter to sign the release papers and for us to get out of there!

While we were waiting, a reporter from the *St. Louis Post-Dispatch* came and interviewed us. She was thrilled to discover that John would be released while she was there to capture it. Jason also contacted KSDK, Kay Quinn's station, to alert them and they sent out a news crew right away.

Finally, at ten o'clock that morning the nurse walked in with the release papers and a cart to carry John's things. "Here you go." I was surprised they didn't offer a wheelchair—but I think we all knew there was no way he was going to be rolled out. He was going to walk.

He grabbed his basketball from the team and led the way out of his hospital room without ever looking back.

Jason, who had arrived earlier that morning, pushed the cart filled with stuffed animals his friends had given him, the photo of his classmates holding the WE LOVE YOU, JOHN! sign, flowers, and other miscellaneous stuff that we'd collected while there. John's nurse and I followed behind. I couldn't stop smiling, I felt so grateful for what God had done. When we got down to the lobby to exit the building, the newspaper photographer and the KSDK cameraman jumped in front of us and began filming John as he walked out of the building.

John had entered the hospital sixteen days before this moment. The entire medical community believed he would be wheeled out of the hospital for the morgue that same day. But after ten days in the PICU, and six days in a step-down unit, he was walking through the hospital doors without hesitation and under his own physical strength—completely normal, totally healed.

CHAPTER 23

Why Him?

I'm hungry," John said as soon as he and I were tucked securely in our car. "Let's go to O'Charley's."

"As you wish," I told him and shook my head with laughter.

Monica, from Cardinal Glennon's public relations department, knew that John loved O'Charley's, so as a treat, she'd called the nearest one and told them about John's story. The manager was delighted and offered to comp John's next meal there.

I suppose I shouldn't have been surprised that my teenage son would want to eat right away. If he wanted to grab food at one of his favorite restaurants, I wasn't going to refuse. After all, this was a time to celebrate. So I invited Jason along and we headed to O'Charley's, where John ordered his favorite meal—chicken strips and steak fries. He cleaned his plate.

Then we went home. Walking into the house was like entering a sanctuary; it felt so calm. *Okay, he's home*, I thought, and I could have cried with relief. *Things are going to be all right. Things are good now.*

Brian hadn't made it home yet, so we both took in the quiet.

"I'm tired," John told me. "I just want to go and lie down."

"Okay, sweetie. Get some rest."

Later that afternoon, Brian's cousin Dave arrived unexpectedly.

"Hi," he told me. "Sorry I missed John at the hospital. I didn't realize he was being released today."

I told him that we'd just found out the previous day, but we could not have been more thrilled. "John's sleeping right now."

"That's okay. I just wanted to make sure he got this." Dave held out his hand. In it was a tie.

That's odd, I thought, but I accepted it. "Thanks. I'll make sure John gets it."

"It's from Dr. Garrett. I stopped by the hospital and ran into him. He was sorry that he missed John and so he passed this to me."

I unfurled the tie to see Michael Jordan's smiling face staring up at me. I burst into laughter, remembering that on the Wednesday when John awoke for the first time, Dr. Garrett had promised to give John his Michael Jordan tie if John would promise to get better and get out of the hospital. Both had kept their word.

"Thanks, Dave. John is going to love this!"

When Brian arrived home, John was still asleep. Brian didn't want to wake him, so he simply went into his room and saw that he *was* really there and that he was okay, and then returned to the kitchen.

"What a ride, right?" I said, feeling like a deflated balloon. All I wanted to do was sit and veg out. Brian looked the same. So that night while John slept peacefully in his room, Brian and I simply turned on the television to relax and unwind. As far as we were concerned, the drama of John's accident was behind us and we could return to our normal, boring, everyday lives.

As Brian flipped through the channels, he saw Kay Quinn, the NBC local affiliate anchor. She was sharing the story of John Smith's remarkable recovery.

"Well, I guess we should buckle up," I told Brian. "The media requests are really going to come pouring in now."

Thursday, February 5, 2015

John slept all the way through until morning. Brian looked in on him before he left for work, but didn't want to wake him. When John finally got up, I made him French toast for breakfast and then I drove him to the rehab hospital—much against both my and John's wills. But I had signed the agreement, and if I didn't follow through, they could have a social worker from the Department of Child and Family Services show up at our door and remove John from our house.

John complained the entire way, and when we pulled into the parking lot, his grumblings grew louder. "I don't know why I have to do this. It's stupid. I'm fine!"

"I know you are, John. But this is what they require, so let's just go in and get it over with."

A nurse met us in the visitor's waiting room, got him signed in, and then led us to another room where they would begin their therapy session. The room felt depressing and sad. It wasn't terribly large and felt crowded. At least five therapists were there working with elderly patients who had obviously suffered from strokes or brain damage. Watching them was somewhat like watching a train wreck, in that you don't want to look but you can't help it. I felt terrible for those people and what they had suffered—but my son didn't belong here.

The therapist decided to start with cognitive therapy, so she asked John to repeat whatever she said. But her voice was soft and the room was crowded and noisy. I was right there and I couldn't catch what she was saying. John scrunched his face, trying to hear what she said so he could repeat it back to her, which made his response times a little longer and awkward. But also, there was so much going on in the room that he was getting distracted. *I* was getting distracted, so I could understand his problem! Instead of him telling her that, though, he kept trying to work through it—I think because he hates to admit that he can't do something.

Finally, the therapist felt that she had seen enough. She turned to me. "I'm afraid your son has some cognitive damage."

"Yeah, he does *not* have cognitive damage," I told her. "There is nothing wrong with his brain function."

She smiled in the most patronizing way, then stood. "Let's go check some of his other functions. Follow me, please."

Oh, I was hot.

She led us down a long hallway toward a small cafeteria area.

"If you'll sit here for a few minutes...I'm going to confer with a few other therapists and then I'll be right back."

John sat across from me, and as soon as the therapist left, he said, "I'm not staying here. I don't need to be here, and you cannot make me do this. I'm not doing it."

He wasn't saying, "I don't want to do this" or "Please don't make me do this anymore." He was obstinate and he was *not* going to do it.

I rummaged through my purse until I found the car keys, which I handed to him. "Just go and get in the car. I'll be there in a few minutes." I watched him walk—perfectly normally—out of the cafeteria, and I waited for the therapist to return.

After a few more minutes and still no sign of her, I called Jason. "I cannot believe they think John's best 'recovery' would take place here. They're just crazy," I told him as soon as he answered.

"Joyce," Jason said in his calmest voice. "God has not brought us this far not to meet this need also. Let's pray about it." Right away, he began to pray. I appreciated the fact that he didn't give some vague "Let's pray" and then hang up the phone. When he said, "Let's pray," he meant right here, right now. "God," he said, "we know that You promised to heal John completely. You have not brought us this far not to take care of this need for physical therapy, too. Please show us today what You want. Open the door that needs to be open, close all doors that need to be closed. Give Joyce and John peace right now. Guide their paths. Thank You for all You have done up to this point. We ask this in the mighty and powerful name of Jesus. Amen." The phone line went silent for a moment to let the words of the prayer sink in. Finally, he said, "God has everything under control—even this. He'll take care of it."

I knew he was right and I knew I was letting my little controlling self get in the way. I needed to take a deep breath and calm down. Sometimes, we moms can go into Mama Grizzly Bear modes and go on the attack when we feel someone might possibly harm our babies. I knew that I had taken on that role several times. I wasn't going to apologize for that—because I know that's part of our role as mothers—to protect at all costs. But I also knew if I wasn't careful, that part of my personality could take over and I could steamroll right over what God was already working on.

Throughout the hospital stay we'd had great people, but a few had gotten my goat, so to speak. Those were the times when Jason would kindly remind me of the truth: "We do not wrestle against flesh and blood, but against the rulers, against the authorities, against the cosmic powers over this present darkness, against the spiritual forces of evil in the heavenly places" (Eph. 6:12). As I encountered these people, I needed to remember who we were really fighting against. I needed to keep my eyes on the spirit realm and not fight the battle in the physical realm. Jason would often say, "We run out of strength very quickly when we fight the battle in the physical. You need to look past the person in front of you and battle in the spirit."

I'll admit, sometimes that was tough to do.

I took another deep breath and waited for the therapist to return.

When she finally came back, before she could say a word, I started in as kindly but firmly as I could. "This isn't going to work out and we won't be back. We're going to make other arrangements elsewhere." As I stood and headed for the exit, I thought, *Okay, she's calling social services now, and I'm in deep doo-doo.* I figured a cop would be sitting in my driveway when we got home.

"God," I said aloud as I walked past a row of cars to mine, "I need You to show up in this. You've brought us this far. You know that John shouldn't be here. Work this out for him, Lord."

I dropped into the driver's seat and looked at my son, who was crying.

"Okay, it's done. We're not coming back here. I don't know where we'll go, but we'll figure out something." I paused. This poor kid had just been through seventeen days of trauma—they didn't need to add to it. "What do you want to do now?"

"I want to go to school. I want to see Mr. Caimi." Jason Caimi was John's physical education teacher. I was surprised that he wanted that, but I also knew that he and Mr. Caimi had a good relationship.

Well, now he was going to get his wish. If John wanted to see Mr. Caimi, then that was what I was going to make happen. I turned the key in the ignition, backed out of the parking space, and headed for John's school.

We arrived at about 11:30 a.m. Just as we were walking into the main entrance of the school building, Marie Glenville, our Mama G, was heading toward the doors and carrying three large tin containers. Marie collected all sorts of tin cans and containers to ship necessities to soldiers stationed overseas, and she worked with the school for collections. As soon as she saw John, she dropped the cans, which made a loud crashing sound that echoed throughout the atrium and down the hallway and brought curious seekers out of every doorway in the area. Mama G and John threw their arms around each other and we all sobbed. She was sobbing for joy—but I was sobbing over the physical therapy dilemma we now faced.

When she finally looked at me and saw that I was crying, too, she said, "What's wrong with you?"

"I have to have a therapist for John and I can't find one, and I don't know what I'm going to do. I'm going to have social services on me."

She looked strangely at me for a moment. "Why don't you call Dave Meers? He's a partner with a rehab clinic."

Her words were like a lightning bolt into my brain. How could I have forgotten about him? Dave Meers was the head coach for Christian High and had watched my son play basketball since John was in the fifth grade. John looked forward to playing for Dave when he got into high school. God had placed

Marie right where He needed her to be. She provided exactly the answer we needed. Once again, another miracle. I was amazed to watch how God had even this under control—the day after John was released from the hospital, and I was scared to death of what was happening, but God had already taken care of it all.

February 6–28, 2015

We got John connected with Dave Meers, and John was much happier. For three weeks his physical therapy included doing basketball endurance drills until everyone signed off and he was completely released.

John also returned to school for half days two weeks after his hospital release, and two weeks after that, he was able to return full time. That brought with it some semblance of normalcy—but it also brought a celebrity spotlight he wasn't completely comfortable with. Girls showing him attention was one thing he didn't mind—but the media, the constant references back to his accident, and the unwanted attention were difficult for him to manage.

Brian, Jason, and I tried to protect John as much as we could from the frenzy, but once Kay Quinn's story hit the airwaves, all bets were off. Every major morning show, afternoon and evening talk show, celebrity show, and everything in between wanted John as a guest. We limited what we allowed, because we didn't want to wear John out—but also because John just wanted to get back into his school routine, play basketball, and hang out with his friends.

But everyone knew his story, so everywhere he went, people would want to hug or touch him, ask him questions, relive with him the experience.

"Mom, why can't we just move on?"

"I know" was all I could answer. As much as we could, Brian, Jason, and I all kept bringing the focus back to God. "Let's use what happened to keep pointing people to God and how good and faithful He is."

The most difficult pressure came from the people who were so excited for him and would tell him, "God must have saved your life for you to do amazing things!" and "God's got great things in store for you."

"What am I supposed to say to that?" he would ask me and Brian.

What, indeed.

Not all people were well-wishers, however. A few kids would see John and comment, "Hey, there, it's the Miracle Boy!" or "Learned how to swim yet, Miracle Boy?"

One person in particular, an adult we'll call Logan, caused him a great deal of grief. One day Logan cornered him and said, "Why do you think you were chosen to make it through this and somebody else wasn't? What's so special about you that God answered your prayers but didn't answer mine when one of my family members died last year?" Doing it in private would have been inappropriate enough, but this person chose to confront him in front of some of his peers.

"Well, John?" Logan asked again, when John didn't answer. "Why do you think God allowed you to live and He lets other people die?"

I understand Logan had recently lost a close relative—and I comprehend the unfairness of it. Death is a terrible, horrible thing. It isn't fair any way you look at it. I also recognize that people's grief sometimes makes them do or say things that are crazy and rude and unsuitable. But to ask that kind of a question to a *fourteen-year-old* boy—in front of his friends—was beyond inappropriate.

I didn't find out until a couple days later when his friend Emma was visiting and told me what had happened. It was such an unthinkable and ridiculous story, I almost didn't believe her—but Emma doesn't lie.

"Is this true?" I turned to John and waited for him to laugh and say what a joke they'd played on me.

But he didn't laugh. He didn't answer at all.

"John?" I wasn't about to let this one go.

He sighed and finally admitted that it was as Emma had stated.

Immediately I met with Logan and had a friendly little conversation about what in the world this person could have possibly been thinking to expect a child to know the mysteries and mind of the Sovereign Creator God.

"I don't even understand that issue of why God chooses some and not others. Theologians talk about that. They write books about it. Why would you place a fourteen-year-old child in that kind of a situation, putting him on the spot like that, and make him feel guilty because he's alive, when God gave him the miracle?"

As an adult, Logan should have known better. If Logan wanted to ask those kinds of questions, then the best route would have been to confront me or Brian or Pastor Jason. We also couldn't have answered the question, but we could have at least dialogued in a grown-up manner. But I made it clear that Logan was not to provoke John, who didn't ask for any of this to happen to him.

"You can't reason why your loved one isn't with you," I told Logan, "and it has nothing to do with my son. So how do you expect my son to answer a question like that? *I* can't answer that."

I told Logan about some friends of our family's who had a child, Mitchell. If there were ever a perfect kid in the world, he was it. Obedient, kind, thoughtful. This kid had an unbelievable level of faith—stronger than most adults have. They dubbed him "the unstoppable child." And he got leukemia. "I never prayed so hard for anyone in my whole life as I did for Mitchell. He and John were basically the same age," I told Logan. "Mitchell fought long and hard, but eventually the leukemia took his life. It crushed me because I just knew God was going to heal this child. I mean, why *wouldn't* He? Mitchell was an amazing boy with so much potential. When he died, I knew in my heart and my head that Mitchell was in a better place where he'd never suffer again, where he was whole and healthy. But knowing those things didn't lessen the ache I felt."

Tears welled up in Logan's eyes as I continued: "I don't know why God decided to answer my prayers for John when He didn't answer my prayers for Mitchell. I can't explain that. I'm not God. The only thing I know is that He is sovereign."

"I never looked at it that way," Logan said. "And I'm sorry. I shouldn't have done that to John. You know, when you go through the grieving process, sometimes your mind goes places it shouldn't go."

I wasn't thrilled that John had to endure these situations, but I was grateful for the lessons they provided on accepting God's mysteries and praising Him for who He is. We worked hard to stay close to John and spent a lot of time talking him through everything he had and was experiencing. God was using all these things to help shape John into the kind of Christ-like character that would please Him. As John wrestled through it, I watched God become increasingly more real, profound, and intimate to him. The truth is that I praised God when He saved John because I knew God was good and faithful and loving and true. But had He not saved John, God would still be just as good and faithful and loving and true. That's what I wanted John to remember.

CHAPTER 24

"There's Science and There's God. This Is God."

Sunday, March 8, 2015

Hurry up, John," I yelled toward John's room. "We don't want to be late."

This Sunday was John's and my first time back to First Assembly Church—and the entire service was focused on thanking and celebrating the first responders and their work in John's life.

We were all nervous and excited. I knew it would feel good to be back in church and to see so many friends who had vigilantly prayed for and supported us, but I wasn't sure how John would handle all this focused attention.

Jason had worked hard to get all of the first responders to attend, inviting the Lake St. Louis police department, the Lake St. Louis and Wentzville fire departments, the paramedics, Dr. Sutterer, the ER medical team from St. Joseph Hospital West, and Dr. Garrett from Cardinal Glennon. I was overwhelmed and grateful they'd all said yes.

I checked John's outfit—he had on the Michael Jordan tie Dr. Garrett had given him. We all looked presentable, so it was time to go. John fidgeted a bit on the drive over, anxious and unsure of what would take place.

"This is going to be good, John," I told him. "Just think of all these people God strategically put in place to save your life. Pretty amazing."

As soon as we walked into the building, some of the church's security team escorted us to a side prayer room where we met with Dr. Garrett to have prayer before the service.

Dr. Garrett offered to pray. He talked about the miracles throughout the Bible and how once again God had given us a miracle, and he thanked God for it. His words made me cry. After thinking this man was stoic and harsh when I first met him...how I had misjudged him! He was a quiet, gentle man who was so kind and caring. He melted my heart with his humble prayer.

When we entered the sanctuary, I was almost overcome by how electric it felt. We got chills! It was so exciting to sense God's presence that way and to look at the capacity crowd of a thousand people. There wasn't an empty seat. We took our place at the front just as the service began. After everyone sang a few worship songs, Jason got on the platform and gave a brief introduction to John's story, then called the first responders onto the stage. Person after person filed up the steps and crowded onto the platform, and my heart skipped a beat. *All these people, Lord. You put all these people exactly where You wanted them to be. Thank You, thank You.*

"This morning you will see a tapestry of miracles that God put together with John," Jason said as the group continued to fill the stage. "The medical professionals did an incredible job, and they partnered with God to see this play out."

Then he asked specific first responders to give their perspective. First up was Tommy Shine, the firefighter who found John's body. Tommy recalled rushing to the lake and methodically poking around until he located my son. "We're going to call it what it is—the miracle on ice happened," he said. "We were able to pull that young man out, who was lifeless. I mean, it's a harsh reality. He was lifeless.... At the end of the day, did we expect to find him? Absolutely not. You hope for the best. You train as hard as you can, but you never really expect it to happen until it does. And then, for me, it's amazement, shock, and awe."

Next Chief Mike Marlo, the Wentzville Fire Protection District chief, spoke.

He shared his part of the story and thanked the first responders, then he said, "Been in this business thirty-eight years, and I will tell you there's divine intervention. This was divine intervention, and I really believe that."

As the crowd applauded, Jason asked him, "Chief, with your experience, what would you have thought the outcome was going to be?"

"The one child who self-rescued—obviously we knew he would be fine," Chief Marlo answered. "The other child whom Lake St. Louis rescued, we knew would be fine. But the child who was submerged for up to twenty minutes—that one does not normally turn out the way it did. And that's what I call divine intervention."

I looked at John. He hung on every word.

The next to speak was Dr. Sutterer. As he told of his experience, I got chills. This was the point when I had entered the picture—and to hear the background of what had taken place stunned me. I hadn't heard most of this until then. I inhaled deeply, trying to take it all in. Dr. Sutterer talked about how cold and lifeless John's body was, how his temperature read at eighty-eight degrees, and how everyone in the room knew this was a grave situation. He explained that after trying everything to resuscitate John, they finally decided it was time to officially call his death.

"I brought Joyce in," he said. "I wanted her to see everything that we were doing and that it was not having any effect. He was gone, and I was getting ready to kneel down next to her and say, 'I'm sorry. Your son passed away.' But when she came in the room..." He paused and shook his head. "It still just leaves me...It's indescribable. I don't have words for what happened at that point. She started praying, and she started praying loudly. People on the other side of the emergency department—"

Cheers and applause erupted, as people all around the room jumped to their feet. Even Pastor Jason and Dr. Sutterer stood and clapped.

"I'm thinking we might just want to stay standing," Jason said and laughed.

Dr. Sutterer told the group that I was "crying out to God with a specific request: 'Lord, send your Holy Spirit to save my son.' And inexplicably that's when his heart started again. Probably the biggest question I've gotten asked since all of this transpired is, 'Was this a miracle?' I hear everybody say, 'Well, the cold water saved him.'...I'm not an expert on miracles. I'm an expert on emergency medicine. People don't come to me for miracles. They come to me for emergency medicine."

"Maybe they will now," Jason kidded.

Dr. Sutterer laughed. "No. No, that's not going to go on my card."

"We could work together," Jason said.

"My job here is just to lay out the facts. The experts on miracles can look at all these time stamps and how long John was underwater and how long he was pulseless, and I don't think that there's any doubt. And even with the fact that his heart came back, I was thinking, *I changed the place where he's going to die.* He would go see Dr. Garrett, and he would die at Cardinal Glennon in ICU. For him to have a total recovery and not some seizure activity or some brain damage or anything like this total recovery, it's unbelievable. It's miraculous. It just doesn't happen like that. And the fact that it happened at the very moment when his mother was crying out in prayer, that right there, you just—" He paused again, as though he were searching for the right words. "I wish everybody could have been there at that moment just to see what happened," he said. "You just can't explain it. There is no explanation." He continued to share his story, and then finished by saying, "There was no controversy in the sequence of events. If we put it into a medical algorithm, we'd say, 'Patient's dead. Mother prayed. Patient came back to life.'"

The crowd erupted again with laughter and applause.

Finally, it was Dr. Garrett's turn to share. After thanking the first responders, he stated, "As I started to hear about this tragic accident that had happened and all the circumstances that surrounded it, medically our hopes were not high. But this is a miraculous story of a miraculous gift from our heavenly Father to a young man, a fourteen-year-old boy named John Smith. And it's a story that many choose not to believe when they first hear it. Nonetheless, it's true." Then he began to list everything that had happened from a medical perspective in John's body. His list grew longer and longer and was more and more stunning. Brian and I had never heard all of these things when we were in the hospital with John—of course, I realize that he might have told us that first night in the conference room, but I shut him down!

Then again, I was grateful that I *hadn't* known. Would I have believed as firmly as I did? Could I have held to the faith? Or would that list of John's problems have been just the thing to get the enemy's foot in the door of my mind and place doubt?

And still Dr. Garrett continued the litany of what had happened to John's body! As he spoke, Brian grabbed my hand. This was hard on him, too, to hear what he had suspected but had never fully known until this moment. Then John grabbed my other hand. I looked at both of my men. Tears were streaming down all our faces as we listened to the overwhelmingly long list of reasons John should not be alive. Everything sunk in as it really hadn't before: *that John survived was impossible.*

And yet, here he sat next to me, breathing, squeezing my hand, crying, fully alive! Dead, and by the third day awake; seven days later, the ventilator came out; seven days after that, he literally walked out of the hospital with no assistance. He needed no medications. He had no side effects. Anyone who knew John before the accident and didn't know about the accident would never know that there *had* been an accident! He was exactly the same!

I had to force myself not to heave loud sobs. God had taken what was impossible and had said, *But I'm going to show you that I AM. I AM an all-powerful God who can do what I say I can do.*

At the end of the long list of everything that happened and the time line in which it all occurred, Dr. Garrett said, "I've been criticized by some on the Internet for using the word *miracle*. They say I should know better because I'm a doctor....I firmly believed that Jesus performed many miracles when He was here on earth and that the Bible details some of them. There have been miracles since. And what happened in this case—John Smith himself is a miracle."

After that, Jason called us onto the stage. As we walked up, over the thunderous applause, several girls shouted, "We love you, John!"

Brian and I spoke briefly about the miracles we witnessed and how appreciative we were to our church family for their prayer support. Then it was John's turn to speak.

He admitted that he didn't remember anything, and then he started thanking specific people. As he named each one, he became more and more emotional.

This is the first time he's heard his own story, I realized, and I found myself needing to dab at my eyes, too. Until this service, I don't think he had really grasped what had happened to him.

"I'd just like to add," Brian said, "God doesn't save people halfway, and He didn't cure John halfway. The other night he was in the backseat of the car with one of his friends, and they were texting and talking about girls and listening to music. And it was so normal. . . . It was like a day three months ago. And for him to go in and out of the hospital. Dr. Garrett talked about how grave all his bodily functions were, and sixteen days after he went under the water in a frozen lake at Lake Ste. Louise, he was walking out under his own steam. I don't know how anybody can say that's not a miraculous thing. The Lord is the same yesterday, today, and forever. End of statement."

I was so proud of Brian. He'd had a long journey of faith through this experience. And he was absolutely dead-on right.

March 9–April 30, 2015

I awoke with a start. John was screaming at the top of his lungs. I ignored the aches and pains from my rheumatoid arthritis, threw myself out of my bed, and rushed into John's bedroom.

He was soaked with sweat, his eyes wild, and he kept screaming.

"John! John, it's okay," I said, grabbing his arms and trying desperately to calm him down. "Just breathe. It's okay. I'm here. You're all right."

He placed his hands to his throat and rubbed, his eyes turning from a wild stare to a panicked expression.

"I was..."

Before he uttered the words, I knew what he was going to say, and my heart sank into my stomach.

"The water...I was under the water...so cold..." He'd started to hyperventilate as he tried to tell me what had happened. "Then burning heat....They were bobbing up and down and I was in the water." He swallowed hard as tears flooded his eyes. "I was inhaling the water!"

"It's okay," I said, taking him into my arms and rocking him back and forth. *God, help him forget. Don't let him remember any of this. Please, God.*

It took several minutes before he calmed down. I finally got him to lie back on his bed and I prayed over him.

"Don't leave," he begged.

"Not on your life," I told him. He had a recliner in his room, so I settled myself there. As he closed his eyes to sleep, I closed mine to pray.

The following evening, the nightmares returned. And the night after that, and the night after that. For many nights, it was always the same—feeling the icy cold that turned to scorching heat, submerging, seeing the muddy, murky, filthy water floating past his face, struggling to get out, inhaling the water, and then waking up with screams.

After the first few nights of rushing into his room, I decided to sleep in his recliner so I could be close to him and comfort and pray over him as soon as the nightmares started. I pushed the chair against his bed, so that when he became restless, I could touch his head and pray peace over him. Many nights we'd sit and talk because he was terrified to fall asleep—certain the nightmare would return.

I knew this was a spiritual assault on him, so I doubled down on my prayers and asked Jason and our church to pray for him. And one night the nightmares just disappeared, never to return.

The timing was interesting because right around the time they disappeared, we had a scheduled appointment with Dr. Gibbons, one of the neurologists at Cardinal Glennon.

Dr. Gibbons performed his typical exam, asked John how he was doing and if he had any residual effects from the accident, which John told him he didn't. And then Dr. Gibbons said, "Well, really, there's no reason for you to come back anymore. Actually, the only reason you had this appointment is because I wanted to see you again! Do you know how amazing you are? You are still the talk of the hospital, and you are Dr. Carter's favorite subject. If he can get anybody in a corner for fifteen minutes and talk to them, he's going to be talking about you." And with that, the good doctor gave his final sign-off for John. We were now completely finished with everything medically related from the accident. I heaved a sigh of relief, laughed, and thanked God again for His work in John's life. It felt good, finally, to be back to normal.

John also started to have horrid headaches and complained about his vision. I didn't think it was a residual of the accident, but I had no idea what to think, so we took him to get an eye examination.

As the doctor looked at John's eyes, he furrowed his brow and then leaned back in his chair. "I know this can't be right, but I would be remiss in my practice if I don't send you to have this checked out," he said. "The bowls of his optic nerve are so large it looks like he's in the starting stages of glaucoma."

So we went to see an ophthalmologist. We let her know about John's accident, so her assistants took a bunch of pictures of the inside of John's eyes and captured even the smallest blood vessels at the core.

We waited for the ophthalmologist to study the photos, and soon she entered the room and sat on a stool next to John. She told him that he needed a new prescription, since it had been a while since he'd had his eyes checked and that was more than likely the cause of his headaches. Then she turned to another subject. "So how long were you unconscious?"

"I wasn't unconscious," John said in an indignant tone. "I was dead."

"Okay. How long were you dead and without oxygen?"

"I was without a heartbeat for more than an hour."

Her eyes widened. "Amazing."

"What are you talking about?"

"The smallest blood vessels in the body are in the eyes. So when you have oxygen deprivation, those will be the first blood vessels to rupture." She paused, "You don't have one ruptured blood vessel in your eyes at all."

I laughed. God was still showing us the work He had done behind the scenes. Even though He had healed John completely, we still could continue to praise Him for His work.

And the glaucoma scare? It turned out to be nothing. The bowls of John's optic nerves were extra large, which is a sign for glaucoma, but it was also something John was just born with.

July 4, 2015

To celebrate Independence Day—but really, to take advantage of seeing their nephew—Janice and Don drove to visit us for a few days. We were planning a quiet holiday celebration with a nice meal and then watching the fireworks later. But John awoke with pain in his abdomen. He complained about it, but I thought it might be gas, so I told him to let me know if the pain grew worse. Janice and I were in the kitchen making food for the evening. Per his usual routine of giving me only bits and pieces of information and not fully disclosing how badly he was hurting, I didn't think much more of it until he walked into the kitchen and announced, "Are you going to take me to the hospital or what?" I knew then that it was serious. So off to our favorite place he and I went again. On the way, I called and told Brian, who was working that day doing instant replay video work at the St. Louis Cardinals baseball game, a job he held in addition to his work at Boeing.

As soon as they pulled up John's history and saw what had happened earlier in the year, a flurry of people came rushing, because they weren't sure what was wrong with him and if it had anything to do with the accident. It was not long before Janice and Don arrived.

"What are you doing here?" I asked, stunned that they'd come.

"I didn't know what was going on, but I feel that I should be here, too, since after all, I am his 'mother,'" Janice said.

I laughed, thinking back to the day in the hospital when one of the doctors had confused us and taken Janice to be John's mom.

Not long after my sister and brother-in-law showed up, my son Charles made an appearance.

John had texted him on the way, but we didn't expect him to come! "What's going on?" he said, looking worried.

Let the circus act begin, I thought as we all crowded into the small ER room where John was.

Soon a nurse came in and gave John a morphine shot.

And the hilarity ensued. Don, Charles, and John all tried to crack jokes and see who could snort their laughter the loudest. We had no idea how paper-thin the walls were and that everything we were saying and laughing about was echoing in the next room and out to the nurses' station!

Soon Jason showed up. "You know, John, the hospital doesn't give out frequent flier miles." We all laughed again, and then he prayed with our family.

It didn't escape my attention that this round in the ER was a far cry from the last time when everyone had heard me getting desperate with God. I believe we were the ER's entertainment for this evening.

At four thirty that afternoon, the doctor diagnosed that John's appendix was ready to rupture, and so they needed to do emergency surgery, which they did. The next morning a nurse walked into the room and told us that they just needed to finish up some paperwork and they could release him. She began typing on her computer.

"Okay, our patient is . . ." She waited for his name to pop up. "John Smi—" She jumped a foot from the computer, as though something had just electrically shocked her.

"You're John Smith? You're *John Smith*?"

"Yeees." He drew out his answer as though not sure where she was going with her question.

"John Smith who fell through the ice?"

"Yes."

"I was at Cardinal Glennon going through my nursing classes there, and every morning our professor would come in and want to talk about things that were going on with John Smith! He'd always end the class with 'There's science and there's God. This is God.'"

I sat amazed. Months later, the medical community was still talking about John Smith and having to admit that he was a miracle.

Thursday, February 11, 2016

The Christian Middle School's ninth-grade team ran onto the basketball court and headed toward our side of the room. This was a home game, so Brian and I sat where we normally did and looked across at the visitors' side. Tonight we were playing St. Charles High School. Although many middle schools only go up to eighth grade, Christian's went up to ninth, so our team was technically playing a high school team. About halfway through the team's lineup came John wearing his team's colors and his freshman number 14. He looked so serious— as if he were playing for Duke University during March Madness. I had to laugh. His competitive streak was in high gear—especially because a good childhood friend of his, Gavin Cannon, was playing for the other team—a team he also would have been playing for had he not attended a private school.

This game might have been important for John to win because he wanted to beat his friend, but it was important to me for an entirely different reason. Almost a year ago to the day, Brian and I had sat in the home bleachers and watched our son and his teammates play an outstanding game in which John made the winning shot. And the next day he had died.

One night, as Jason and I had talked about how God was going to complete this miracle while John was still in the PICU at Cardinal Glennon, I predicted that God would demonstrate John's total healing on the basketball court. Now here we were. He'd played great through this season, but this was the game that he was the most concerned about.

John and Coach Pat Turner had talked about how they should approach the St. Charles team, and the coach had assured John that John could pretty much call the game as he felt he needed to. With that leadership mantle now on his shoulders, and having talked smack for weeks with Gavin, I could tell John was itching to get in and play. He was focused but fidgety. His legs bounced up and down, he swung his arms backward and forward, and then he pulled his legs up to his bottom and wiped his shoes off with the palms of his hands. That last ritual drove me nuts—I could only imagine what gross things he was touching. But all the boys were doing it because they had seen NBA players do it. "Oh! Well, I guess that makes the germs less germy and gross," I'd told John when he'd given that explanation.

I spotted Gavin on the other side, wearing a big 24 on his shirt. He had found John and nodded. Then he mouthed, "We're going to win" and smiled. I knew that fed John's fire. Gavin and his brothers had lived in our neighborhood, and they'd all played basketball together since the third grade. But John had never been able to beat Gavin. It was time to even that score.

The game started and I immediately heard John and Gavin yell out, "I got twenty-four!" "I got fourteen!" They were going to guard each other. John got off the first shot and ran his cocky little self down the court as our side cheered. He was trying to act cool, but I knew he was doing somersaults inside his body. He maneuvered and twisted and turned and dribbled and shot as well as—if not better than—before his accident. As the game went on, it seemed as though John was pretty much able to do what he wanted with the ball. By the end of the first half, the score was thirty-six to seventeen, and John had scored half of those thirty-six points. Our team was on fire!

During the halftime break, John made his way into enemy territory to greet Gavin's family. Gavin's dad shook John's hand, complimented him on how well he was playing, and then said, "Now knock it off."

As the third quarter began, Christian High School's junior varsity and varsity basketball team had arrived and were sitting right behind Brian and me. I loved hearing them chant and cheer on my son. It was as if John could hardly miss. He completed eight out of eleven attempted three-point shots. It seemed the more John and his team's shots hit, the more frustrated the St. Charles team became, and they kept missing their shots. John's team came together and moved up and down the floor in precision, guarding one another well.

Into the fourth quarter, our team wasn't losing any steam. In fact, the fans could hardly contain their enthusiasm. Even the junior varsity coach was on his feet and cheering.

Wow, God, I prayed as I stood with the rest of the crowd and yelled my encouragement to our boys on the court. *We've come full circle*. God had completed the work and restored John better than before.

The final score was sixty to twenty-nine. John outscored the other team by himself by one point. I'd say we worship a mighty powerful God.

Epilogue

February 2017

In the two years since the accident, Brian and I—and all the medical experts—have seen nothing left over from what happened to John. Not one thing. He's the same sensitive, sweet, eye-rolling adolescent he was before. It's interesting, because when we take John for his checkups or see any of his doctors for unrelated issues, they all continue to ask him the same questions—"Any residual effects? Any *anything*?"—as though they still can't process the fact that John was dead and now he lives just as normal and healthy as before. As though the thought of a supernatural, unexplainable phenomenon called a miracle is still impossible—that there has to be a scientific, medical explanation for why John survived the way he did.

To which I easily and joyfully respond, "There is. He's called God."

Many people believe, though, that John survived not because of a miraculous work of God's hand but because he was submerged in cold water, which basically froze his brain and organs, thereby protecting them. That sounds promising—only it isn't possible. The water wasn't cold enough, his brain would have had to freeze before the rest of his organs, and he couldn't have been dead for more than an hour. The truth is that he had too many obstacles for him to have been able to survive a cold-water drowning, according to the medical experts. Only one other adult survived a cold-water drowning—a skier whose head broke through the ice when she fell. Her body remained outside of the water. With each attempted scientific explanation, the experts are forced to respond with a "Yes...*but*..."

"I'll go toe to toe with anybody who tells me there's not a God," Alex told me. She was the ER nurse who, along with Gigantor Keith Terry, worked so long and hard giving John CPR. "I know there's a God. I've seen what He does. I've seen Him raise a child from the dead."

People have asked John if God visited him that day in the ER. I supposed they're asking if he saw a great white light or angels or a long tunnel. They want to know if he visited heaven when he died. He didn't experience any of those things. But he wasn't supposed to. Everyone else in that room was meant to experience God's presence and power.

And we all did. In fact, what happened that day in the ER was so astounding that several people on staff gave their lives over to God because of it. Alex was one of them.

We recently saw Dr. Ream and Dr. Garrett and thanked them both for their help during John's stay at Cardinal Glennon.

"John definitely had the criteria for a miracle," Dr. Ream told us. "Lots of families toss that word around, but there really isn't a good explanation other than that."

"It was an awesome experience. So I thank you guys," I said.

"Yes," Dr. Ream agreed. "Let's not repeat it, though."

"I'm all for miracles, but yes, no repeating," said Dr. Garrett and laughed.

"Once and done!" I assured them.

And yet people still struggle to believe. As I've listened to people dissect and try to leave God out of the equation, I shake my head in amazement. We didn't just experience one big miracle—we experienced miracle after miracle that created one big miracle.

- The firefighters just "happened" to do their ice rescue training a week before John fell in.
- Tommy Shine just "happened" to sense a holy nudge to move a few steps in the opposite direction and found John's body.
- Dr. Sutterer just "happened" to decide to hold off on calling time of death.
- I prayed and John's heart just "happened" to start to beat again at that moment.
- Dr. Garrett—a drowning and hypothermia expert—just "happened" to work at the hospital where John needed critical care.
- John swallowed a lot of nasty lake water and had it in his lungs, but the lung culture just "happened" to come back sterile.
- Every time John faced a challenge and we sent out the word for people to pray, John just "happened" to overcome that challenge.
- John just "happened" to recover with no side effects.

Those aren't coincidences. No, God put together everybody He needed to perform this miracle. And the miracle isn't about us. The miracle is about what God is capable of doing.

But the miracles didn't stop with John:

- The paralyzed three-year-old Jackson just "happened" to be close to death when we prayed for him and he recovered fully.
- The drowned three-year-old Remie just "happened" to be close to death when we prayed for him—and he also recovered fully. Eight weeks after the accident, he was released from the hospital. A year later, he was doing well in preschool, was full of energy, and was living a life that the doctors never would have believed.

Even our church saw miracles when people began to believe and pray.

- During the service at First Assembly Church that first Sunday after John's accident, one man who had broken his foot and had been in constant pain with it found that the pain disappeared and his foot had reset itself. And the X-rays later proved it.

- The following Tuesday another man who, earlier that week, had been hospitalized with a massive, deep brain bleed, similar to what had killed his father seven years before, survived and was healed. His doctors still call him a miracle and admit that they had never expected him to recover at all, let alone as well as he had.

- A woman who had polycystic tumors on her kidneys, which had caused her to go into kidney failure, and who desperately needed a kidney was able to find a match in her son and today is well and healed.

- And a woman with stage four cancer left that Sunday morning church service without a trace of it remaining in her body. This baffled her doctors.

As people saw John's miracle and the power of prayer, it gave them hope! And with that hope, they believed that if God could—and did—hear the prayers of just an average mom and heal just an average fourteen-year-old boy, then He could do the same for them. For months afterward, we continued to hear amazing stories of how people began to pray and they were healed of chronic depression, anxiety, fibromyalgia, heart blockages.

All miracles! And they have the medical records to prove it. But it hasn't just been physical healing. People have experienced spiritual and relational healing. Many of John's classmates have sought me out to tell me how this experience changed their lives. I heard from a pastor friend who called to tell me, "I'd gotten to a point in my faith that I didn't think God did miracles any longer. This has just turned me on ear."

It was as if God opened the windows of heaven and poured out miracles upon our church family. It was as if God said, "Ask me! Watch what I can do!" It was as if God was serious when He said to King Solomon, "If my people who are called by my name humble themselves, and pray and seek my face and turn from their wicked ways, then I will hear from heaven and will forgive their sin and heal their land" (2 Chron. 7:14). Having experienced a miracle, I can confidently say that's a great trade-off to get my son back!

When I went into that ER room that day, I wasn't looking for a miracle. I was simply a desperate mom who was asking her God to do something for her son—believing that God could actually do it. And every day after that, I continued to believe that God was still able to do what He said He could do— heal, restore, bring light to darkness, bring joy from pain, turn mourning into dancing.

One of the most frequently asked questions I receive is, "Did you ever doubt?"

No, I didn't. I can honestly say I never had a moment when I doubted that God would heal John. That's not to say that I didn't have moments of stress and anxiety. I can believe an airplane will safely fly me across the country, but when we hit major turbulence, I can still feel frightened and stressed!

But here's why I didn't doubt—and it's so simplistic and childlike. I never doubted because I *chose* to believe that God is who He says He is. Period. Either I believe that or I don't. There's no halfway with God. Doubt is my saying to God, "Sorry, but I just don't believe that You are capable of handling this particular situation." When I prayed and John's heart started, that was enough proof for me that God had heard, He was working, and He would continue to work.

My biggest frustration, honestly, was being exposed to people who *did* doubt. They decided that they were going to "protect" themselves and try to comfort us by saying, "It looks bad, so let's not get our hopes up." Just because something *looks* bad—even appears hopeless—doesn't mean we don't have hope. The storm on the Sea of Galilee looked bad, but Jesus calmed it. Lazarus, being dead and buried for four days, looked—and smelled!—bad, but Jesus raised him. An interesting side note here: Do you know why Jesus took four days before he raised Lazarus from the dead? The Jewish people believed that anyone could raise a person from the dead in two days. But only the Messiah could raise a person from the dead past three days. It just shows us that God really does have a purpose in how He works everything.

God's specialty is making the impossible possible. I could sit with you for hours and go through every little thing that God did to weave together this one massive miracle, but the thing that amazes me the most is how he used the prayers of so many people to accomplish what no mortal could.

A few weeks after John was released from the hospital, we were at the doctor's office for a checkup. As we sat in the waiting room, a woman walked in. I have to admit, by this point, we'd been in front of so many cameras and talked to so many people, all those faces just started to fade in and out. So when she saw me and smiled brightly, I flung open my mental filing cabinet and started flipping through every file trying to figure out if and how I knew this person.

"Hi!" she said to me as she headed toward the sign-in desk.

I'm in trouble, I thought. *I don't have a clue who this lady is, and she obviously knows me.* I tried to smile and act as though we were old friends. "Hello!" *Please, Lord, do not let her come back and talk to me, because I am going to be so embarrassed when I don't know who she is.*

Sure enough, as soon as she finished checking in, she came back to us. "How are you? And how are you doing, John?"

I just could not summon up how I was supposed to know her.

"I know you don't know me," she said, smiling. "But I want you to know this. I live across the street from where they pulled John out of the water. When I came outside and saw what was happening with John, I knew things were desperate. I'm a believer, and I want you to know that I went back into my house, got on my knees, and started intercessory prayer for John."

I was stunned and so grateful to know that prayers were already going up to God before I even entered the ER room and prayed my own desperate prayer.

Often, God asks us to partner with Him in making miracles happen. In what way? Through prayer. Too many of us turn to pray as a last resort: "Well, we've tried everything so let's pray."

Recently I was watching the movie *The List* and heard a quote that sums up our all-too-often problem with prayer: "God's children and his enemies both make the same mistake. They both underestimate the power of prayer."

Can God heal completely with just one prayer? Absolutely. But often, for whatever sovereign reason, He wants us to be active participants in His work. He wants us to pray and keep praying. He wants us to consider prayer as the first resort—and the continual resort. It's all about God's perfect timing and purpose. Just as He did with Lazarus, He does with us.

He wants us to pray and pray and then pray some more—"without ceasing" (1 Thess. 5:17). He wants us not just to pray crisis prayers—but to pray, as the apostle Paul told us, "on all occasions with all kinds of prayers and requests" (Eph. 6:18 NIV). He wants us to "ask, and it will be given to you; seek, and you will find; knock, and it will be opened to you. For everyone who asks receives, and the one who seeks finds, and to the one who knocks it will be opened" (Matt. 7:7–8).

I discovered why that's so important. Because if I make prayer a habit, then I see God at work all the time. If I see God at work all the time, that builds my trust in Him, so that when the crisis comes, my faith is already strong, my trust is already solid, and I have no need to doubt. I can much more easily believe that God is who He says He is, because I've experienced it over and over. And in turn my prayers become filled with worship and thanksgiving, not just asking for things.

The truth is that my prayer wasn't so unique and I wasn't such a great saint that God listened. God wants to answer all of our prayers. Anybody can pray and get a miracle. It's how you approach God. I've joked before that I've prayed for more people who have died than who have lived. God answered my prayer not because I'm some giant in the faith. But I did one thing right— I stubbornly, bullheadedly believed.

I think sometimes people want God to do something for them, so they think they can just pray and God will pull out this magical wand and everything will be okay. Yes, God can do that. I mean, He spoke this world into existence. So why can't He heal cancer? He can. Why can't He deliver my prodigal child from drugs? He can. Why can't He save my marriage? He can. But if the only times we want to speak to God is when we expect Him to do something about the bad thing happening in our lives, we potentially set ourselves up for disappointment.

I don't know why God chose to save my child but doesn't choose to save someone else's. I don't presume to speak the sovereign mind of God. Only He knows. But I do know this: He is good; He is always good. And whatever He does or does not do, whatever He allows to happen, doesn't change His compassionate and kind character. He sees the big picture when all we see is a piece. He is still in control. He is still good. And someday when we see Him face-to-face, we will understand it all. We will understand all the whys—and they will all make sense.

In the meantime, we have the privilege to go on this journey and watch what God does. As Pastor Jason likes to say, "Lord, you drive and I'll ride." And when we do, hold on tight, because you and I will see the most impossible things become truly possible.

AFTERWORD

Jason Noble
Senior Pastor, First Assembly Church, St. Peters, Missouri

When I arrived at the hospital on January 19, 2015, I had no idea how desperate the situation was. Throughout my career as a pastor, I have been called on to visit patients and pray for miracles. But this day was different. Though an incredible desperation filled the air, a resolve was just as strong—that we would believe for *nothing less* than God turning an impossibility into the fact of making John Smith whole again. None of us really knew just how dire John's situation was, or how certain the doctors and medical community were that John was not going to make it.

This was a time for Joyce and Brian Smith—along with our entire First Assembly Church community—to choose not to go by what we heard or by what we saw, but by God's promises. This was a time to hold on to God's Word. And this was a time to test the real power of prayer. So we did. We spoke the truth of Scripture, we prayed, and we refused to allow any negative talk or thoughts to enter John's room. We focused on the truth of God being a life-giving God.

From that first night on, God impressed upon me that I was not to leave John's and Joyce's side. That I needed to be there to encourage, strengthen, and support the Smith family. God has not released me from that calling. I will have a deep heart connection with Joyce, John, and Brian for the rest of our lives. I'm thankful that Joyce allowed me to have a front-row seat to witness what God has done in John's and his family's life. And I'm grateful that you, too, have discovered the story.

Nothing you read has been embellished. When God does something this incredible, no embellishment is necessary. What happened to John Smith is one of the most well-documented miracles in the medical community.

After reading this book, do you believe that God can make the impossible possible? It's easy to say that God can still do miracles, but what about when you are in the middle of a crisis and you desperately need one? Do you believe He can *really* do what you are asking Him to do? What about when you have prayed and nothing seems to happen? Does your faith turn into doubt? Do you simply accept that what you need is an impossibility?

I have always tried to encourage people to believe that God *can* do miracles. I don't know *how* He's going to work it, but I know that He always answers every cry for help—especially when the situation seems most desperate, dark, and hopeless. If this is where you find yourself, then this story is exactly what you need. It's a true story about how a mom, a pastor, and a faith community firmly held on to the belief that God can make the impossible possible.

Many people want a formula for a miracle. But there isn't one. Every miracle God does is different. He knows exactly what we need and has a purpose for everything He does. But we *can* position ourselves to receive a miracle. That was exactly what we did. We prayed first.

So many times I hear people say, "Well, I've done everything I can do, now I guess I should pray." They look at prayer as a last resort. I want to challenge you to pray *first* and invite God into your situation. He can do incredible things when He's invited.

Another important part of positioning ourselves for a miracle is to staunchly and doggedly speak life. Scripture tells us that the power of life and death is in the tongue (see Prov. 18:21). Speak life over your situation. Hold on to every promise that God has given you through Scripture. If God can do it for John Smith, He can do it for you.

As you pray to make the impossible possible in your life, I encourage you not to put God in a box. So many times we pray and tell God how to answer our prayers. But in His sovereign grace He always answers us with the best answer and the best solution—*His* answer and *His* solution. In Isaiah 55:8–9, God tells us that His ways are not our ways, and His thoughts are not our thoughts. He works and thinks differently from how we do—and His answers are always so much better than ours. We must remember the greatest miracle of all is eternity. John Smith has been temporarily healed, which we are thankful for. But John will experience the ultimate healing as he stands before God and God welcomes him into eternity. If John had died that day, it would have still been a miracle—but not the one we were hoping for. He would have experienced ultimate healing and an eternity with Jesus in heaven. We can't forget that death is sometimes as much a miracle as life is.

Miracles are all around us. Every breath we take is a miracle of life. The more you look for them, the more you'll see God's miraculous work in *your* life. But you have to look for it, you have to expect it, and you have to appreciate it.

I'm thankful that Jesus is close to the brokenhearted and crushed in spirit. He doesn't promise us that it will be easy, or even that it will be what we hope for. But God's plan is always the best plan. And He always promises to go with us and help us through every impossibility that we face.

If you don't know the Lord, I encourage you to make a decision to give your life to Him. It's the best decision you can make. I'm not sure how people make it without Jesus through moments like the one you've just read. The Bible says to be saved all you have to do is believe in your heart that Jesus came to save you and that you need a savior, and then confess with your mouth, or say a simple prayer: "Jesus, I need You. Come into my life. Save me. Forgive me of my sins. My life is Yours. Please take all the broken pieces of my life and make me whole. Thank You for loving me, even when I wasn't so lovable." If you pray that prayer, it's as simple as that. Jesus comes into your life and begins to change your heart and mind. Get a Bible and start reading about how amazing God is. Find a good church that will walk beside you on this new journey. And make prayer a daily conversation with God.

I do my best as a pastor to create a *Do it again!* environment in our church in which we pray, "Lord, we know You can do miracles. We know You can make the impossible possible. We read about Your miracle-working power through-out Scripture. Do it again! Don't let it just be something we read about, let us experience it today!"

Experience it we did. This modern-day resurrection story captures all that God did with and through Joyce, Brian, and John Smith. And I hope it has changed your perspective on how God works. I hope you saw His miracle-working power.

I encourage you to believe for the impossible. Because with God, *anything* is possible!

The best is yet to come.

AUTHOR'S NOTE

I'm still amazed by how God continues to work this miracle. Even when we think things have calmed down and we can get back to our lives, God shows up to say, *We aren't quite finished here yet!* (This book being one of those!) And more people get to hear about God's impossible possibilities. All I can say is that I'm so grateful to be part of this adventure—not that I'd like a repeat performance, however.

As I was working on this book, I was stunned to hear and learn still new things about John's condition during those first days and other things that happened, as well as about other people who heard the story and had their lives changed by it. It reminds me that I will probably never truly know the depth and scope of what God did during that time. And I know people who are still trying to process what they experienced in their part of the miracle—and to that I say, "God isn't finished with you!"

Those sixteen days in the hospital and the days that followed are forever seared into my brain. And yet, in some ways, they're a blur. Many people helped me as we did our best to piece together a correct time line of when things happened and on what days. Some of those conversations or events may have actually occurred at a different time, in a slightly different way, or on a different day—but they did happen. I apologize for anything we incorrectly stated. Please know that any inaccuracies are purely our own and not connected with family, friends, first responders, or any medical personnel.

APPENDIX A

Clinging To Scripture

Prayer and Scripture were the tools that we used to fight the spiritual battle for John's miracle. Whenever the doctors said John wasn't going to make it, and gave us the worst-case scenarios, we made the decision not to go by what we saw or heard, but by what we knew and what God had promised us through the Bible. Throughout our time in the hospital—and even afterward—we constantly claimed the following Scriptures.

Whenever you face an impossibility, cling tightly to these verses—no matter what you see, go by what you *know*: that with God *anything* is possible.

God's Promises To Protect

"Because he holds fast to me in love, I will deliver him; I will protect him, because he knows my name. When he calls to me, I will answer him; I will be with him in trouble; I will rescue him and honor him."

(Psalm 91:14-15)

"When you pass through the waters, I will be with you; and through the rivers, they shall not overwhelm you; when you walk through fire you shall not be burned, and the flame shall not consume you."

(Isaiah 43:2)

The Importance Of Speaking Life

"Death and life are in the power of the tongue, and those who love it will eat its fruits."

(Proverbs 18:21)

"What comes out of the mouth proceeds from the heart, and this defiles a person."

(Matthew 15:18)

"We destroy arguments and every lofty opinion raised against the knowledge of God, and take every thought captive to obey Christ."

(2 Corinthians 10:5)

Prayers For Healing

"Is anyone among you sick? Let him call for the elders of the church, and let them pray over him, anointing him with oil in the name of the Lord. And the prayer of faith will save the one who is sick, and the Lord will raise him up."

(James 5:14–15)

"Pray without ceasing."

(1 Thessalonians 5:17)

"Pray in the Spirit on all occasions with all kinds of prayers and requests."

(Ephesians 6:18 NIV)

"Ask, and it will be given to you; seek, and you will find; knock, and it will be opened to you. For everyone who asks receives, and the one who seeks finds, and to the one who knocks it will be opened."

(Matthew 7:7–8)

For Peace

"To set the mind on the flesh is death, but to set the mind on the Spirit is life and peace."

(Romans 8:6)

For Hope

"I know the plans I have for you, declares the LORD, plans for welfare and not for evil, to give you a future and a hope. Then you will call upon me and come and pray to me, and I will hear you. You will seek me and find me, when you seek me with all your heart."

(Jeremiah 29:11–13)

On Spiritual Warfare

"We do not wrestle against flesh and blood, but against the rulers, against the authorities, against the cosmic powers over this present darkness, against the spiritual forces of evil in the heavenly places."

(Ephesians 6:12)

APPENDIX B

Dr. Sutterer's Letter

The boy had been pulseless for greater than twenty minutes when we brought his mother into the room. I remember her sitting down in front of him, in front of the half dozen nurses, the respiratory techs, the paramedics, and techs who were fatigued from the prolonged CPR. We had at least two emergency physicians assisting in resuscitation along with a pharmacist and many other department personnel. She was crying, as is to be expected, wailing that her son had just passed away. And then she cried out, "I believe in a mighty God and He can perform miracles. Lord, please bring John back to us. God, please send your Holy Spirit to heal this boy!"

We continued to resuscitate this young man knowing the situation was grim. Being underwater for more than twenty minutes, coming to the hospital without a pulse, and at a temperature that is incompatible with life. We performed CPR for another twenty minutes after he arrived at the emergency department. None of the prognostic indicators looked good. But a mother's love and, more importantly, a mother's prayer can overcome all obstacles. God's sovereignty knows no bounds. Lazarus was in the tomb for three days. Jarius's daughter was reported dead by the ruler of the house. The son of the widow from the town of Nain was being carried out of the town in a burial ceremony.

This John, whom you know and love, was on the gurney in front of me at that very moment with no signs of life, dead. I had exhausted all interventions in my scientific armamentarium without even a hint of success. All the resources of this world were being thrust upon this young man with no indication except the cold reality of a young life snuffed out before our very eyes. But the interventions of modern medicine are not what John's mother was counting on. Spiritual warfare is what she called this. No sooner did John's mother call on the Holy Spirit to bring her son back to him that the monitor started that rhythmic beat, a pulse could be felt in his groin and his carotid artery. After the numerous resuscitation attempts with medicines and CPR to pump blood in place of the heart's natural beating. Breathing via a plastic tube pumped through a hand-squeezed bag. Warming devices in place and heated IV fluids being pumped into his veins. All ineffective. What was effective was when John's mother called the Holy Spirit.

The Holy Spirit came in that room and started that boy's heart once again. We had been actively warming him from the 88-degree temperature of his arrival up to 94.6 degrees. That's when his heart was jump-started by the Holy Spirit listening to the request of a praying mother. Immediately his temperature plunged back to 88 degrees, showing us the futility of our CPR compared to the efficiency of the natural beating heart as designed by God. Blood was moving through his body, sending the icy fluids from his extremities back to his core, plunging his temperature dramatically. Cold as he was, he was alive. Even starting to try to take his own breaths as we readied him for the helicopter flight to Cardinal Glennon Children's Hospital.

I don't know if Lazarus was ever the same after he came back from the tomb, how long he lived, and whether he suffered with the ailments that caused his death. I don't know if the centurion's daughter ever fully recovered completely from her episode that preceded her first death. We would inquire, did she have any neurologic deficits? It is not recorded if the widow's son returned to his same pre-death productivity. I also don't know that John Smith will ever be the same as he was before he fell through the ice. But I know that God can do more than we ever imagined. I know that God has given us a gift, even if it is only for a few days. I was privileged to witness a miracle. I was preparing myself to give a mother the final bad news that her son was gone from this world. She had more faith in God than I did. She called on God, and God brought him back.

God, thank You for the gift of each day that You give us with the ones we love. We look forward to each hour You chose to give us with those we love. God, hold us up in this difficult circumstance. Thank You for covering us with the saving blood of Jesus Christ, which saves us from our sin and ushers each of us into everlasting life with You in heaven.

Amen.

Kent Sutterer, DO
Emergency Department
SSM Saint Joseph Hospital West

ACKNOWLEDGMENTS

The past couple years have been one of the most trying and yet exciting times in my family's life. We are so grateful to have the honor and privilege to share this miracle with the world. Our prayer is that those who read the account of God's handiwork on these pages will experience a God of love and hope, but most of all, a God who still does what we think is *impossible*.

That said, first and foremost, I want to give all praise and glory to my God and Savior, Jesus Christ, for sending the Holy Spirit to answer this mother's prayer of desperation, which restored breath and life to our dead son. There is no detail that God had not already made provision to cover. He handled every single need that presented itself over those sixteen days—and far beyond when John walked out of the Cardinal Glennon Children's Medical Center on his own two legs, completely healed.

I could write another book on all those who have been such a big part of this miracle, but I must keep it to a couple pages. I believe I speak for Josh Rieger's parents, Cindy and Kurt, and Josh Sander's parents, Bob and Mary, when I say that we can never thank the first responders enough for saving our sons from the icy waters of Lake Ste. Louise. These brave people put their lives on the line every single day for our safety. There are not enough words to thank them for their selfless service. Our gratitude also goes to Jamie Rieger, Josh Rieger's sister, and Ron Wilson for making the 911 calls. And of course to Josh Sander and Josh Rieger for immediately trying to help John at their own risk.

Thank you to the Lake St. Louis police department—in particular to Rick

Frauenfelder and Ryan Hall, who jumped into the icy waters without wet suits, thinking not of their safety but only of saving our boys' lives. Also a huge thank-you to the other officers onsite, who helped tremendously: Tyler Christeson, Cody Fry, and Detective Sergeant Bret Carbray.

Thank you also goes to the Lake St. Louis fire department, who were so quickly on the scene and at work.

Thank you to Wentzville's district fire chief, Mike Marlo, and his sweet wife, Kathy, who have been such great friends and supporters of our family.

Thank you also to firefighters Joe Marrow and Mike Terranova, who went into the water.

And last but not least—thanks goes to Capt. Tommy Shine. Words are not sufficient enough to thank Captain Shine. He has been such a blessing to us even after finding John's body so quickly. He is my hero. He has given me many laughs and helped John through the overwhelming attention with his wit and humor. Tommy, you are one in a million and I love how you embody the "never give up" spirit.

Thank you to the heroes from the St. Charles country ambulance Medic 9, Jeremey Hollrah and his crew, who worked tirelessly on our boys to get them prepared and transported to the hospital in record speed. I thank God for each and every one of you mentioned or not mentioned. We honor you for all the excellent work you do to serve our community.

To the crew at St. Joseph West. What can I say that would even come close to being a proper acknowledgment? Alex Gibbons, John's charge nurse, you are precious to me. Keith Terry, you worked so hard doing CPR on John and telling him he was not going to die on you. Those are *awesome words of life*! Dr. Sutterer, you are such a godsend, thank you for not calling time of death before I got there. Words cannot express my gratitude. Dr. Bauer and all those from the medical staff, thank you for your tireless dedication and for not giving up on our son. To the precious nun who stayed by my side—you were my angel.

To the Cardinal Glennon PICU staff: *You are the best!* Dr. Garrett, you are the most kind, gentle, caring doctor—how could I have misjudged you? God put you right where you needed to be and worked through you to lead and guide and do what was necessary for John to live. Dr. Ream, not only are you a fantastic doctor, but you were my anxiety relief! You always knew what to say to alleviate my stress. Remembering your dry wit and humor during those difficult days still brings a smile to my face. You and Dr. Garrett worked tirelessly, giving your best for our son. Dr. Carter and Dr. Gibbons, thank you for seeing us through our remaining days at the hospital. To the PICU nurses—your dedication is award winning. To all the staff at Cardinal Glennon Hospital, a big *thank-you*.

Friends and family are the backbone of every community. Thank you to our basketball family and coaches, Kevin and his dad. Thank you, Nancy, Keith, Pat, Colleen, and the rest of the staff at Christian Middle School and Christian High School and students and their parents, who came night after night to the hospital. Thank you to our friends, family, and staff at First Assembly Church St. Peters and surrounding-area churches, who prayed and supported us, who visited the hospital and brought countless meals. You'll never know how much we appreciated it.

For Emma Riley and Chayla Gilkey, who spent many nights sending me Scriptures that got me through the tough times. I love you both.

For Marie Glenville, Mama G. You are priceless.

For Margret and Jeanenne, thank you.

My sister, Janice, and brother-in-law, Don. For all you did and always do, I can never say this enough: I love you.

I love my sons Joe, Tom, Charles, and their families. You are incredible and I'm blessed to call you mine.

Thank you to Brian's sisters and family—Miriam, Ken, Jane, Tom and Laura, and Cheryl and Gary.

Thank you to Dave and Sharon and your family, and to Mark and Cathy. Love you guys.

Thank you, Melissa Fischer, for all the nights you stayed with me at the hospital. To you and Keri Munholand and our Bible study ladies—love you.

A huge thank-you to Pastors Brad and Beth Riley, or as John would say, "Papa" and "Mama Riley." We are so thankful God brought you back into our lives and for making us part of your family. Also to Mark and Cami Shepard for loving John, and the sweet note from Megan Shepard. Love you guys. Thank you, too, Wayne and Arlene Hogue, for always being there for us.

I also want to thank Rev. Sammy Rodriguez for all he has done to promote this miracle and for giving us the connections with DeVon Franklin, so we can share this story with the world.

To Dupree Miller's Nena Oshman for doing an excellent job brokering our book to Hachette/FaithWords, we are so grateful you wanted to share our amazing story—it has been an exciting ride. We so appreciate our editor, Christina Boys from Hachette/FaithWords, for being so sweet and kind working with us to make this book the best it can be.

Thank you to Tim Vandehey for writing our proposal, which secured a wonderful contract with Hachette/FaithWords. It was a pleasure working with you.

I would also like to thank God for sending us the amazing writer, Ginger Kolbaba, who wrote one of the most anointed manuscripts in a record time of eight weeks. You are *the best*! I can't thank God enough for bringing you across our path. You have been the ideal person to do spiritual warfare with; you are a mighty warrior.

I also want to say how much I appreciate my husband, Brian, and son John, who have held down the fort for the past months while I wrote and held many conference calls. I love you both to the moon and back.

I also have to thank all the people around the world who prayed for our son's recovery!

Kay Quinn, what can I say? You are the best of the best in news reporting. Your coverage of John's story on KSDK TV 5 was award-winning. Your integrity is second to none. Thank you from the bottom of my heart!

Michelle Wilson from *The 700 Club*, I'm so thankful God sent you to tell John's story. You are a beautiful woman of God.

Last, but *for sure* not least, thanks to Pastor Jason Noble and his sweet and beautiful wife, Paula, and their family for supporting us through the past few years. Paula and Jason, thank you for your endless hours of editing our manuscript to make sure it was accurate and that no embellishments had been added. Jason, for all the endless hours you spent at the hospital and in making sure this process was continually moving us forward. Thank you for getting us to this point and beyond. Thank you, thank you, *thank you*! I thank the Lord every day that He sent you guys here to walk through this journey with us. What an honor to share this experience.

ABOUT THE AUTHORS

Joyce Smith was born in Wichita, Kansas, but because of her father's work for a tool-and-die company, she grew up in Ohio and lived in eight different states as well as Canada and Germany. She worked for twenty-five years in accounting, but feels her biggest accomplishment has been as a wife and mother—one of the toughest jobs, with the lowest pay but with the most rewards. She and her husband, Brian (her Prince Charming), live in St. Charles, Missouri. They have four wonderful sons and five beloved grandchildren. Joyce keeps busy with attending her youngest son John's school and basketball events, enjoys cross-stitch, crochet, and decorating, and loves speaking to audiences about what God has done—and continues to do—for her family.

Ginger Kolbaba is an accomplished, award-winning author, editor, and speaker. She has written or contributed to more than thirty books, including *Your Best Happily Ever After*, and more than four hundred magazine and online articles. In the publishing industry for more than two decades (she started *very* young), Ginger is the former editor of *Today's Christian Woman* magazine and *Marriage Partnership* magazine, and is the founding editor of Kyria.com, all award-winning resources of Christianity Today International. You can visit her at www.gingerkolbaba.com, Facebook.com/GingerKolbabaAuthor, or Twitter @gingerkolbaba.